EZ

FLASH MX

Animation
ActionScript
Gaming

For Macromedia Flash

Bradley Kaldahl M.S.Ed

Printed in Victoria, Canada

A cataloguing record for this book that includes the U.S. Library of Congress Classification number, the Library of Congress Call number and the Dewey Decimal cataloguing code is available from the National Library of Canada. The complete cataloguing record can be obtained from the National Library's online database at: www.nlc-bnc.ca/amicus/index-e.html

TRAFFORD

This book was published *on-demand* **in cooperation with Trafford Publishing.** On-demand publishing is a unique process and service of making a book available for retail sale to the public taking advantage of on-demand manufacturing and Internet marketing. **On-demand publishing** includes promotions, retail sales, manufacturing, order fulfilment, accounting and collecting royalties on behalf of the author.

Suite 6E, 2333 Government St., Victoria, B.C. V8T 4P4, CANADA

Phone	250-383-6864	Toll-free	1-888-232-4444 (Canada & US)
Fax	250-383-6804	E-mail	sales@trafford.com
Web site	www.trafford.com	TRAFFORD PUBLISHING IS A DIVISION OF TRAFFORD HOLDINGS LTD.
Trafford Catalogue #03-0987		www.trafford.com/robots/03-0987.html	

10   9   8   7   6   5   4   3   2

To my son Thomas
My little dinosaur :)
Love "AaaDee" (Daddy)

Acknowledgments:
I could not have written this book without the loving support of my spouse Sonia, daughter Samantha and son Thomas.

Prof. Fred Howell, my dept. chair, mentor and friend. I continue to learn from your example and dedication to students.
Dean Ed Roberts. I am grateful to have you as an advocate.

To my friends and colleagues who captivate me with their knowledge and expertise.
Profs. Deborah Solomon, Mike Cantwell and Mike O'Conner.

Special thanks to Jill Weinstein who was kind enough to provide comments and suggestions for the initial projects and proof.

Bruce Bachelor & Sarah Campbell at Trafford.

A special thanks to my students. Your creativity, enthusiasm, and willingness to explore continues to amaze me.

Special thanks to the companies that provided software (and hardware) for review:
Macromedia (Flash, Director and Fireworks).
Erain (Swift 3D).
Sorenson (Squeeze).
Dazzle (Hollywood DV Bridge and DVD Complete).

SECTION 3 USING OTHER APPLICATIONS WITH FLASH

Condensed Table of Contents

SECTION 1 ANIMATION

SECTION 2 INTERACTIIVITY & ACTIONSCRIPT

Expanded Table of Contents

Chapter 4 - Symbols and Tweening   27

Chapter 5 - Shape Tweens   35

Chapter 6 - Shape Tweened Type   39

Chapter 7 - Exploding Light Animation   43

Chapter 8 - Spinning Type 49

Chapter 9 - Multi-Layer Animations 51

Chapter 10 - Later Explosion 57

Chapter 11 - Spinning Letters 63

SECTION 2   INTERACTIVITY & ACTIONSCRIPT

Chapter 18 - Interactive Presentation

Chapter 19 - Button Sounds

Chapter 20 - Controlling Timeline Sound

Chapter 21 - Dynamic Text Fields

Chapter 38 - Flash Video Project   203

Chapter 39 - Swift 3D Tutorial   207

Chapter 40 - Using Swift 3D in Flash   211

Chapter 41 - Fireworks for Flash   213

Chapter 42 - Photoshop for Flash   217

Chapter 43 - Freehand for Flash   221

Chapter 44 - Illustrator for Flash   223

I hope you will have as much fun using this book as I had in writing, teaching and exploring new ideas. The previous edition of this book still has the highest user rating of all Flash books available (as of this writing). As with the previous edition the projects maintain the same brevity and simplicity in order to allow the reader to understand the concept quickly as well as explore and apply the procedure in real world applications.

The design of this book is based on a few simple academic concepts.

1. Information is presented in a logical progression. While this makes clear sense to educators I have discovered that some young publishing executives do not seem to appreciate this concept. If you have struggled with other Flash books you may be pleased and a bit surprised at how easy it is to learn Flash using this book.

2. This book incorporates the concept of drill and practice for topics that are more difficult, but attempts to do so in a way that is exciting and presents new creative ideas. For example there are several projects on using tweens. Each project presents a different visual effect but the ultimate goal is to provide enough practice with this concept before moving onto more advanced topics.

3. The projects have been classroom tested with a diverse range of individuals. This not only means that the projects work but also that the projects have incorporated extensive feedback in order to avoid reader frustration. If I had a nickel for every time I got stuck halfway through a software tutorial I would be a rich fellow. It is inevitable that the writer who knows the software, at times, accidentally jumps over a key element. Because these projects have had extensive classroom testing you should find that even questions

WHAT MAKES THIS BOOK USABLE

that might occur are addressed while you are working through the project.

On the other hand I always appreciate reader comments and suggestions. If you find a project that needs refinement please feel free to let me know.

4. Additional Exploration. At the end of most chapters you will find suggestions for additional exploration. While the tutorials may provide an introduction to a concept it is through your experimentation that a concept can attain personal meaning and ultimately be used to achieve your objectives.

THIS BOOK HAS 3 SECTIONS

The book is divided into three primary sections:

1. The first part of the book (chapter 1-14) is devoted to the basics of Flash and animation techniques. In my classes, the midterm project is to create an animation on a topic such as dreams, nightmares, love, or some other abstract concept.

2. The second section of the book is devoted to interactivity, and more advanced topics using movieclips and ActionScript. In my classes, the final project is to create an interactive game prototype. Even though some users may not be interested in the career area of gaming it is a good portfolio piece and helps to reinforce a solid understanding of Flash and basic ActionScript.

3. The final section of the book is devoted to using external applications in order to prepare, optimize, and import content into Flash. There are four tutorials on video capture and compression. There is a chapter on using Swift 3D to create Flash content and a chapter that provides some clever ActionScript to control 3D content. There are also basic tutorials for Fireworks, Photoshop, Freehand and Illustrator.

One misconception that I encounter in the classroom is the statement "I want to create a Flash only web site." The statement implies that Flash is an independent web technology.

It is a legitimate request but it does not reflect the true nature of the web and how Flash exists on the internet.

Abbreviated history: The internet was around before the World Wide Web (HTML) existed. The internet was (and still is) a connection to multiple computers. Before HTML the user would have to type in keyboard commands using VAX, UNIX, or some other computer language in order to gain entry into computer hosts that existed on the internet.

HTML was a revolutionary step in changing the internet from a keyboard driven interface into a graphical (use my mouse and click) interface. To restate, HTML allowed us to more easily navigate the internet.

HTML was just the beginning. Over time new technologies have been layered on top of HTML to provide additional features. Some of the technologies that are now overlaid on top of HTML are DHTML, XML, Javascript, CSS, just to name a few. In addition to new technologies that have been added on top of HTML there are also plug-ins which allow your web browser to display content that is not built into web standards. Flash requires a plug-in. Most new browsers already include the Flash Plug-in. You may wonder why Flash (which is so widely used) has not become a standard web technology. Keeping Flash as a plug-in allows Macromedia the ability to update and maintain this technology without going through a web standards committee and also keep upgrades confidential until they are ready to release.

File formats and the Flash SWF format:
File formats are like packages that contain different information. For images used on the Web you might save them a JPEG or a GIF, but if you wanted to be able to open the image in Photoshop (with all layers intact) you would save it as a PSD file (Photoshop Document). Flash uses the same type of convention. A file that can be opened and edited in Flash is saved as an FLA file. When you choose File - Save in Flash you are saving the file as an FLA. Before a Flash animation can be placed on the web it is converted into an SWF file. This procedure is discussed in the chapter on Publishing Flash for the Web, and is actually very easy to perform.

UPLOADING TO THE WEB

A word about placing SWF files on the Web:
A Flash SWF file must be imbedded into a HTML document. An SWF file is similar to placing a JPEG or GIF image into a web page in that you must upload the HTML web page and the SWF file. As you will see in the chapter on publishing for the web, Flash will create the HTML document for you while it is producing your SWF file. You could use Macromedia DreamWeaver or Adobe Golive to produce your web pages and insert Flash content.

Flash can also produce a self running application for both PC and Macintosh. This provides the exciting prospect that you can create a software application that can be burned onto a CD and sold.

Uploading content to the web:
This book will show you how to "publish" your Flash work in a form that is ready for web uploading, i.e.: generating an SWF file that is imbedded in an HTML web page.

This book does not discuss the specific procedures that your Internet Service Provider (ISP) requires for uploading your content as this may vary based on the ISP you choose to use. Your ISP should be able to provide specific details on, tools, utilities, and procedures for uploading your content into your site. It is best to search the site of your ISP first and if stuck email your ISP to get advice and suggestions.
There are also many resources on the web that cover this topic. While performing a Yahoo search for "uploading web pages" I found a variety of pages that address this topic. One that does a great job of addressing the tools needed by either Mac or PC users who have FTP access to their web site is...
http://www.utexas.edu/learn/upload/
This site not only provides step by step guidance but also provides links to popular tools available on the internet.

Conventions for using this book:

Finding a topic or procedure:
You will note that there is not an index at the back of the book. A hands on training book does not readily lend itself to an index. Looking up the word movieclip and seeing it referenced throughout the book is actually more confusing than productive.

As an alternative there are two separate tables of contents. The first simply provides a listing of the title of each chapter. The second table of contents is comprehensive and includes primary section, chapter topic, and the margin notes from each chapter. By glancing at the section, chapter and margin note you should be able to more easily look up the topic or procedure you wish to perform, in addition you can see the topic in reference to corresponding topics to determine if you need to go back a few steps.

Action Steps:
❑ Action Steps are the actual instructions to perform in Flash (or other application). Throughout this book, all "action-steps" will have a checkbox ❑ in front. In addition you will note extensive use of screenshots. While many chapters can be completed just by looking at the screenshots you will benefit by taking the time to read the text.

Menu commands:
Menu and sub-menu commands are shown using a dash. For example to describe how to save a document using the Save command found under the File menu it is shown in the book as File-Save.

Scripting:
Scripting is shown in the courier typeface to set it apart from the other text of this book. For example...

```
on(rollOver) {
    gotoAndPlay (1);
}
```

Frame by Frame Animation

CHAPTER 2

This chapter introduces the topic of frame by frame animation. As you get further into Flash you'll find that frame by frame animation is not used frequently but there are times where it is essential.

Historically all animations were produced one frame at a time. This required an enormous amount of effort and patience, as you will see in this project.

For this project you will create a simple 10 frame animation of a ball that bounces. Remember that the goal of this book is to quickly and simply show you how to use Flash. It is up to you to expand on the idea using your own creativity.

While creating a frame by frame animation you will learn about the tool palette, stage, timeline, onion skinning and other palettes in Flash. In addition to learning some of the tools and palettes, the most important benefit is to gain comfort with the use of a timeline. The biggest obstacle most novice animators encounter when working with a timeline are the concepts of frames and keyframes. Once you understand what a keyframe is and how to add one to the timeline the rest of Flash becomes much easier to understand.

❏ Launch Flash

❏ Choose the menu command Window-Panel Sets-Designer.
This will reset all the palettes to their default locations.

SET UP

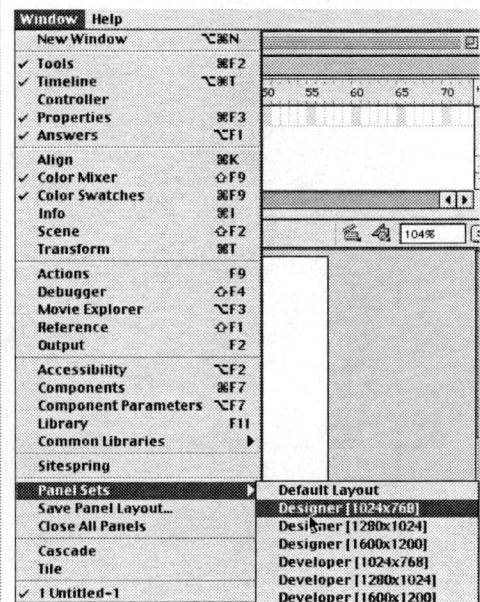

©*BRADLEY KALDAHL 2003*

First Look Around

Layout

Animation Basics

With all the palettes reset to their default locations your monitor screen should resemble the diagram displayed below.

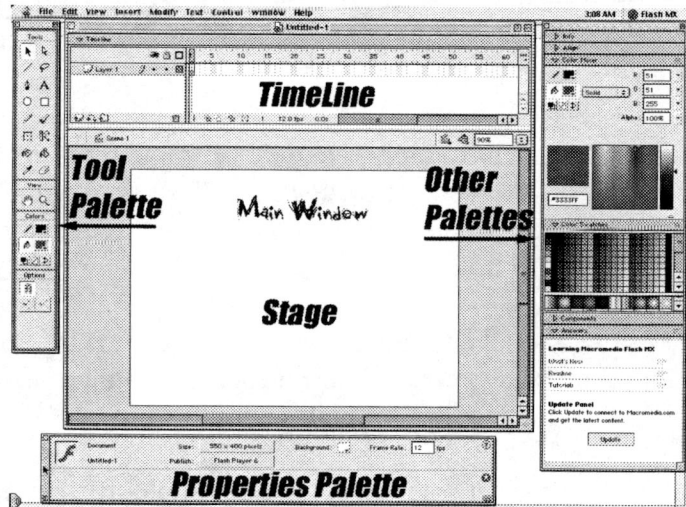

Note: The Properties palette is context sensitive and will change based on what you are doing.

The main window contains both the timeline and the stage. The tool palette (on the left) displays a variety of tools. I'm sure you can guess at the use of some of them simply by looking at the icon. Options for each tool are displayed either on the lower half of the tool palette or on the Properties palette or other palettes displayed on the right side of your monitor.

The main window contains two different areas. The upper half displays the timeline. It allows you to create movement over time for animation.

Below the timeline is the stage. This is the area where animation takes place and represents what the user will see. This is also the area where you will draw, position, and create your animation.

Animation Basics
One way to create a simple animation would be to use a notepad or even this book.

For Example: Lets say that on the first page of this book you draw a circle at the bottom of the page. Then on the next facing page you draw the same circle but moved it up a little. Then, on the next page you moved it further up and so on until you reached the last page where the circle was at the top of the page. If you flipped through the pages rapidly the circle appears to move ie: it is animated.

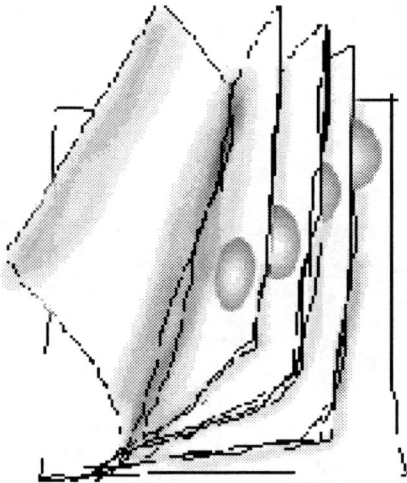

Frame 6
Frame 5
Frame 4
Frame 3
Frame 2
Frame 1

Flash works on the same principle. To create the same animation in Flash we would start with the first frame. Frame number 1 of the timeline is the same as page 1 in the book example above, so place a circle at the bottom of the stage. Frame number 2 on the timeline represents page number 2, so move the circle a little closer to the top of the stage. With each frame move the circle closer to the top until you reach a frame where the circle is at the top of the stage. When you play the animation back, you are seeing the illusion of the object moving from the bottom to the top of the stage.

So each frame of the timeline represents the page numbers or one small point in time of the movement of our animation.

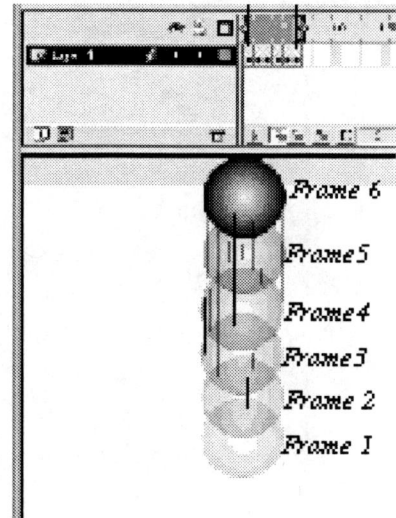

FRAME BY FRAME PROJECT

For the first part of this project you will create a 5-frame animation where a ball begins in the center of the stage then moves (frame by frame) to the top. The purpose of this project is to experiment with the timeline in Flash and produce a simple frame by frame

The Project

Tool Palette

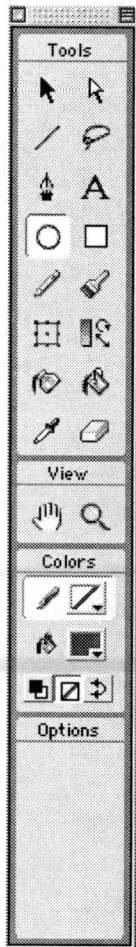

Setting Fill & Line Color

animation of a bouncing ball. This will also give you an opportunity to explore some of the basic procedures used in Flash.

❑ With the Flash application running and your panels set to Designer(1024x760).

❑ Select the oval tool on the tool palette and note the color options available on the lower half of the tool palette.

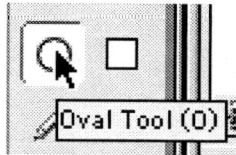

❑ Set the line ✏ to none ▨ (no line) and the fill 🪣 to red.

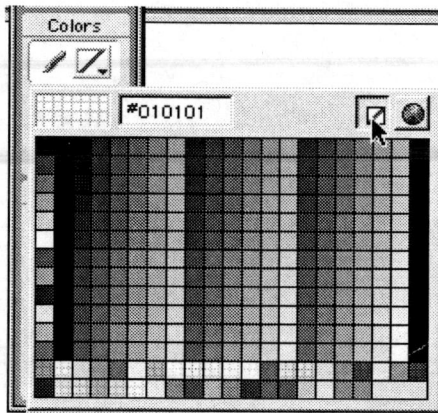

#010101

Select the color pop-out swatch, then choose from the available colors.

#FF0000

© Bradley Kaldahl 2003

❑ Draw a circle on the center of the stage.

To draw with the oval tool, click and drag diagonally on the stage.

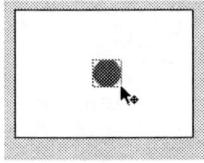

❑ Click on frame 2 of the timeline .

❑ Select the Insert-Keyframe command from the menu bar to insert a new keyframe.

Insert	Modify	Text	Contro
Convert to Symbol...			F8
New Symbol...			⌘F8
Layer			
Layer Folder			
Motion Guide			
Frame			F5
Remove Frames			⇧F5
Keyframe			
Blank Keyframe			
Clear Keyframe			⇧F6
Create Motion Tween			
Scene			
Remove Scene			

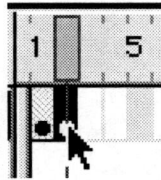

Note: The F6 Key can also be used to insert Keyframes.

❑ Select the solid pointer tool [↖] from the tool palette and drag the circle a little toward the top of the stage.

❑ Click on frame 3 of the timeline

❑ Select the Insert-Keyframe command from the menu bar. **Keyframe   F6**

❑ With the pointer tool [↖] still selected drag the circle a little further toward the top.

❑ Click on frame 4 of the timeline.

❑ Insert a new keyframe. (Select the Insert-Keyframe command from the menu bar.)

❑ With the pointer tool [▲] still selected drag the circle further toward the top.

❑ Click on frame 5 of the timeline.
❑ Insert a new keyframe.
❑ With the pointer tool still selected drag the circle to the top edge of the stage.

You have just completed your first simple animation in Flash.

Test the animation and see how it looks...

❑ Choose Control-Loop Playback.

TESTING PLAYBACK INSIDE FLASH

Control	Window	Help	
Play			↵
Rewind			⌥⌘R
Go To End			
Step Forward			.
Step Backward			,
Test Movie			⌘↵
Debug Movie			⇧⌘↵
Test Scene			⌥⌘↵
✓ Loop Playback			
Play All Scenes			
Enable Simple Frame Actions			
Enable Simple Buttons			⌥⌘B
Mute Sounds			
Enable Live Preview			

Control	Window	Help	
Play			↵

❑ Then choose Control-Play, to see the animation in progress.
You should see the ball appear to move to the top edge then abruptly jump back to the center of the stage. Ideally we would want the ball to appear to strike the top edge of the stage and then bounce back towards the center.

© BRADLEY KALDAHL 2003

❏ To stop the animation from playing choose Control-Stop *(or hit the return key on your keyboard).*

❏ Retouch the animation to create smoother movement. *You may need to click back on each separate keyframe to reposition the ball so there is an equal amount of space and the ball moves more smoothly.*

After tweaking and testing the animation:
Continue buildingthe animation so the ball returns to the starting point in the center of the stage.

❏ Click on frame 6 of the timeline and then, insert a new keyframe. Move the ball slightly back to the center of the stage.

❏ Click on frame 7 insert a new keyframe and move the ball further back towards the center.

❏ Continue this process until the ball has moved from the top of the stage back,to the center of the stage.

❏ Test the animation again to make sure it works properly. Choose Control - Play.

To add some interest to the animation use the following steps, to make the ball get larger as it moves to the top:

❏ Click on frame 1 to select the object at that point in the timeline.

❏ Use the solid pointer tool, ▶ click on the ball on the stage, then click on the Free Transform tool ⊞ on the tool palette. *(See diagram)*

RESIZING OBJECTS USING FREE TRANSFORM

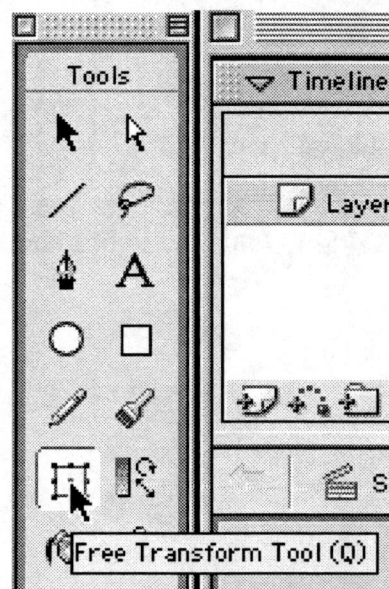

FREE TRANSFORM

ONION SKINNING

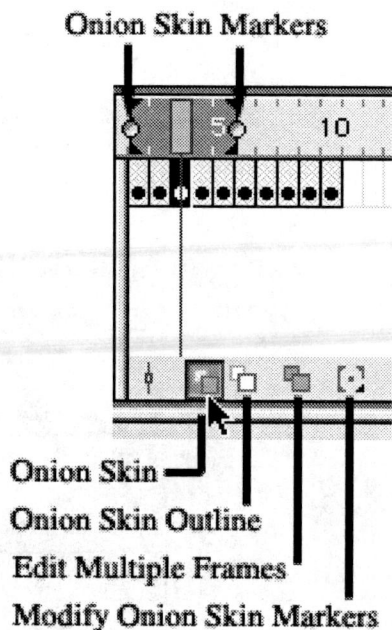

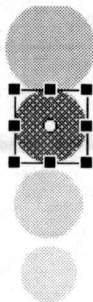

Onion Skin Markers

Onion Skin
Onion Skin Outline
Edit Multiple Frames
Modify Onion Skin Markers

❑ The ball object should now have resize handle bars.

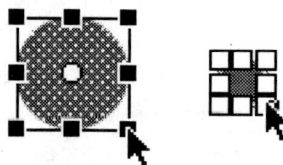

❑ Drag a corner handle in, to make the ball smaller.

❑ Click on frame 2, and use the Free Transform tool ⊡ to make the ball small but a little larger than frame 1.

❑ Continue by clicking on the next keyframe, then clicking on the ball on the stage, and using the Free Transform tool to make the ball a little larger in frames 3, 4, and 5.

By now you are most likely saying I wish there was some way I could see where the ball was in the previous frame to know where to position it or how big to make it in the next frame.
Onion Skinning: Have you ever worked with tracing paper, otherwise called onion skin paper? That is what onion skinning is about.

❑ Click on frame 3 on the timeline.

❑ At the bottom of the timeline window there are three different onion skin options.

Select the first option as shown.
With onion skinning turned on you can see several other frames that are lighter than the current frame.

❑ Select the modify onion skin markers button to change the settings. By default Flash uses onion 2, which shows the two frames before and after the selected frame. Change the setting to onion 5 to see the results.

© BRADLEY KALDAHL 2003
Frame by Frame Animation

❑ You can also grab and drag the onion skin marker handles to control which frames you are seeing.

❑ Try the onion skin outline button.

❑ To turn onion skinning off click the button again. *They toggle like on and off switches.*

❑ Finally the last onion skin option to try is Edit Multiple Frames. Using this option you can edit the ball on several frames at once without clicking through individual frames on the timeline. This is a great time saving feature when working with frame by frame animation but can also get a bit confusing because you can select multiple frames.
In the next three steps we'll use the onion skin feature to touch up the growing ball animation.

❑ Click on frame 3, choose the Edit Multiple Frames button, then select the Modify Markers button and set it to onion 2.

❑ With the pointer tool, click on any one of the balls, (make sure only one ball is selected) then select the Free Transform tool from the tool palette.

❑ Resize and reposition each ball until you are happy with the size and placement.

To finish the animation we want the ball to shrink as it moves back towards the center.

❑ Use onion skinning to assist with placement and repeat the previous steps to make the ball shrink as it returns to center.

❑ Turn onion skinning off, then choose Control-Play to test the movie.

Exaggeration Adds Interest
A part of what makes animation fun and more interesting is exaggeration. In the real world a ball would

Animation Technique: Exaggeration

flatten slightly when it strikes a surface. In the world of animation we want to exaggerate the impact.

If you have ever seen the Road Runner cartoon, when poor Wile E Coyote realizes he is about to blown up, his eyes become 3x's larger, and pop out of his head. When he falls from a cliff and hits the ground he sinks 3 feet into the earth. We intellectually know this is not real, but because it is animation it becomes more interesting. When the anvil falls and hits Wile E. in the head, if you watch this in slow motion, his entire body is almost flattened, and expanded sideways to emphasize the impact, and then of course he gets a bump on his head that raises two feet in the air. If we wanted a realistic image of a ball striking a surface we might grab the camcorder and film it. With animation we want to emphasize the unreal quality. In a way animation is the ideal medium for surrealism (beyond realism).

In this next step we will exaggerate how the ball would look when it strikes a surface.

❑ Select the **frame** where the ball appears to hit the bottom (frame 10).

❑ Click on the ball on the stage then select the Free Transform tool ⊡

❑ Stretch the ball so it appears to flatten when it Hits the bottom. See diagram.

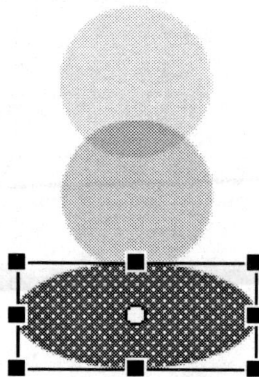

❑ After the ball hits the bottom and flattens it would most likely wobble. In frame 1 make the ball shorter and wider. Then in frame 2 give it less exaggerated flatten effect. See diagram.

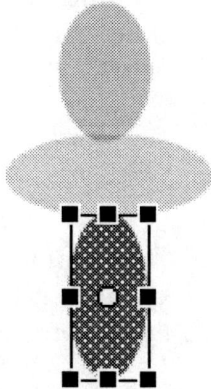

❑ Test the animation to see if the effect works.

❑ **Save this project** as "ball bounce" we will be using it in the next chapter.

WOW! we have just covered a huge amount of infor-mation, and if you are new to Flash you definitely need a break!

Take a few minutes to rest your mind. When you come back, before continuing on, take a moment to review this chapter (just skim it). These are the basics of working with Flash, creating objects, using the timeline, and adding keyframes, onion skinning to view object placement, testing playback and making revisions, resizing and exaggerating objects to create interesting animated effects.

After you have had a chance to review the chapter try one of the "Further Exploration" projects, to see if you are comfortable with the information covered.

Further Exploration:

1. Create an animation where a ball drops in from the upper left corner and bounces out in the upper right. Use onion skinning to help with placement. Use ex-aggeration to make it look as if the ball hits the sur-face hard.

USE FURTHER EXPLORATION TO IMPROVE YOUR SKILLS

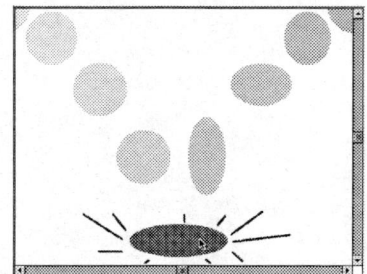

2. Create a 10 frame animation with a single line that appears to twirl. To make this effect work use the Free Transform tool ⊞ .

In each frame rotate the line a little further than the previous frame. Use onion skinning to help with rotation placement.

3. See if you can create a 2-frame animation of a bug that appears to be walking. You may use this animation later on when creating a game project.

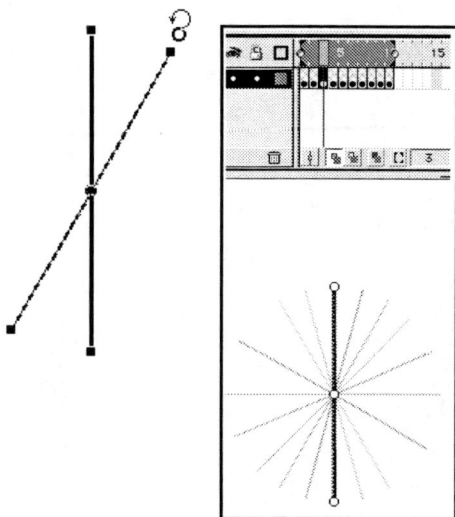

Basic Game Graphic

Some tips for creating a bug walking:
Create the bug object in frame 1 then choose Insert-Keyframe to create an exact copy in frame 2. In frame 2 use the eraser tool to remove the legs then draw them in their new position. Use the Lasso tool to select the bug's head, then use the free transform tool to rotate and reposition the head slightly. Use the Lasso tool to select the entire bug then move it up a bit to emphasize the body movement the bug might make when walking. Loop the animation to see what the bug might look like over several frames.

Remember the goal is to learn and have fun so, do not be afraid to experiment and try your own ideas.

NOTE: Later we will talk about how to take a 2 frame animation and encapsulate it into a movieclip. Once encapsulated as a movieclip it will continue to loop over and over and can then be animated using some of the techniques we will discuss in the following chapters. **Save everything that you produce!** It may be useful later on!

Frame by Frame Animation

This chapter will provide a brief intro to the palettes, tools, and features in Flash. A lot of Flash interface information is covered in this short project so take your time and make sure you are comfortable with these tools. This chapter does not provide a lot of action but it does provide important interface information.

❑ Launch Flash

❑ Choose the menu command Window-Panel Sets-Designer(1024x760).

❑ The first palette to explore is the Properties Palette.

FLASH PALETTES

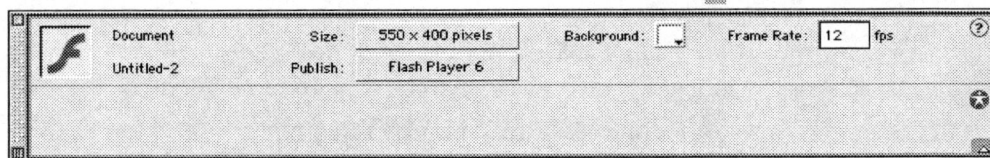

Document	Size:	550 x 400 pixels	Background:	Frame Rate: 12 fps
Untitled-2	Publish:	Flash Player 6		

❑ If your Properties Palette does not appear as shown above then choose the Expand / Collapse triangle (shown below) to expand the palette.

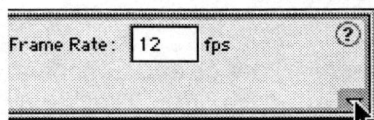

Frame Rate: 12 fps

Expand/collapse the information area

About the Properties palette: This is a new in Flash MX, and it makes sense. The Properties palette is context sensitive, meaning that it will change based on the tool you select and the object you select on the stage. When you want to perform a particular function you SHOULD find the options displayed on the property's palette. While there may be times that the

SETTING THE BACKGROUND COLOR

Tools

Solid Ponter Tool

Background:

CHANGING LINE THICKNESS USING THE PRPOERTIES PALETTE

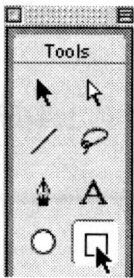

Tools

Tools

FILL VS LINE

function you seek is not displayed on the Properties palette, I expect that any missing features will be included in future versions of Flash.

❑ With the Solid Pointer tool selected, use the Properties palette set the background of this document to gray.

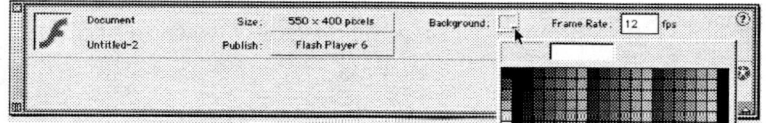

❑ Select the Rectangular tool ▢ from the Tool palette.

❑ Note that the Properties palette has changed.

❑ Set the line color to solid blue with a thickness of 10 points. Set the fill color to red.

❑ Draw a square or rectangle on the stage.

Understanding Flash Objects :

❑ Select the Solid Pointer tool

❑ Click on the center of the square.

• Note that when selected, it changes and appears to have a texture.

• Note that you can move the center "fill" independent of the "outline."
• If you moved the center red fill you can put it back to its original position by choosing Edit-Undo.

❏ Click ONCE on the RIGHT side of the blue line.
• Note that Flash does not select the entire outline but only one portion. It can be moved independent of the rest of the outline.

❏ CLICK and DRAG on the TOP edge of the line and note that Flash allows you to "bend" the edge. You can return it to its original shape by choosing Edit-Undo.

❏ Using the solid pointer tool, [pointer icon] drag around the object on the stage to select it (as shown in the diagram). You will know that the entire object is selected because it will have a texture.

Controlling Size and Placement.

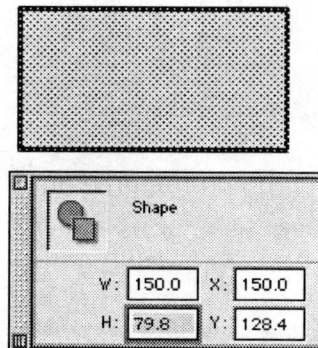

❏ Once the object is selected, look at the Properties Palette and notice the width w: and height H:.

You can use this feature to control the exact size of your object from frame to frame.

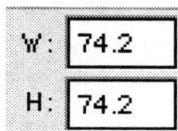

W: 74.2

H: 74.2

❏ Note the X and Y coordinate options.
Your X & Y coordinates will not match the diagram below but it is helpful to know that if you set both the X & Y to zero (0) the object should appear in the upper left corner of the stage.

VECTOR LINE EDITING

SELECTIONS WITH THE POINTER TOOL

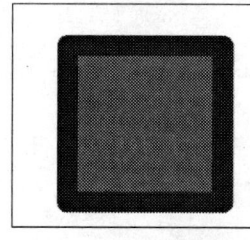

SIZE AND PLACEMENT

X & Y Coordinates

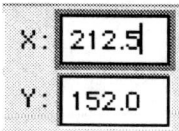

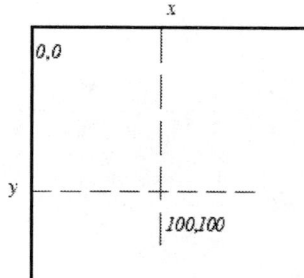

X: 212.5
Y: 152.0

x

0,0

y

100,100

Modify Fill & Line Settings with the Properties Palette

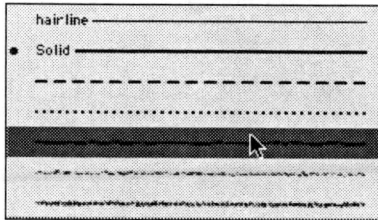

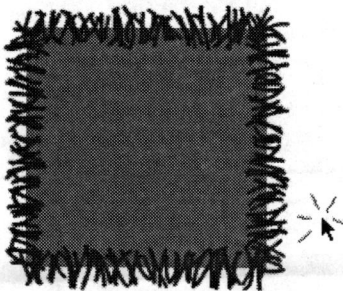

hairline
• Solid

If you increase the value of X the object will move to the right. If you increase the value of Y the object will move down on the stage. While this information may not seem significant now, later when you begin to work with Actionscript it will be helpful.

Changing the Line and Fill settings using the Properties palette.

❑ With the entire object still selected, look at some of the line settings available on the Properties palette; dashed, dotted ragged stippled and hatched.

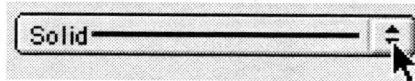

Solid

New in Flash MX— you have some limited control over how these line effects are applied.

❑ After selecting any line style choose the custom
Custom... button.

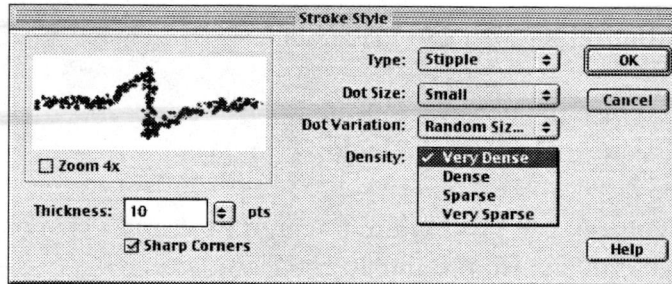

Stroke Style			
	Type:	Stipple	OK
	Dot Size:	Small	Cancel
	Dot Variation:	Random Siz...	
	Density:	✓ Very Dense	
☐ Zoom 4x		Dense	
		Sparse	
Thickness: 10 ⬦ pts		Very Sparse	
☑ Sharp Corners			Help

The options are cool but I would prefer to see sliders and a live preview rather than predefined pop-out menus but HEY, I'm not complaining, because it is better than what we had in Flash version 5.

❑ After applying a new line style you will need to accept the change by clicking OK then click on a blank area of the stage to actually see the effect applied.

Click on a blank area of the stage to see the effect applied.

Changing the fill.

❏ Using the solid pointer tool, [pointer] drag around the object on the stage to select it again.

❏ Select a GRADIENT FILL COLOR from the Properties palette.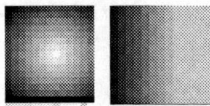

(What is a Gradient? A gradient is a transition from one color to another.)

Gradients will apppear as swatches with either a lighter/darker center or lighter/darker edge.

Modifying a gradient fill.

On the right side of your monitor there is an array of palettes. The Color Mixer is the third palette down (as shown).

❏ If it is not already selected, set the Fill Selector to Radial.

❏ With the object still selected on the stage, experiment with the inside color and outside color slider tabs on the color mixer to see the results.

Creating a Custom Gradient.

❏ To change the inside color of the gradient click on the inside color tab, then click on the color selector to pick a different color.

❏ To change the outside color of the gradient, click on the outside color tab, then click on the color selector and pick a different color.

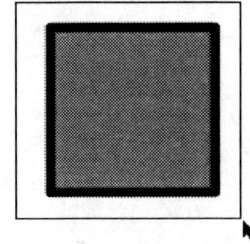

GRADIENT OPTIONS

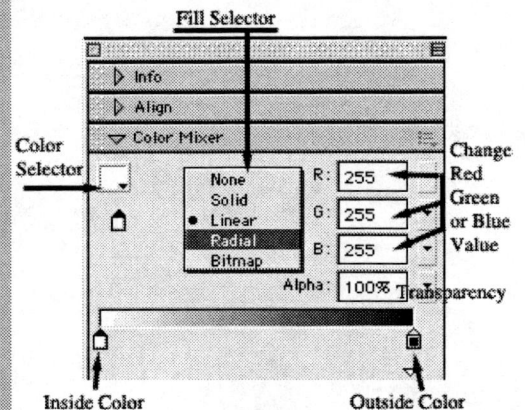

Inside Color

Outside Color

Exapand Color Mixer

Alpha Color

Alpha: 58%

❏ You can change the Alpha or transparency of any color to make it translucent.

Gradient Bar

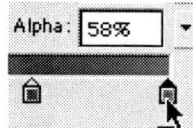

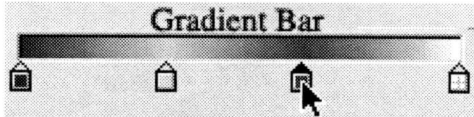

Gradient Bar with four color tabs.

❏ You can add additional color tabs to the gradient by clicking in the area below the **gradient bar.**

❏ You can remove color tabs by dragging them down and away from the **gradient bar.**

Saving a Custom Gradient

Saving a gradient

Once you create a gradient that you like you may want to save it for future documents.

In the upper right corner of the Color Mixer there is a light gray icon that produces a pop-out menu.

▽ Color Mixer

❏ Click on the pop-out menu and select Add Swatch.

▽ Color Mixer	
✓ RGB	
HSB	
Add Swatch	

✓ **RGB**
HSB
Add Swatch

❏ Now that you have added the swatch to the Color Swatches, click on the pop-out menu on the Color Swatches palette and choose **Save as Default**. This will add your gradient to the default color swatch's palette and make it available for all future documents.

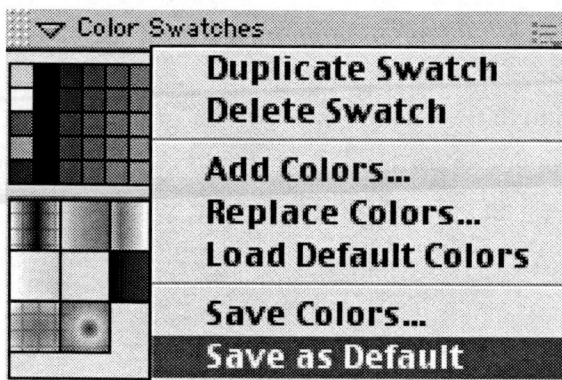

▽ Color Swatches

Duplicate Swatch
Delete Swatch

Add Colors...
Replace Colors...
Load Default Colors

Save Colors...
Save as Default

Distorting a gradient

The following feature is new to Flash MX and is useful for creating certain visual effects with your gradient.

❑ Select the Fill Transform Tool from the tool palette.

❑ Click on the gradient until you see a circle around the object that resembles the following diagram.

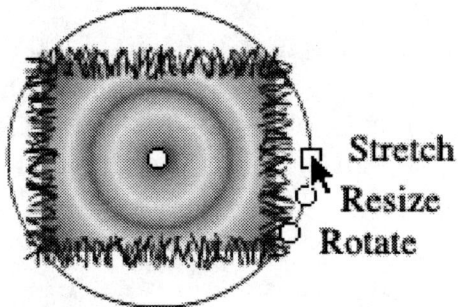

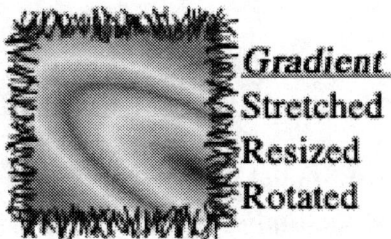

Stretch
Resize
Rotate

Gradient
Stretched
Resized
Rotated

❑ The Fill Transform circle has 3 different handles. The square handle allows you to stretch the gradient, the 2nd handle resizes the gradient inside the line, and the 3rd handle rotates the gradient.

Painting In Flash.

The last item to be covered in this chapter is painting. While Flash is a vector based program what I really enjoy is that you can create vector information in the same way that you would with a simple paint program.

PAINT TOOLS

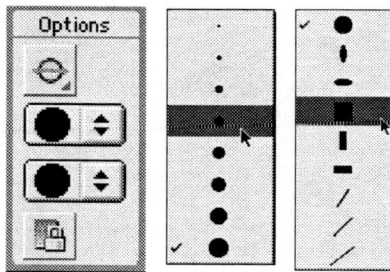

Options   *Size*   *Shape*

Effects

❑ On the tool Talette select the Paint Brush tool

❑ After selecting the paintbrush tool, look at the bottom of the tool palette to see the options for this tool. Brush Size, Brush Shape, and how the paint effects the object.

❑ Select your prefered brush size and brush shape.

❑ Experiment with the Brush effects. This is definitely not the kind of thing you can do in Photoshop.

We have covered a lot of information in this chapter and you have not had an opportunity to produce much content. Experiment with some of the Additional Exploration topics to discover more about the graphic tools provided in Flash.

Additional Exploration:

1. Create a graphic....
Bird, Fish, Frog, Dog, Desert Sunset, portrait, or other. Save your work, you may want to use it later.

2. See if you can use the gradient palette to create a short frame by frame animation of a sunrise or sunset.

3. Using the Paintbrush tool create a frame by frame animation that appears to grow over time. The animation can be of a plant, hair, tree, toenail or anything else that grows.

4. Create an animation where the outline of an object grows over time. You can accomplish this effect by setting the line thickness of an object from frame to frame over time.

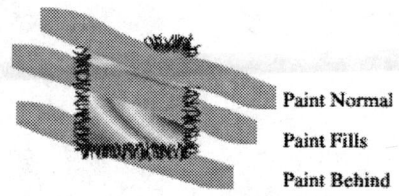

Paint Normal
Paint Fills
Paint Behind

Two Flash features that save time and make the animation process easier are symbols and tweening.

Symbols:

One of the reasons that Flash has become popular is the use of symbols which make the creation process easier. What is more important they dramatically reduce the final file size. Smaller file size means a shorter download time for the Web browser. Creating a symbol is easy and will be covered in this short tutorial. A symbol can be used 100 times in the animation, **but** when the final product is distributed on the web, the Flash plug-in only needs to download the original symbol once.

Tweening:

Tweening is common in most sophisticated animation applications. Historically when producing something like a Disney animation, the primary artist would produce the key frames of the animation. For a ten second animation there might be twenty or more key frames that would capture the most critical points of the animation. Then an aspiring animation artist, or "Tweener," would produce the frames in-between the key frames. Computer tweening is by no means as sophisticated as an aspiring animation artist. Tweening will not take two pictures of a person who is walking, and change leg, arm, and head position to create the in-between frames. On the other hand, if you have a ball symbol on the left side of the stage, then insert a keyframe on frame 10 with the ball symbol on the right side of the stage, Flash can generate the transition frames in-between. This is only one example of the power of tweening, as you will see in the chapters that follow.

ANIMATION TECHNIQUES WITH SYMBOLS AND TWEENING

THE PROJECT

❏ Launch Flash, create a new document.

❏ Choose Window-Panel Sets-Designer [1024x768] to rearrange the palettes.

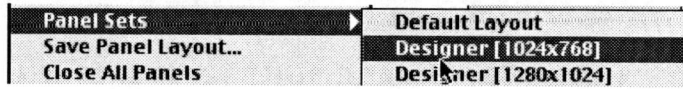

Panel Sets	Default Layout
Save Panel Layout...	Designer [1024x768]
Close All Panels	Designer [1280x1024]

❏ Create a ball object on the stage.

❏ Click on frame 1 in the timeline to select the ball. *Clicking on the key frame will select both the fill and the line for the ball.*

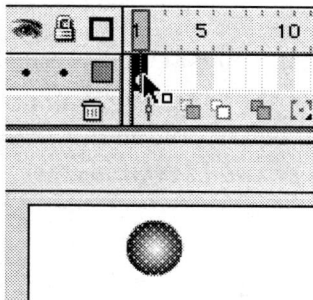

❏ With the ball object selected choose Insert-Convert To Symbol...

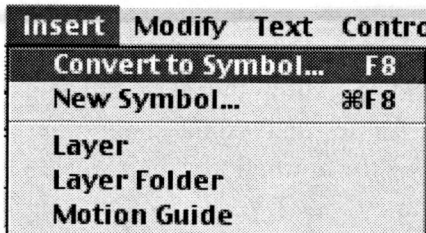

Insert	Modify	Text	Contro
Convert to Symbol...	F8		
New Symbol...	⌘F8		
Layer			
Layer Folder			
Motion Guide			

Note: If your Convert to Symbol dialog looks different from the example shown then click on the Basic button. [Basic]

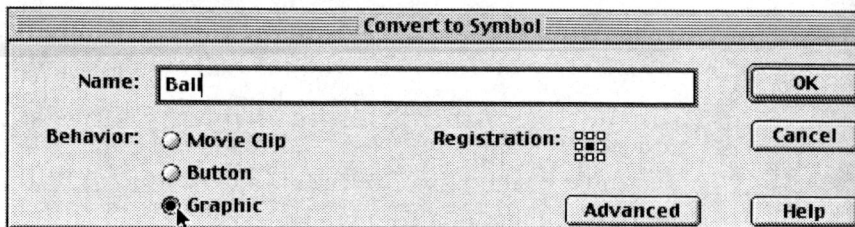

CREATING A GRAPHIC SYMBOL

Convert to Symbol

Name:	Ball		OK
Behavior:	○ Movie Clip	Registration:	Cancel
	○ Button		
	● Graphic	[Advanced]	Help

❑ Enter a name for the symbol and choose graphic, then hit OK.
Note: Flash has 3 different types of symbols, graphic, button, and movieclip. Later chapters will cover the other symbol types.

Once converted into a symbol its appearance on the stage changes. It is contained in a light blue box and also has a center point.

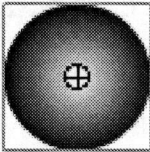

❑ Delete the ball from the stage, by selecting at with the pointer and using the Delete key on your keyboard.
Converting an object into a graphic symbol also places a copy of the symbol in the Flash library.

❑ Select the Window-Library menu, to display the library palette and to view the symbol.

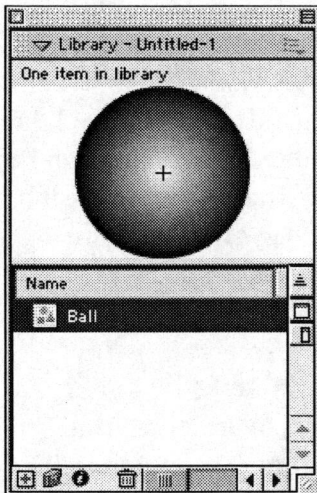

About the symbol editor: Because the ball is saved as a symbol it cannot be edited on the stage. To edit the ball you would need to open it in the symbol editor.

ACCESSING SYMBOLS FROM THE LIBRARY

Window	Help	
New Window		⌥⌘N
✓ Tools		⌘F2
✓ Timeline		⌥⌘T
Controller		
Properties		⌘F3
✓ Answers		⌥F1
Align		⌘K
✓ Color Mixer		⇧F9
✓ Color Swatches		⌘F9
Info		⌘I
Scene		⇧F2
Transform		⌘T
Actions		F9
Debugger		⇧F4
Movie Explorer		⌥F3
Reference		⇧F1
Output		F2
Accessibility		⌥F2
Components		⌘F7
Component Parameters		⌥F7
Library		F11
Common Libraries		▶

THE SYMBOL EDITOR

To enter the symbol editor, double click on the graphic symbol in the library or double click on the ball on the stage. You can tell you are in the symbol editor by looking at the left corner, of the main window, below the Timeline.

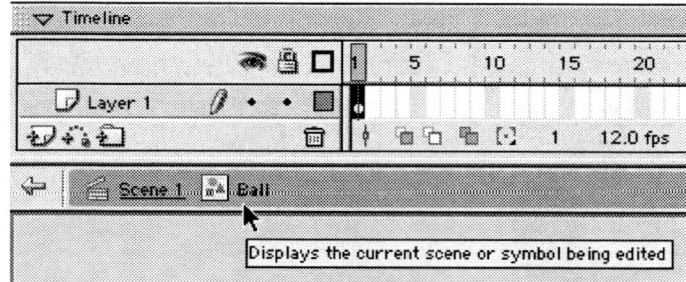

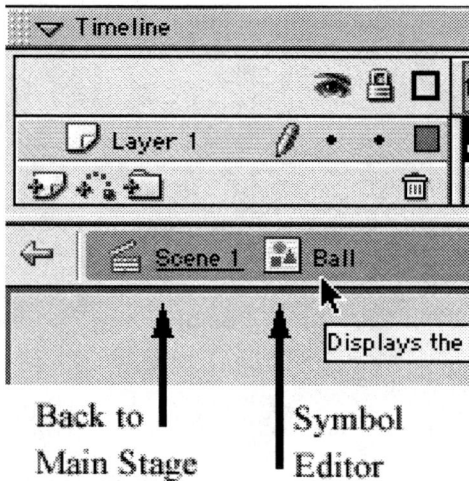

To exit the symbol editor, click on the Scene1 button. This will take you out of the symbol editor and back to the main animation stage.

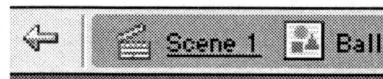

Back to Main Stage | **Symbol Editor**

Important: If you are working in Flash and it appears that your animation has vanished, look below the time line to see if you accidentally entered the symbol editor. It is one of those things that can be disconcerting while you are first learning Flash but will become second nature as you grow more comfortable with this application.

Tweening: Flash will generate the transition frames in between two keyframes.

❑ On the main animation stage drag the "Ball" graphic symbol from the Library palette onto the left edge of the stage.

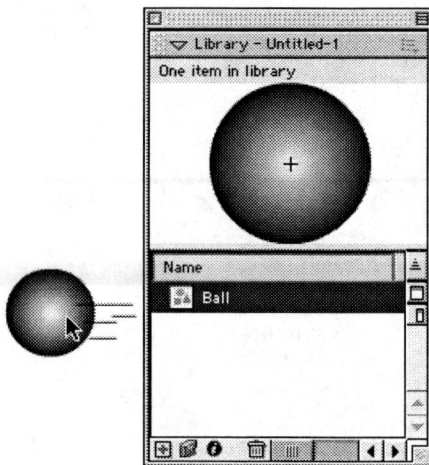

Symbols & Tweening

❏ Once the graphic is in place on the stage, click on frame 10 in the timeline.

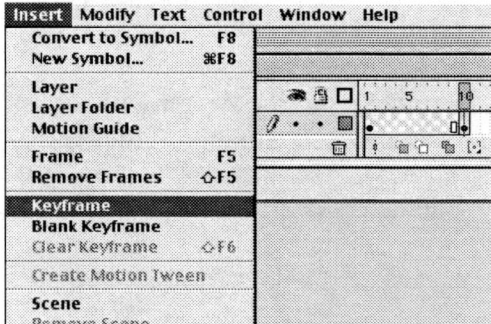

❏ Choose Insert-Keyframe, to insert a new keyframe at frame 10. See diagram.

❏ With frame 10 still selected drag the ball (which is on the stage) to the right edge of the stage.

❏ Click on keyframe 1 and you'll note that the ball returns to the left edge of the stage.

❏ With frame 1 highlighted select the Property palette.

❏ Select the tweening pop-out menu and select Motion. *Note: We will discuss the motion tween ooptions later.*

❏ After tweening has been turned on, you should now see an arrow between keyframe 1 and 10 on the timeline.

❏ Select Control-Play to test the animation.

MOTION TWEEN

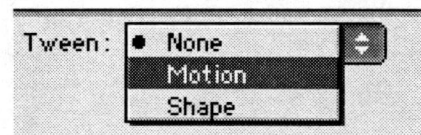

TWEENING SIZE

Important: In order to create a MOTION tween the object MUST be a SYMBOL.

Any of the 3 Symbols (graphic, button or movieclip) can be used for a motion tween.

If you attempt to create a motion tween with an object that is not a symbol the timeline will display a "broken tween" [broken tween image] in order to let you know there is a problem.

A working motion tween displays in blue with an arrowhead at the end of the tween. [motion tween image]

Changing Size over time.

❑ Click once on frame 10 in the Timeline.

❑ Choose the Free Transform tool [:]

TWEENING COLOR AND TRANSPARENCY

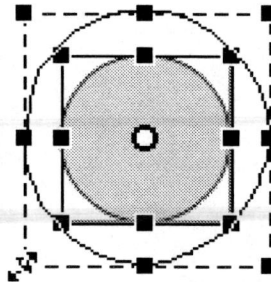

❑ Use the handle bars that appear around the object to increase the size.

Changing Color over time.

❑ With the Properties palette visible, Select the Color tab.

© BRADLEY KALDAHL 2003

❏ Select a tint color and set the transparency to 25%.

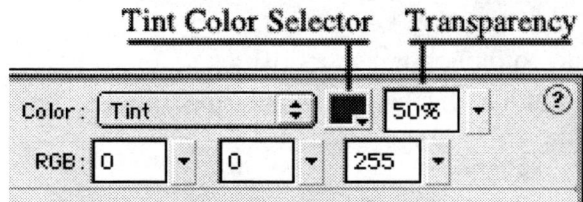

Tint Color Selector   Transparency

Color: [Tint] ▲▼ ■▼ [50%] ▼   ⑦
RGB : [0] ▼   [0] ▼   [255] ▼

RGB sliders to tweek the color

❏ Play the Animation again.
Remember you can loop the animation by selecting the command from the Control menu.

❏ Experiment with some of the other effects options, size, and rotation before closing this project.

SAVE EVERYTHING!! Anything you create or produce in Flash should be saved, no matter how simple. Later we will discuss how you can re-use symbols and animations.

A simple ball moving from left to right may not seem like much now, but later, when saved as a movie clip and combined with animated type and images, it may add an element of interest and be exactly what you are looking for. I frequently find that simple experimental animations are exactly what I need to compliment a complex project. Rather than recreate that simple animation over from scratch it is quicker to re-use pieces from previous works.

Additional Exploration:

1. Create a new graphic symbol.
If you are successful it should appear in your library palette.

ADDITIONAL EXPLORATION

ADDITIONAL EXPLORATION

2. Create a tweened animation where the object remains static but fades in and out over time.

3. Create an object that starts off small and semi-transparent and grows in size and opacitity until it covers the entire stage.

4. Create type fading in and changing color as it moves from the bottom to the top of the stage.

5. Import a PNG or JPEG scanned image. Convert it into a graphic symbol. Use the Transform tool to make the image change size over time.

If you are not sure how to create a PNG image in either Photoshop or Fireworks then use the tutorial provided in the last section of this book.

6. Using the imported image from above, use the colors options on the Property palette to make the image change color and transparency over time.

CHAPTER 5

Shape Tweens

You are going to love this feature! It is so wild!

This short project explores a feature called Shape Tween. Shape tweening can produce organic transformations from one object to another. I encourage you to explore and experiment with this feature. I have seen some incredible art produced using this technique. You do need to be aware that very complex shape tweens (or multiple shape tweens) can slow your user's computer, especially older computers.

In the previous chapter we converted the "raw vector object" into a symbol to create a motion tween. The shape tween is different. In order to create a shape tween the object MUST NOT be a SYMBOL. Shape tweens only work with raw vector graphics. When the shape tween is created correctly you will see a green background on the timeline ▮⬚⬚⬚⬚⬚▮ and a solid arrow between the two keyframes. If there is a problem with the shape tween you will see a dashed line on the timeline. ▮- - - - - - - -▮

❑ Launch Flash and create a new document.

❑ Choose Window-Panel Sets-Designer [1024x768] to rearrange the palettes.

Designer [1024x768]

SHAPE TWEEN

THE PROJECT

❑ Use the Properties palette (at the bottom of your screen) to set the background color of the stage to black.

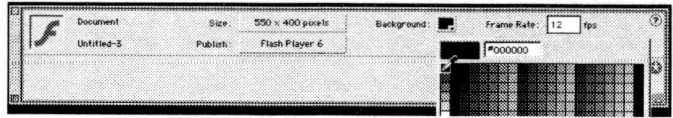

PENCIL TOOL OPTIONS

❑ Select the pencil tool ✏ and choose bright green as the line color ✏ ▢ and smooth as the pencil option ⌇, as shown in the diagram.

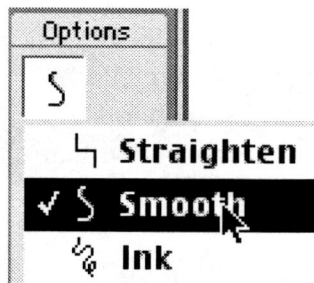

❑ Draw a simple object in the upper left corner of the stage, such as the example shown below.

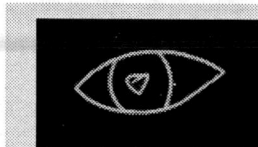

Remember that you can change the line thickness and stroke style using the Properties palette.

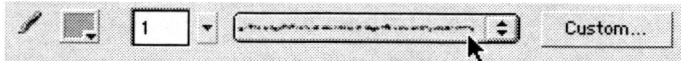

TIMELINE SHORTCUTS

F6 adds a normal keyframe and the F7 adds a blank keyframe.
Control-click *on the timeline with the Mac or* **Right-click** *on the timeline with the PC, to display a menu of timeline options.*

❑ Click on frame 20 of the timeline then insert a **blank** keyframe at frame 20.

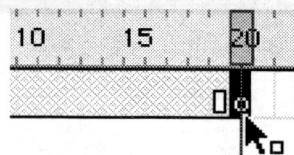

© BRADLEY KALDAHL 2003

Shape Tweens

❑ With frame 20 selected (in the timeline) draw an unfilled circle in the lower right corner of the stage.

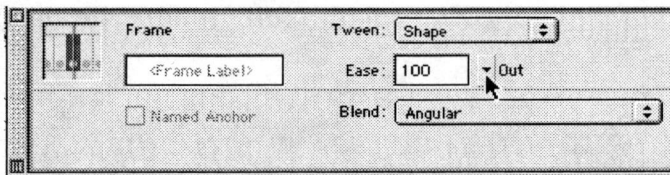

Turn the fill option off and change the line color and thickness for the circle using the Properties palette.

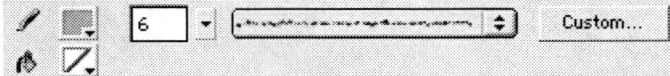

SHAPE TWEEN COMMAND

❑ Select frame 1 in the timeline. In the Properties palette set the tween to Shape.

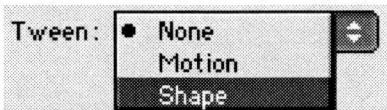

❑ Choose Control-Play to test the animation.

❑ Experiment with the Ease and Blend options to see if you can note the effect.

EASE AND BLEND TWEEN OPTIONS

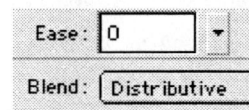

You may be asking yourself. "This is great but can I do it with a scanned photograph?" The answer is "no, BUT" if you can convert your scanned bitmapped image into a vector then a shape tween is not only possible but also graphically enticing. In a later chapter we will discuss how to use Flash to convert a scanned image into vector format.

Tweening Tips

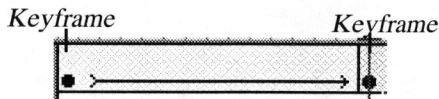

Keyframe   Keyframe

Arrow indicates tween
Blue = Motion
Green = Shape

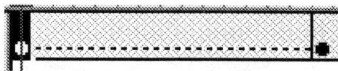

A motion tween was applied when the objects were not symbols

Shape vs. Motion Tween

Use Motion tweening when you need a controlled change from keyframe to keyframe. If you are changing the object's position, size, rotation, or color you should use the motion tween, even if the object is not moving. Shape tween produces very organic but unpredictable in-between frames.

Additional Exploration

Flash provides different visual information on the timeline based on the type of tween that you use. A motion tween is displayed as blue with an arrow and a shape tween displays as green.

Tweens only work from keyframe to keyframe. The idea behind tweens is to produce frames IN BE-TWEEN 2 keyframes. If you ever attempt to create a tween and see a dashed line instead of an arrow the problem lies in either the beginning or ending keyframe. Motion tweening will only work if the object is a symbol whereas shape tweening will only work if the object is not a symbol.

The shape tween feature can produce some interesting effects. The fact that it is called a "Shape" can be misleading, especially when the alternative is called the "Motion" tween.

Additional Exploration:
Choose any of the following experiments to get familiar with shape tweens.

1. Create a shape tween between a solid line and a square.

2. Create a shape tween between the outline of a square and a hand drawn smiley face.

3. Create a 100 frame shape tween of a seed into a tree.

4. produce a shape tween from a cat into a dog (or vice versa).

5. Create a shape tween of the Sun into the Moon.

6. Draw a gradient circle on frame 1, insert a standard keyframe on frame 30. (This will copy the gradient circle). Click on frame 1 and use the erasor tool on the circle as shown. Apply a shape tween.

CHAPTER 6

Shape Tweened Type

If you worked with the additional exploration section in the previous chapter you may have tried to create a shape tween using type. Type in Flash is interesting: because it is not treated as a raw vector graphic, yet it is not a symbol either. To perform a shape tween the text must be converted into a raw vector shape by "breaking it apart." Once the text is broken apart it is no longer editable as type so you can no longer select it with the text tool and add in new letters. When type is broken apart it becomes editable as a graphic which means that you can apply gradients to it, paint or erase parts of the letters, or manually reshape the vector information.

CONVERTING TYPE INTO RAW VECTOR GRAPHICS

Gradients on Type

Paint or Erase on Type

Reshape Type

Raw Vector Type does not Rely on a Font

Project

Breaking type apart (or converting it into vector shapes) offers another advantage. As a vector graphic it is no longer dependent on the FONTS the user has on their computer. If you are using a few letters (or words) of an unusual font, you may want to "break" the type into a vector graphic to insure that they will display on your user's computer. The other option is to imbed the font outlines in your document, but that is a subject for another chapter.

Project:

❑ Create a new Flash document with a background color of white.

❑ Choose Window-Panel Sets-Designer to reset the palettes.

Designer [1024x768]

❑ Select the text tool from the tool palette.

❑ Note the Properties palette now displays type information.

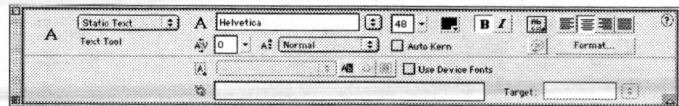

❑ Set the Properties palette to Static Text, choose the font you want to use, select a large point size, and pick a color for your font.

❑ Click on the stage (to set the insertion point) and type in your name.

❑ Select frame 30 on the timeline and insert a **blank keyframe**.
Remember you can Option-Click (Mac) , Right-Click (PC) or use the F7 key to insert the Blank Keyframe.

❑ With frame 30 selected click on the lower right corner of the stage (to set the insertion point) then choose the Properties palette and change the font and size.

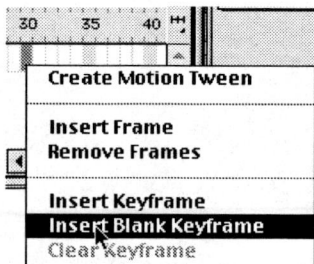

❑ In the lower right corner of the stage type in the word "Flash."

If you tried to perform a shape tween at this point the type would vanish after frame 1 and the new type would appear on frame 30. In order for Flash to produce a shape tween you will need to break the text apart, which is easy to do.

❑ With frame 30 selected choose Modify-Break Apart. See diagram.

Flash

This converts the type into individual letters.

Break Apart ⌘B

❑ Choose Modify-Break Apart again.
The type now appears as a vector graphic with a "grainy dotted appearance."

❑ Select frame 1 and choose Modify-Break Apart to convert the type into individual letters, then choose Modify-Break Apart again to convert the type into a raw vector graphic.

❑ With frame 1 still selected set the tween option on the Properties palette to Shape.

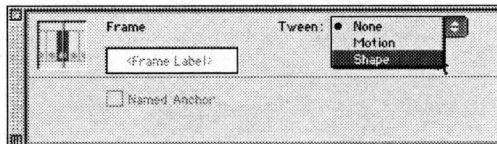

❑ Test the movie using Control-Play.
Shape tweening type Tips

CONVERTING TYPE TO VECTOR

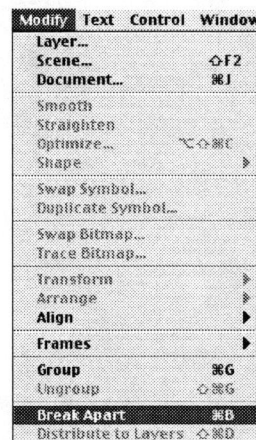

Note: Both Frame 1 and frame 30 must be "broken" converted in to raw vector graphics in order for the shape tween to work.

If you are changing the color of the type from the first to the second keyframe and the type vanishes or the tween is not as exciting as you would like try one of the following.

1. Use the same color in the first and second keyframe. Break the type apart so it is in vector graphic format. After it has been broken apart use the pointer tool to select the type in keyframe 2. Use the Fill palette to change the color.

2. Shape tweening appears to work better with lines than with fills. Sometimes the shape tween is not very interesting. Select the first keyframe, then select the pencil tool and set it to the same color as the type. Draw lines inside the type on keyframe. Keep the lines inside the type to avoid distorting the type. Select the ending keyframe, and with the pencil tool set to the same color as the type in the ending keyframe, draw lines inside the type.

Additional Exploration

1. Create a shape tween from type into an object.

2. Create a shape tween from an object into type.

3. • Create a 30 frame shape tween between type and a background image that covers the entire stage such as a "desert sunset".
• Test the movie to see how it plays.
• Click on Frame 15 in the Timeline and hit the F6 key to insert a new Keyframe in the middle of the animation.
• Test the movie again to see how it plays differently.

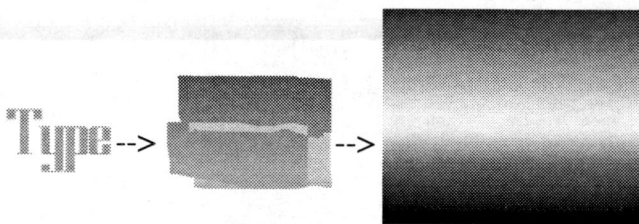

Type-->

-->

Shape Tweened Type

In this project you will create an explosion of light.

In the last two projects you worked with raw vector graphics creating shape tweens. This project uses a motion tween and therefore requires a symbol. If your fuzzy on creating symbols you want to glance back at chapter 4.

I have taught this project countless times and it still fascinates me. There is something about an explosion of light that is esthetically engaging. Light has always been such a powerful tool in the arts. I can imagine this technique being used to portray a brilliant mountain sunrise, an explosion in a web based game or a solar explosion.

Technically this animation downloads fast because it only uses a single graphic symbol. While it downloads fast playback speed will depend on your computer.

❑ Launch Flash and create a new document.

❑ Choose Window-Panel Sets-Designer to reset the palettes.

Designer [1024x768]

❑ Use the Properties palette to set the background color to black.

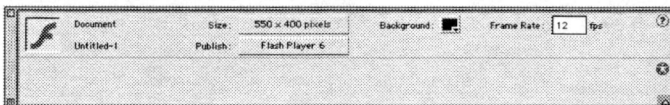

| Document | Size: | 550 x 400 pixels | Background: | Frame Rate: | 12 | fps |
| Untitled-1 | Publish: | Flash Player 6 | | | | |

EXTENDED MOTION TWEEN ANIMATION

THE PROJECT

❑ Select the oval tool on the tool palette ⬭

❑ On the Properties palette set the stroke to none.

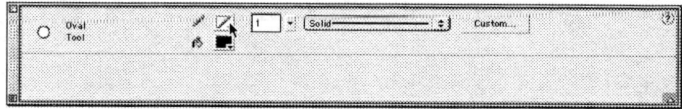

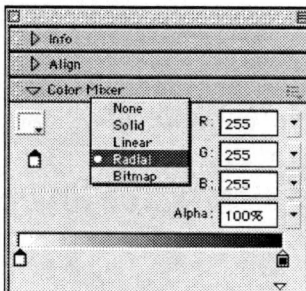

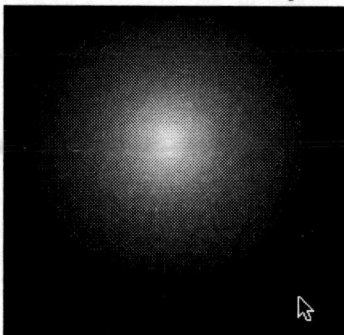

❑ Create a Radial gradient on the Color Mixer palette.
❑ Set the left color tab to white, this represents the inside color of the gradient.

❑ Set the right color tab of the gradient to black and set the Alpha to 0.

❑ Draw a circle on the stage. Hold the Shift key down while drawing the circle to make it symmetrical.

If all went well you should have a soft sun-like object on a black background. The fact that the outer black edge was set to transparent helps to soften the edges.

❑ Click on frame 1 of the timeline to select the object.

❑ Choose Insert-Convert to Symbol.

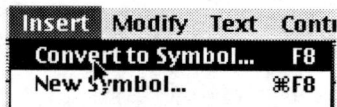

❑ Create a graphic symbol and name this symbol "Light."

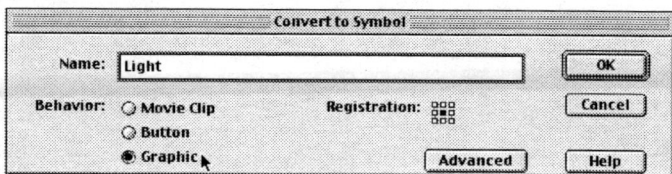

Exploding Light Animation

❏ With frame 1 still selected choose motion tween from the Properties palette.

Choose the Free Transform tool ⌖ from the Tool palette and make the graphic small on the stage.
At the beginning of the animation we want the light to appear as a small dot.

❏ Insert a keyframe at frame 20.

❏ With the Free Transform tool ⌖ still selected make the graphic a little larger on the stage.
The idea is that from frame 1-20 the light will slowly grow in size then explode quickly from frame 20-35.

Creating the Explosion
❏ Insert a keyframe at frame 35.

In the upper right corner of the stage there is a pop-out menu that allows you zoom-in or zoom-out on the size of the stage.

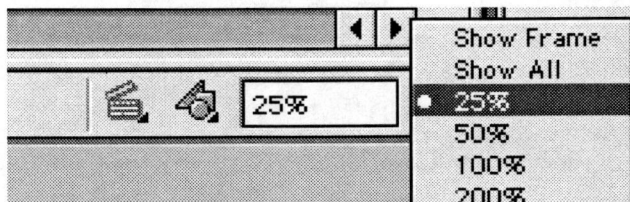

❏ Set the stage size to 25%.

❏ With frame 35 still selected use the Free Transform tool, and increase the size of the light graphic until it completely covers the stage (or larger). Make the graphic wider as well.

❏ Insert a keyframe at frame 60.

❏ With the Free Transform tool still selected drag the upper **left** graphic handle to the upper **right** corner of the stage as shown in the diagram. This will cause an interesting twist effect as the graphic gets smaller

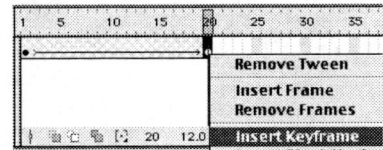

RESIZING THE STAGE

CREATING AN OBJECT LARGER THAN THE STAGE

CREATING A FLIPPED TWEEN

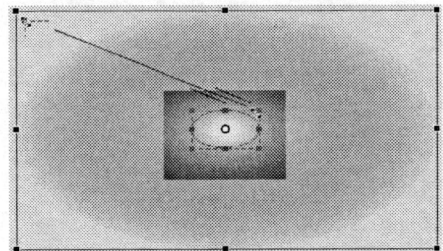

Control | Window | Help
Play   Return
Rewind   ⌥⌘R

Step Forward   .
Step Backward   ,

Test Movie   ⌘Enter

❏ Choose Control-Test Movie to have this movie display in it's own separate window.

❏ Resize the Test Movie window so it covers your entire monitor

❏ To exit the Test Movie player, after viewing the movie, click the close window button.

❏ See if you can add frames to the end of this animation so the sun object appears to slowly shrink back down into a tiny spot of light before it loops back into the explosion.

To make something appear to happen quickly use fewer frames for the transition but expect the transition to be more jerky. To make something appear to happen slowly use more frames for the transition and the transition will appear smoother. To have the sun shrink slowly you may want to add a new keyframe out at frame 130 or greater.

PLAYBACK SPEED

As long as we are discussing animation speed this is a good time to discuss Frame Rate, "frames per second."

Frame Rate: 12 **fps**

Under the Modify Menu-Document (or from the Properties palette) you can "adjust" the frame rate. This is a global setting that effects the entire movie and cannot be change during playback. You might assume that setting the frame rate to high number will guarantee faster playback but unfortunately this is not the case. A complex shape tween, will slow your frame rate to 12 fps or even lower depending upon the complexity of the tween.

REDUCING JERKY PLAYBACK

How can I get rid of the "jerky" playback?
You might notice the jerky appearance more than those who view our product. As an artist, you are working closely with your project and will likely watch it many times. As a result you will notice mi-

nor imperfections that the casual user will not. It is helpful to remember that the casual web observer will see your 10 second animation for 10 seconds. Another internet reality is that the user with the newer, faster computer will experience a better animation than the user with an older, slower computer. With some animations it might be possible to smooth out the animation by experimenting with Motion Trails, as discussed in a later chapter.

Additional Exploration:

1. Revolving Square.
Create a square that covers the entire stage. Convert the square into a graphic symbol.
Insert a keyframe at frame 30. Create a motion tween from frame 1-30. With Frame 30 selected use the Free Transform tool and drag the upper right corner to the upper left.

2. Shape to Motion Tween.
See if you can create a single layer animation that starts as a Shape Tween and eventually turns into a Motion Tween.

3. Fake 3D:
This is a great technique for artists, designers, Bryce users, or photographers who want to display their work on the web. It takes a 2D image and gives it the feel of 3D space. It transforms your artwork into a "visual experience." It allows you, as the artists, to focus the viewers attention on details that viewers might otherwise miss. You will enjoy this one.

❑ Select an image. It can be any type of image but should be large enough to cover the stage.

❑ Convert your image into the PNG-24 file format. If you do not know how to do this then see the last few chapters in this book which discuss using Photoshop or Fireworks to prepare image for Flash.

❑ Import the image into Flash using File-Import.

CREATING FAKE 3D
WITH A 2D IMAGE

Import...   ⌘R

Tween: None
Motion
Shape

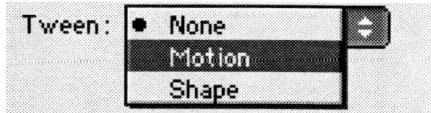

❑ Use the Free Transform tool ⊡ to resize the image to completely covers the stage.

❑ Click on Frame 1, and using the Properties palette,, set the Tween to Motion.

❑ Click on frame 30 and add a new keyframe. Resize the graphic on the stage and make it much larger. Reposition the image so the upper left corner of the image is covering the stage.

❑ Click on frame 60 and add a keyframe. Reposition the image so the upper right corner of the image is covering the stage.

❑ Click on frame 90 and add a keyframe. Reposition the image so the lower right corner of the image is covering the stage.

❑ Click on frame 120 and add a keyframe. Reposition the image so the lower left corner of the image is covering the stage.

❑ Click on frame 150 and add a keyframe. Use the Free Transform tool ⊡ to resize the image (make it smaller again) to completely cover the stage. Reposition the image so it closely matches the position of the image in frame 1.

❑ Choose Control test Movie to see how this effect works.

❑ Try rotating or disproportionately resizing the image to increase the visual impact.

Now that you have seen the basics of this Image Exploration project, create a new document and import your PNG image and create an animation that focuses the viewer on the important aspects and highlights of the image.

CHAPTER 8

Spinning Type

The spinning text project works with a motion tween. The interesting thing about type is that it does not need to be converted into a symbol in order to apply a motion tween. While it does not appear in the library, Flash recognizes it as an object.

❑ Create a new Flash document and set the stage color to black.

❑ Reset the palettes.

❑ Select the text tool [A] from the tool palette.

❑ On the Properties palette choose a font, size, and color (bright green is a good choice).

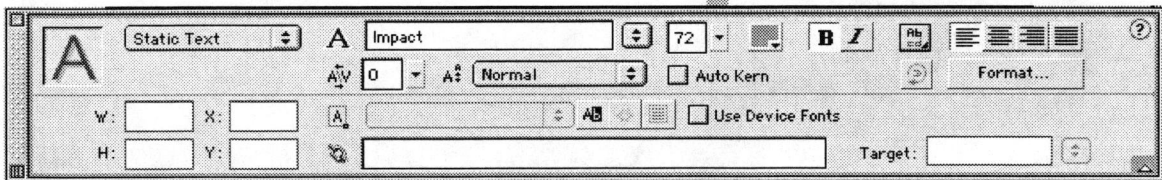

❑ Click on the stage, set the insertion point, and type in your name.

❑ Select frame 30 on the timeline and insert a keyframe.

Insert Keyframe

❑ Select frame 1 on the timeline.

❑ In the Properties palette set the tween to motion.

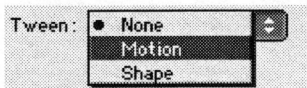

Tween: None / Motion / Shape

GETTING TEXT ON THE STAGE

Tween Options

Rotation

Ease

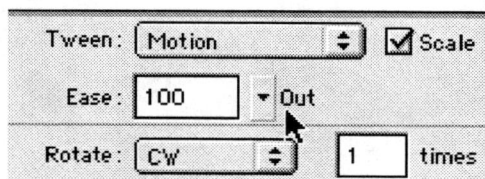

Center Point

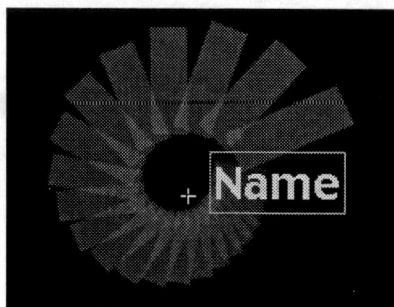

❏ Use the motion tween options on the Properterties palette and set the rotation to CW (clockwise) 1 time.

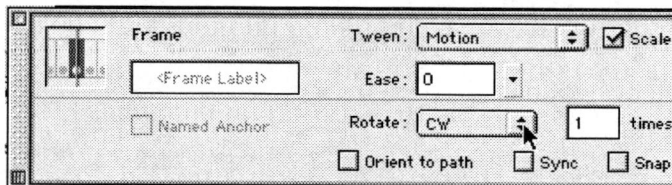

❏ Choose Control-Test Movie to see the effect.

❏ After testing the movie, click on frame 1 and experiment with the easing options on the Properties palette.

❏ With Frame 1 selected choose the Free Tranform tool ⊡ from the tool palette and drag the center point of the graphic to the left edge.

❏ Replay the movie to see the effect.

Additional Exploration

1. See if you can have the type animate across the stage while spinning.

2. Try to make the type grow larger while spinning, then shrink back down.

3. See if you can make the type fade in while spinning.

4. Make the type change color while spinning.

5. Create type that spins clockwise, then slows down, and finally spins counterclockwise, while shrinking and fading.

CHAPTER 9

Multi-Layer Animations

If you are following this book chapter by chapter then you should now be comfortable with the following...

• Keyframes, and tweening.

• The difference between a motion and shape tween and be able to distinguish the difference by looking at the timeline.

• The difference between a raw vector graphic and a symbol and know how to create a graphic symbol.

 • You should also be able to look at the timeline and see if the tween is working or has a problem and be able to problem-solve why a broken tween is not working.

Having some comfort with these foundatrion concepts you will want to expand and add complexity to your animations.

If this book (or course) is your first exposure to Flash then you will be delighted with the additional capabilities layers provide. I you have had previous experience with Flash then you may have been incorporating layers in your previous exploration of Flash and wondering why this book has not approached the subject. The obvious answer is that while layers are essential for complex animations they also add additional "layers" of complexity. *--Sorry for the bad pun.*

WORKING TWEEN

BROKEN TWEEN

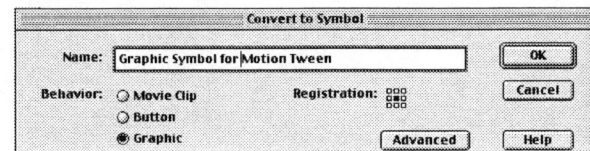

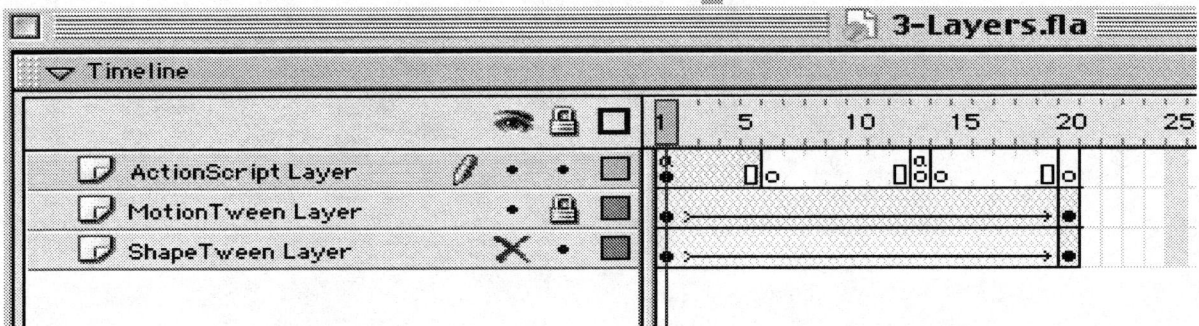

Since many Flash users are familiar with Photoshop the concept of layers is easy to grasp. On the other hand, if you are not familiar with Photoshop (or other applications that use layers), you will gain skills using Flash layers which will help you as you begin to explore other applications.

Flash uses layers in several different ways.

1. It is a way to help organize the parts of your animation into logical pieces.

2. It is a way to help position one object in front of another.

3. It is required to create multiple tweens in an animation. This is important. If you need to use several motion tweens each tween requires a separate layer.

4. It is a way to determine which parts of your movie will be streamed to a customers first, i.e. should they get the bottom layer first while the other layers download or should they get the top layer first.

The following shows many of the features of the layers section on the Flash timeline.

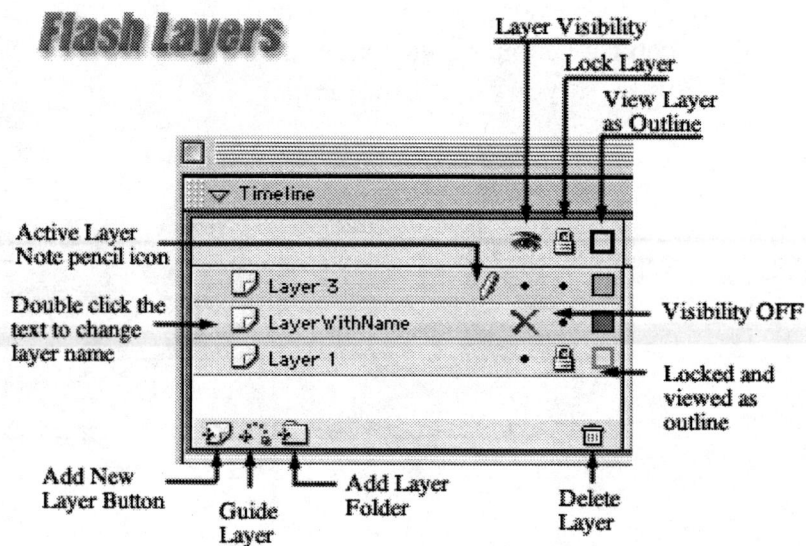

Flash Layers

Layer Visibility

Lock Layer

View Layer as Outline

Active Layer Note pencil icon

Double click the text to change layer name

Add New Layer Button

Guide Layer

Add Layer Folder

Delete Layer

Layer 3

LayerWithName — Visibility OFF

Layer 1 — Locked and viewed as outline

Set-up: Create a new Flash movie with a gray back-ground. A blue ball starts in the upper left corner and fades out as it moves to the lower right corner of the stage.

Set up step by step:
❑ Create a new movie

❑ Set the background color to light gray.

❑ Select the circle tool and create a simple dark blue ball with no line. Place the ball in the upper left corner of the stage.

❑ Convert your ball into a Graphic symbol.

❑ Check the library to make sure the ball exists as a symbol.

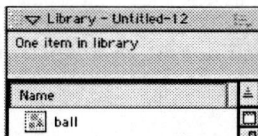

❑ Click on frame 20 of the timeline and add a new keyframe.

❑ With frame 20 selected move the ball to the lower right corner of the stage.

❑ With the ball selected, use the Properties palette to make the ball transparent in frame 20.

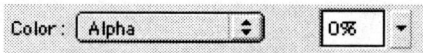

❑ Click on Frame 1 in the timeline then use the Properties palette. Create a motion tween between frame 1 and 20.

If you have problems with the previous steps refer to chapter 4.

You should now have a one layer animation that is 20 frames long where the ball symbol starts in the upper left corner and fades out as it moves to the lower right.

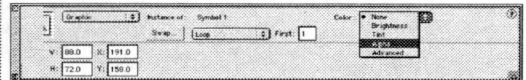

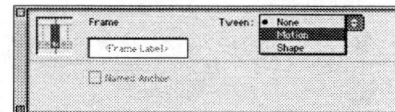

Naming Layers

Locking a Layer and Changing Its Visibility Visibility

Adding a New Layer

Adding Objects to a New Layer

Note: If you accidentally double click on the library symbol Flash will open the Symbol Editor. To exit the Symbol Editor click on the Scene 1 button below the timeline.

❑ Double click on the label of layer 1, until it becomes highlighted. Change the name to "BallLeftToRight".

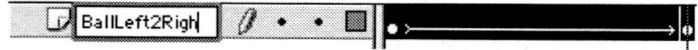

❑ Click on the visibility button for layer 1. *Turn off the visibility of layer 1 to make it easier to work with the objects we will create for layer 2.*

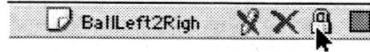

❑ Click on the locked button for layer 1 in order to insure that we do not accidentally modify the animation we have created there.

❑ Click on the insert layer button under layer 1 to add a new layer.

❑ Click on frame 1 in layer 2 (on the timeline) to make sure it is active.

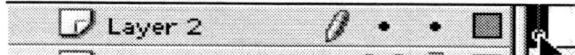

❑ Drag a copy of the ball symbol from the library to the middle of the right edge of the stage.

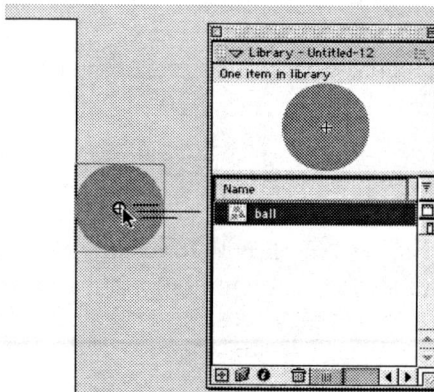

❑ Click on frame 20 of layer 2 on the timeline and add a new keyframe (F6).

Multi-Layer Animations

❑ With frame 20 of layer 2 selected drag the ball on layer 2 from to the left edge of the stage.

❑ Click on frame 1 of layer 2. Select the Properties palette and create a motion tween between frame 1 and 20 of layer 2.

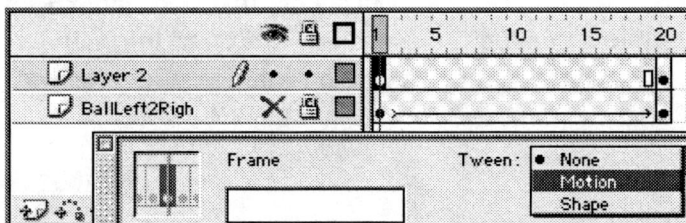

❑ With frame 1 of layer 2 still selected click on the ball on the stage, then choose the Color option from the Properties palette. Set the Alpha to 0%.

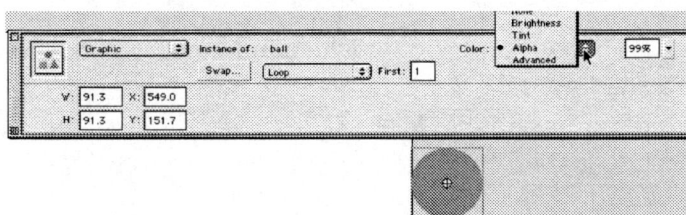

You should now have an animation on layer 2 where the ball starts at the right edge of the stage and is invisible and gradually fades in while it moves to the left edge of the stage, if not, work back through the previous six steps to create the animation on layer 2.

❑ Unlock layer 1 and make it visible.

❑ Test this animation.

If all went well the ball on layer 1 fades out as it moves from left to right, while the ball on layer 2 fades in as it moves from right to left.

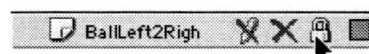

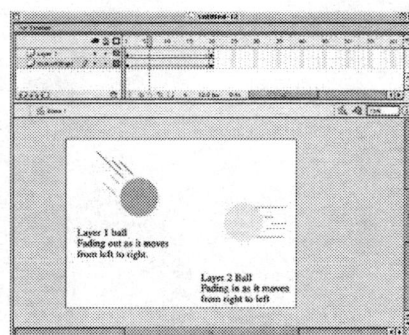

This has been a basic introduction to layer animation. While Flash is capable of tweening, it is important to remember that each layer can only contain a single tween. For example, to have multiple words tweening from different directions, each word must be on a separate layer. If you wanted individual letters to move onto the stage to spell out a word then each letter needs to be animated on a separate layer. Additionally you could have motion tweens on some of the layers while shape tweens are acting on other layers.

FURTHER EXPLORATION

BALL WITH SHADOW

Further Exploration:

1. Create a new layer in which the ball moves to the center by frame 10 then changes direction at frame 10 and exits the stage.

2. Create a new movie with a bouncing ball that has a shadow.
• Create a ball that looks 3D using the gradient tools.
• Use layer 1 to create tha ball bounce part of the animation.
•Add a new layer in order to create a shadow that follows the ball.
• After you get the shadow to follow the ball, work with the shadow to add realistic details. For example the shadow will be lighter and more difuse when the ball is higher and darker with stronger edges when the ball stikes the surface.

3. Create a new movie where two words come spinning in from different directions then drop into place to make a statement.

CHAPTER 10

Layer Explosion

A couple of students asked how to create a shatter or explosion effect with Flash. Since this is an interesting topic and illustrates the concept of synchronizing animation on several layers, I've created this project to demonstrate one possible approach. Of course, with Flash, there is a wide variety of approaches you could explore.

Photoshop users: the concepts covered here are very similar to what you might do in Photoshop if you wanted to create a series of images representing an explosion. First you would create an object. Then you would break the object into pieces, putting each piece into a separate layer. Then you would select each piece, on the different layers, and move them apart a little at a time to create a series of images of the object breaking apart.

To keep this project from getting longer than it needs to be we will use simple objects. I encourage you to walk back through this project later and try creating something more complex. There are some suggestions for further exploration at the end of the chapter.

SET UP

❑ Create a new Flash Document and reset the palettes to Designer 1024 x 768.

❑ Create a circle object filled with red and the line set to none.

Using the Lasso Tool

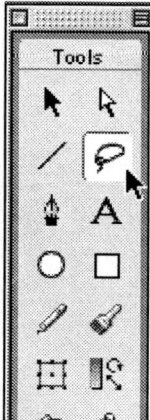

❏   Select the lasso tool and divide the circle into quarters. See example.

❏   Use the pointer tool [pointer] and select one chunk of the circle, as shown in the example below.

❏   With the one chunk selected choose Insert-Convert To Symbol.

❏ Name the selected graphic in a manner that helps to remember its location, such as "leftChunk".

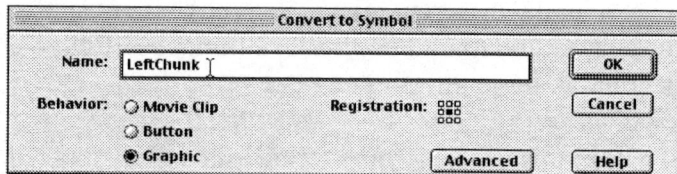

Convert Each Piece Into a Symbol

❏   Repeat the process with the remaining three chunks of the circle. Give each chunk a name that will help you identify its location or purpose.

❏ After all the pieces are converted to symbols, select and delete all the items on the <u>stage</u>.
❏ Do not delete items in the library palette.

❑ Create 3 new layers on the timeline, as shown.

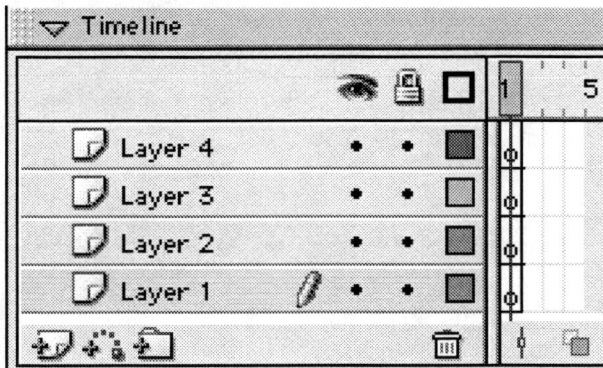

Put a separate symbol (chunk of ball) onto each separate layer as described in the following steps.

❑ **Make layer 1 active** (by clicking on frame 1 of layer 1) and drag the "left chunk" onto the stage.

❑ **Make layer 2 active** (by clicking on frame 1 of layer 2) and drag the "top chunk" onto the stage.

❑ **Make layer 3 active** and drag the "right chunk" onto the stage.

❑ **Make layer 4 active** and drag the "bottom chunk" onto the stage.

❑ Select the pointer tool and reassemble the circle. *You may need to use the directional keys on the keyboard to nudge the pieces into the correct position.*

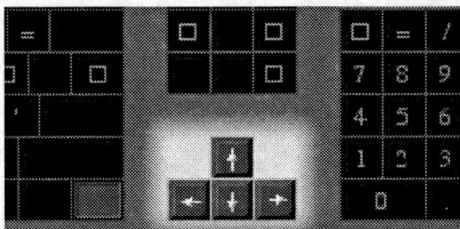

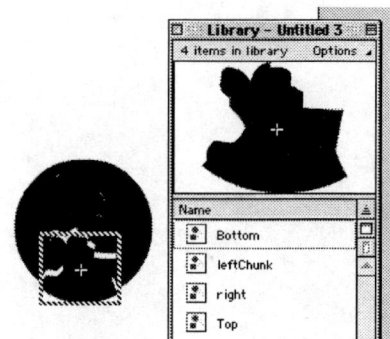

Review: The circle was broken apart, each part converted to a symbol, each symbol placed on a separate layer and then the circle reassembled.

©BRADLEY KALDAHL 2003

MULTI-LAYER KEYFRAMES

❑ Click on frame 40 of layer 4. Hold down the SHIFT key and click on frame 40 of layer 1.
This should have the effect of selecting frame 40 for all the layers at once.

❑ Select Insert-Keyframe from the menu-bar (or F6). Your timeline should now look like the example shown.

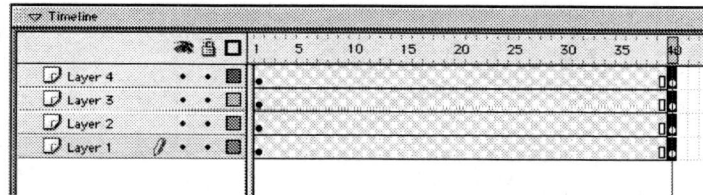

❑ Select the first frame of layer 1 and set the Properties palette to motion tween, as shown below.

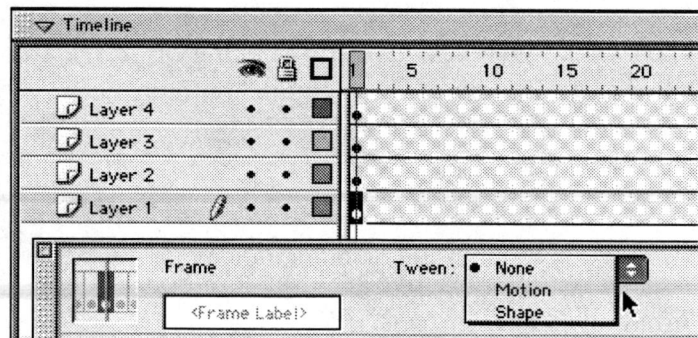

❑ Repeat the above step for the other 3 layers. *Select the first frame of each layer and use the Properties palette to create a motion tween.*

❑ Your timeline should look like the example.

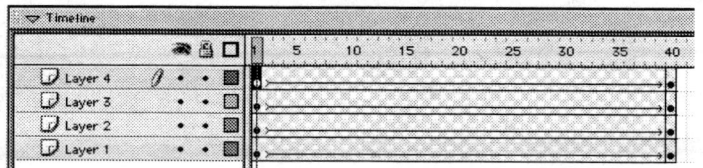

© BRADLEY KALDAHL 2003

Layer Explosion

❑ With frame 40 of layer 1 selected drag the circle chunk off the stage in the direction that you would expect it to move if it exploded.

❑ Repcat the above step (in Frame 40) for the remaining layers. As shown in the diagram below.

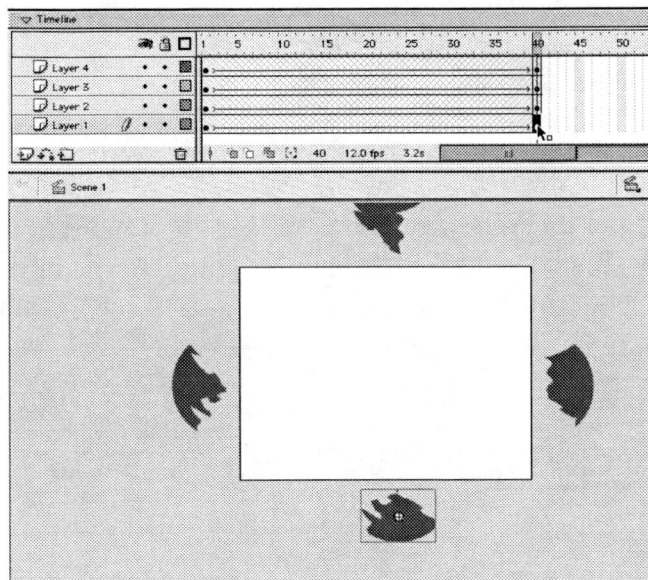

❑ Save this movie.

❑ Choose Control-Test Movie to see the effect.
If all went well you should see each piece of the circle moving outward from the center.

Additional Exploration:

1. Import a Photoshop Scanned image, use the lasso tool to break it apart, and repeat the steps in this project to create an explosion of the scanned image.

2. Try synchronizing the Solar Explosion with this project. Try to time the shatter effect with the solar explosion. To get the best results the solar explosion would occur on layer 1, and the objects will need to be on layers 2 or greater.

FIRST ATTEMPT AT ACTIONSCRIPT

You might be thinking that a complex explosion or shatter effect is going to take much time patience and layers! You are correct. This is the reality of animation. The consolations are that we can use tweening instead of hand drawing each frame and that with Flash we can convert this shatter effect into a movieclip, so it can be re-used, as will be discussed later. You might be thinking that a programmer could come up with an easier solution. This is partially true. A programmer with a solid understanding of physics, logic, high level math, and years of experience with computer algorithms might be able to develop code that could be re-used to create an explosion or shatter effect but the programmer would most likely spend more time developing the ActionScript code then it would take you to create the effect by hand.

3. Using ActionScript to stop a movie when it is done. To keep the movie from looping back to the beginning a bit of ActionScript can help.

Using the ActionScript stop ( ) command.
• Add a new layer to the timeline.
• Click on the last frame of the new layer and insert a blank keyframe.

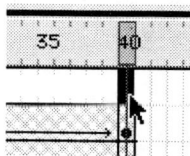

• Click on the new keyframe and choose Actions from the Window menu to display the Frame Actions dialog box, shown below.

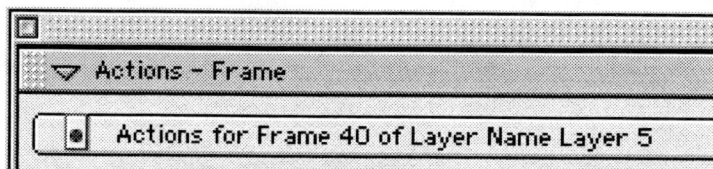

• In the Frame Actions dialog, click on the Movie Actions book to display the various movie actions. Click on Movie Control to display movie control actions. As shown.

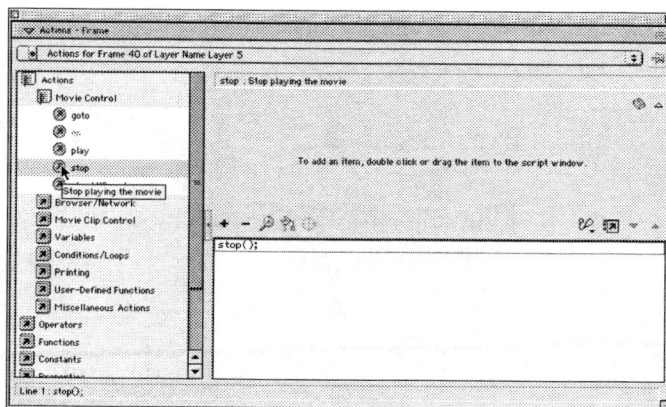

• Double click on the Stop action, shown above.
• Choose Control-Test Movie to see the effect.

This project explores a new feature that allows you to break a text object apart and distribute each letter to a separate layer.

❑ Create a new Flash document and set the stage color to black.

❑ Reset the palettes.

Designer [1024x768]

❑ Select the text tool [A] from the tool palette.

❑ On the Properties palette choose a font, size, and color (bright green is a good choice).
❑ Important: Select the "Use Device Fonts" option on the Properties palette.

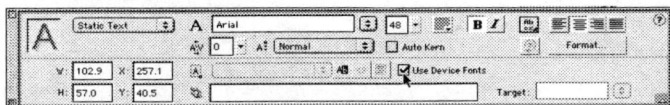

❑ Click on the stage, set the insertion point, and type in your name.

❑ Choose the menu command Modify-Break Apart.

Break Apart   ⌘B

❑ Now that the word has been broken into letters chose Modify-Distribute to Layers.

Break Apart   ⌘B
Distribute to Layers   ⇧⌘D

BREAK APART
DISTRIBUTE TO LAYERS

Break Apart   ⌘B
Distribute to Layers   ⇧⌘D

Flash MX provides 2 new features that can save a lot of time when producing this particualr effect.

UNDERSTANDING FONTS IN FLASH

Is type a symbol or a raw vector graphic? Type is not a symbol (at least not in the sense that it appears in the library pallete), but type is not a raw vector graphic either (as was discussed in chapter 6 "Shape Tweened Type"). A motion tween can be applied to type without converting it into a symbol but the type is dependant on the font in the viewers computer. To avoid error messages when the viewers computer does not have a matching font you can break the type apart into raw vector graphic format and convert each letter into a symbol, or use the option "☑ Use Device Fonts" on the Properties palette, or imbed the font in your document. To find out more about fonts in Flash choose the menu command Help-Using Flash, then do a Search for "Device Fonts."

Expanding the Timeline View

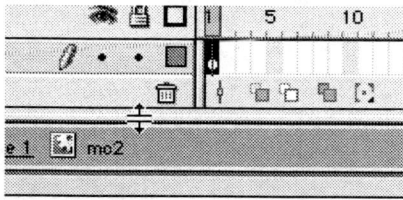

To see all the layers you may need to grab the bar between the Stage and the timeline and expand the timeline area, as shown.

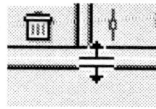

Applying a Tween to Multiple Layers

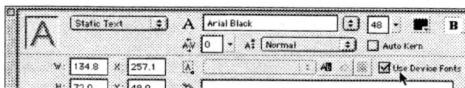

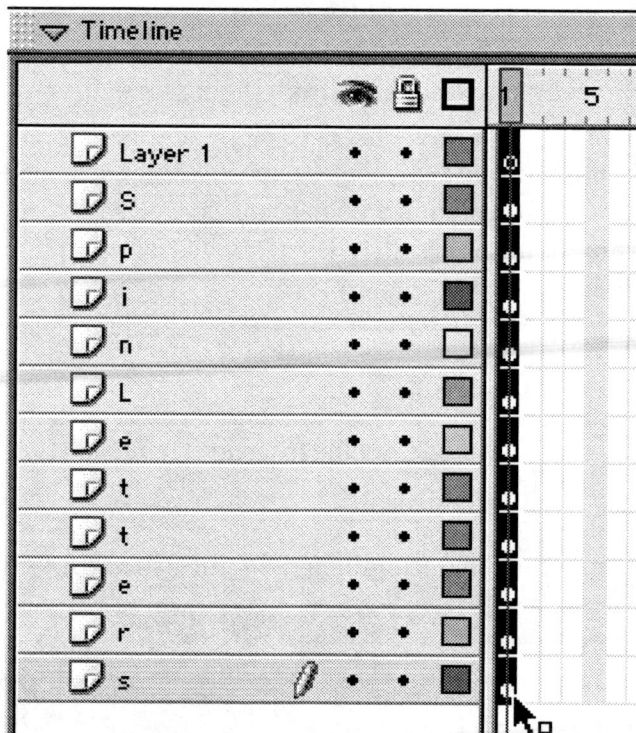

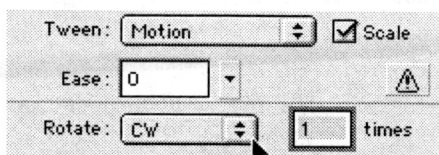

Applying a tween to multiple layers:

❑ Click on frame 1 of the top layer. Then, while holding the shift key down on the keyboard, click on the first frame of the bottom layer. This will select all the layers, as shown.

❑ On the Properties palette set the Tween to Motion, set the Rotate to CW (clockwise), and set the number of rotations to 1.

❑ At Frame 30 on the Timeline, click on the upper-most layer, then hold the shift key down and click on the bottom layer (at frame 30). This will have the effect of selecting frame 30 of all the layers at once, as shown.

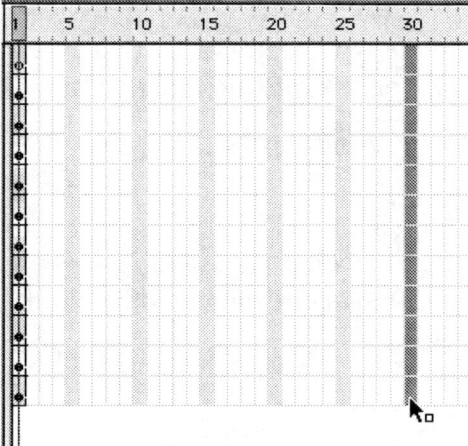

❑ With frame 30 selected on all of the layers, choose Insert-KeyFrame (or use the F6 key on your keyboard).

❑ Choose Control-TestMovie to see the effect.
If all went well then each letter should be spinning.

Spinning Letters

Additional Exploration:

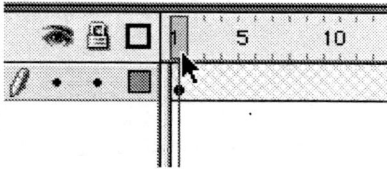

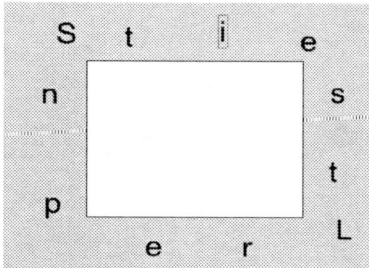

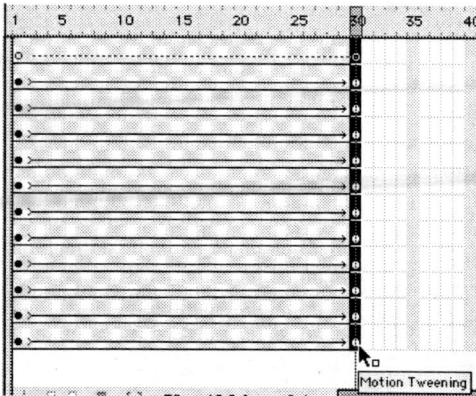

Multi-directional Spinning letters:
What if you want each letter to come spinning onto the stage from a different direction?

1. Select the Pointer tool from the Tool palette.
Click on frame 1 of each individual layer and drag the letter off the stage, see diagram.
(You can also click on the individual letter with the PLAYBACK head ▯ *positioned at frame one.).*

When you test the animation each letter will come spinning in from a different direction to form the word or sentence you created.

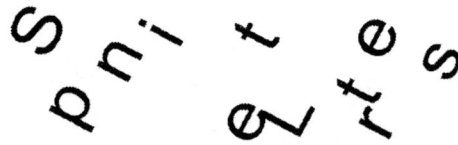

2. Pausing the animation using the Timeline.
If you did additional exploration (1) above then you may want the word to pause for a moment the allow the viewer a chance to read it.

• Select all of the layers at frame 30.
Click on the TOP layer of frame 30. Hold down the SHIFT key and click on the BOTTOM layer of Frame 30. This should select all the layers in frame 30, as shown.

• Select the Properties palette and set the tween to none.

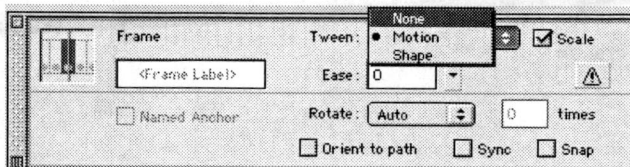

• Add a new keyframe at frame 50.

Click on the uppermost layer of frame 50, hold down the shift key, then click on the bottom layer, to select all of the layers at frame 50. Choose Insert-Keyframe (or F6) to insert a new keyframe. See diagram below.

Since the TWEEN has now been turned OFF the letters will remain static from frame 30 through frame 50. See diagram.

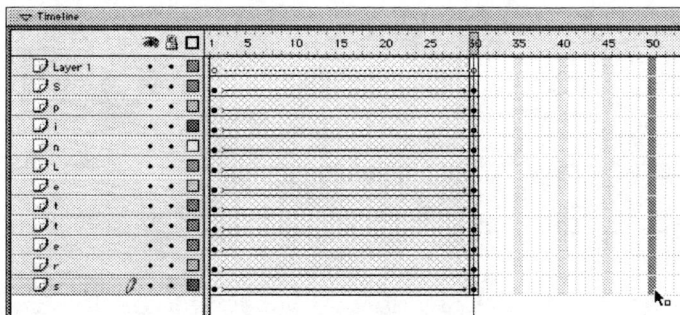

Additional frames without a tween

• Test the animation to see if it worked.

3. Creating a Layer Folder

Assuming that you like how everything is working on these layers you may want to create additional animation. Having multiple layers cluttering your timeline can make development difficult. Flash MX provides another NEW feature that allows you to take all the layers and drop them into a single "Layer folder". This removes clutter from the timeline and allows you to work only on the layers that need attention.

To take all the existing layers and place them in a layer folder try the following steps.

LAYER FOLDERS

• Click on the uppermost layer to make it active.

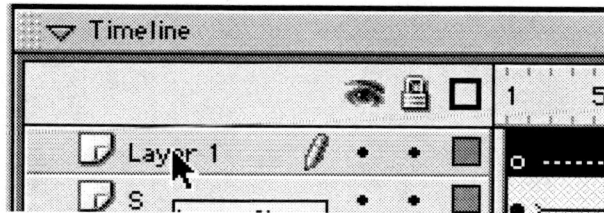

• Choose the Insert Layer Folder icon from the bottom of the timeline.

• You can click and drag each layer into the folder or shift click and drag several layers into the folder at once. Drag the layer/s on top of the new layer that is called Folder.

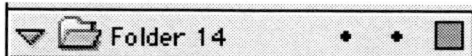

• Finally, to reduce the clutter on your timeline, click on the triangle icon ▽ to minimize ▷ the folder.

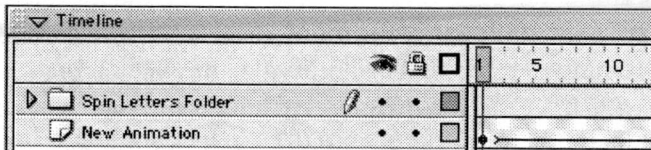

• At anytime you can click on the minimize icon ▷ to expand the folder.

CHAPTER 12

Timeline Sound

Sounds can add a new dimension to your Flash animation. Sounds can portray joy, sadness, mystery, excitement. or they can take us to other locations like a tropical island, a walk on a city street, or a dark damp subway station. Music can convey light and love or darkness and passion. Combine the right sound with your animation and the possibilities are limitless. Adding sound to your Flash animation can transform it. Choosing the right background sound can capture the mood you are trying to convey. The ability to combine sound with your visual art is an art form in and of itself.

In this chapter we will be using a "sound loop" to add impact to your visual art. What is a sound loop? A sound loop is a short bit of music (4-14 seconds in length) that is designed to repeat over and over. Sound adds to download time so a short sound loop is a good way to provide background audio while keeping download time quick.

Although adding a sound file to a Flash animation is easy, the process of finding the right sound that compliments your art can be time consuming. The goal of this short project is to describe how to get sound files into your Flash animation. In a later section we will focus exclusively on sound and discuss different ways that it can be used (and abused) in Flash.

PROJECT

Timeline Sound:

❑ If you have a copyright free sound loop jump to the next step. If not a good place to find copyright free sound loops is http://www.flashkit.com/loops/. There are a large number of sound loops that are under 10 seconds. A sound loop should be under 30 seconds (smaller is better) to be effective as a fast downloading background sound.

ADDING SOUND TO TIMELINE

❑ Launch Flash, open the animation that you want to add the sound loop to, and reset the palettes.

❑ Add a new layer and label it as sound.

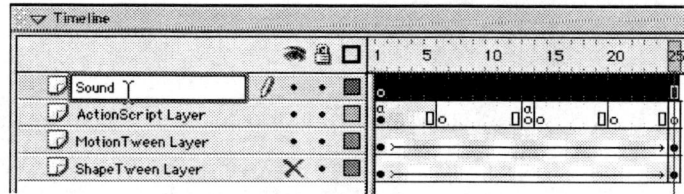

❑ Choose File-Import to Library

❑ Choose Window-Library to display the library palette.

❑ With frame 1 of the sound layer selected drag the imported sound file from the library onto the stage. *Note: you will not actually see the sound on the stage but you will see it displayed in the timeline.*

❑ You will now see the sound file displayed on the sound layer of the timeline.

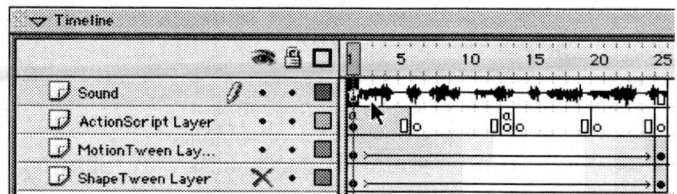

❑ Click again on frame 1 of the sound layer, then look at the properties palette to see the sound options.

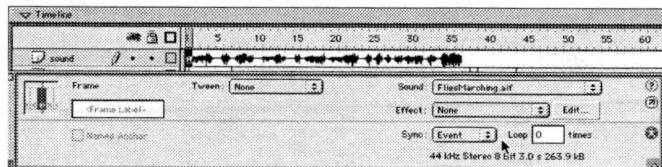

Timeline Sound

❑ Important: Flash provides four options for play-ing your sound. The options are referred to as **Sync**.
NOTE: These four Sync options are the key to successful time-line sound playback. **Event, Start, Stop, Stream.**

Event: When the playback head reaches a particular frame the sound will start. This allows you to syn-chronize sound with a particular frame.
Note: Event is not a good solution for a background sound, because every time the playback head hits the designated frame the sound will start again and overlap other existing sounds. Event is used when you want a sound to synchronize with a particular animation event.

Start: This is ideal for a background sound. The sound will only start when the animation begins and will repeat for as many times as you specify. The sound loop will not overlap on itself.

Stop: The sound will start when the animation stops.

Stream: Use this option when the sound file is large. The sound will begin playing when the user has down-loaded enough information to play the sound file.

❑ Since this sound is intended as a background loop click on frame 1 of the sound layer and set the Sync to Start.

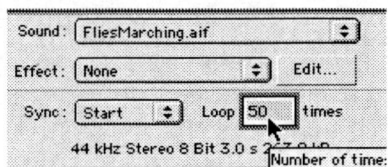

❑ Set the Loop to 50 times.
A Sync of Start and a Loop of 50 should keep your background sound playing throughout your anima-tion. If the sound stops short of the completion of your animation then increase the number of loops.

❑ Test the animation to see if the sound works with your animation.

ADDITIONAL EXPLORATION

SOUND EDITORS

One tool you will need in your Flash arsenal is an inexpensive, easy to use sound editor.

Macintosh:

For the Macintosh I recommend SoundEffects which is a shareware application (http://www.riccisoft.com). It is easy to use for sound editing and recording. It also has some cool filters such as echos, reverbs, and robotize. Try it for free as long as you like to see if it works for you. If you like SoundEffects the shareware fee is only $15.00. The only drawback is that it only excepts sounds in the AIF file format, but there are other freeware and shareware utilities that will convert your audio to the AIF format.

PC:

I predominately use a Mac for my sound editing so I asked a friend, Joshua, who is digital musician (as well as an ActionScript expert) who works mostly on PC.
"The sound editor I use most often is called Goldwave. It's shareware and does just about everything required for wave editing. Great tool!" —Joshua Trout (http://www.amongtrout.com)
You can download Goldwave at http://www.goldwave.com.

Additional Exploration:

1. Download and experiment with a couple of different sounds.

2. Use a freeware, shareware, or commercial sound editing tool to modify the sound to see if it better captures the mood you are trying to create.

3. Create a small voice or special effect sound and experiment with placing it on the timeline using EVENT syncing to have the sound play at a crucial point in your animation.

You may be thinking that this is an opportunity to explore your personal CD collection or MP3's. It is important to note that unless otherwise specified by the company that is publishing the music, you cannot legally use the copyrighted works of others in your Flash product (without permission) if you are going to publish your work on the web or sell Flash applications that you create.

The other question is "what about academic use?" The attorneys I have spoken state that if the work is published on the web, even without any type of compensation, the student is publishing copyrighted work and in violation of copyright law. With so many freeware software loops available at flashkit.com why risk a legal confrontation?

Resource for copyright free sound loops:
http://www.flashkit.com/loops/

Sound Editors:
(Mac) http://www.riccisoft.com
(PC)   http://www.goldwave.com
http://www.simplythebest.net/music.html
http://www.hitsquad.com

CHAPTER 13

Intro to MovieClips

This short project not only introduces the movieclip symbol but also demonstrates a huge time saver for creating animations. As you will see in later chapters movie clips offer a great deal more than what is discussed here. I have made a change from previous publications to provide an introduction to movieclips early on because they can be used to greatly simplify complex animations. This chapter demonstrates how to use movieclips to speed your development process.

For this project we are going to create an animation of a bug walking across the stage.
To start we will create a simple 2 frame animation of a bug walking.

❑ Create a new document and reset your palettes to default.

❑ With frame 1 selected draw a simple bug.

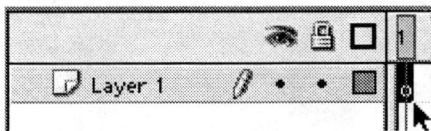

❑ Insert a keyframe **Keyframe** and turn the onion skin feature on.

❑ With frame 2 selected erase the legs and the antenna of the bug and move them to a new position to make it appear that the bug is walking.

SIMPLIFY YOUR ANIMATIONS WITH MOVIECLIPS

THE PROJECT

Onion Skin

TWO FRAME DANCING BUG

The above diagram represents the minor changes from frame 1 and 2 with onion skinniing turned on.

CREATING A MOVIECLIP IN FOUR STEPS

STEP 1

STEP 2

STEP 3

❏ Click again on frame 2 on the timeline and use the up arrow key to move the bug up a few pixels.

❏ To make the effect complete you can use the Lasso tool to select the head and use Transform tool to rotate the head slightly.

❏ Choose Control Test Movie to see the result. It may appear that the bug is dancing rather than walking but the next few steps will complete the effect.

To create a movieclip from an existing timeline animation requires 4 steps.

STEP 1
❏ Click on any frame on the timeline and choose EDIT- Select ALL Frames.

Select All Frames ⌥⌘A

Note: Edit Select All is NOT the same as Select All Frames.

Step 2
❏ Choose Edit-Copy FRAMES

Copy Frames ⌥⌘C

Note: Copy is not the same as Copy Frames.

Step 3
❏ Choose Insert New Symbol.

Insert	Modify	Text	Contro
Convert to Symbol...			F8
New Symbol...			⌘F8

Note: New Symbol is different than Convert to Symbol.

❏ Inside the " Create New Symbol" dialog give the movieclip the name "BugWalk" and make sure you choose the Behavior Movie Clip. Click OK.

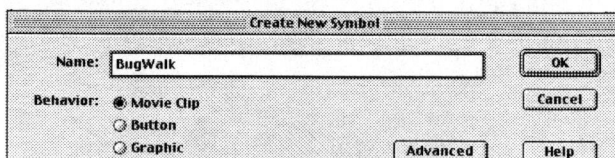

Intro to MovieClips

Step 4

You will now see the movieclip symbol editor, which looks just like the regular timeline.

❑ **Important**, click on frame 1 .

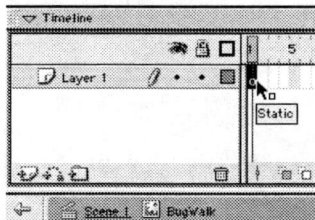

❑ Choose Edit Paste Frames.

Paste Frames ⌥⌘V

Note: Edit Paste Frames is different than Edit Paste.
If all went well you just created a movieclip symbol that can not only be reused but can also be animated.

Animating the movieclip symbol.
❑ Choose Window-Library to display the Library palette.

✓ **Library** F11

❑ In the Library palette you should not only see the movieclip symbol but you should also see a play button which allows you to see the 2 frame animation of the bug walk.

The last part of this project is to animate the clip.
❑ Create a new document.
It is always better to use a movieclip symbol in a NEW document because it helps to avoid confusion.

❑ Drag an instance of the BugWalk clip from the library to the left side of the stage in the new document.

❑ In the new document click on frame 1 on the time-line and set the tween to "motion" using the Properties palette.

OVERVIEW OF **4** STEPS TO CREATE A MOVIECLIP

1. Select ALL of the FRAMES.
2. Copy All of the FRAMES.
3. Create a NEW symbol of the type movieclip.
4. Click on frame 1 of the movieclip symbol and choose Edit-Paste FRAMES.

USE A NEW DOCUMENT TO ANIMATE THE CLIP

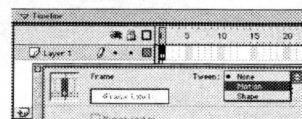

ANIMATING THE MOVIECLIP SYMBOL

ADDITIONAL EXPLORATION

RECAP OF THIS PROJECT

1. You created a very short animation of a bug walking.

2. You converted the bug walk animation into a movieclip.

3. You created a new document and placed the animated clip into the document.

4. You used a motion tween to animate the movieclip.

The process may seem a bit complicated but after you use this technique a few time you will be hooked.

❏ Click on frame 40 on the timeline and insert a key-frame.

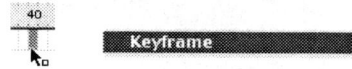

❏ With frame 40 still selected drag the bug clip to the far right edge of the stage.

❏ Test the animation to see the results.
The dancing bug should now appear to walk across the stage.

Additional Exploration:

1. Create a short animation of a ball bouncing up and down, convert it into a movieclip and use it in a new document with a motion tween to have the ball bounce across the stage.

2. Using the example above add a new layer to create a shadow under the bouncing ball. the shadow should get smaller and darker as the ball hits the surface and lighter and more diffuse as the ball rises higher in the air.

3. Create a 2-5 frame animation of a stick figure walking. Convert it into a movieclip and make the stick figure walk across the stage. Use the transform tool to make the movieclip stick figure reverse direction and walk back across the stage.

4. Using example 3 above, add a layer to create a shadow underneath the stick figure to add higher level of realism.

5. Create a 2-4 frame animation of a stick figure that is using the motions to climb. Convert the short animation of the stick figure into a movieclip and animate it to climb.

6. Use a digital camera (or scanned images) to capture 3-4 images of a person walking. Remove the background information using Fireworks or Photoshop. Save the images as background transparent PNG files. Import the images into Flash and create a movieclip.

Animate the movieclip to create a photo-realistic image of a person walking

By now you are ready to publish your work.
Flash makes publishing for the web easy. Flash will generate both an HTML document and an SWF file that can be uploaded to your website.

Flash also allows you to create self-running software applications. I have had some students liken this capability to PowerPoint which can create self-running presentations. I suggest that this capability is more akin to Director which allows the creation of self-running, interactive, scripted, software applications. It is concievable that you could produce a highly involved, multilevel, game that could be burned onto a CD for distribution. Or you could produce an interactive animated software utililty such as a scientific calculator. You could develop an animated organizer or planner to be used in a handheld computer or even used on a cell phone.

❑ Open an animation to Publish.

❑ Save the File to the location you want to create the Flash web movie file. *This is an interesting Flash oddity, since you cannot set the save location in the publish dialog. The save location is based on the location where you saved the original Flash document. Actually in a way it is a usefull feature because it forces us to keep all of our files together.*

❑ Choose File-Publish-**Settings** to get the following dialog box.

PROJECT

GENERAL PUBLISH SETTINGS

ABOUT PROJECTORS

Projectors allow you to create self running software applications. You can create a projector, burn it onto a CD and ship it to your customers. While you can generate a Mac Projector on the PC it will of course only run on a Macintosh computer. Flash will add all of the Operating System instructions for you. The extra code will increase the final file size of the Projector by about 1Mb.

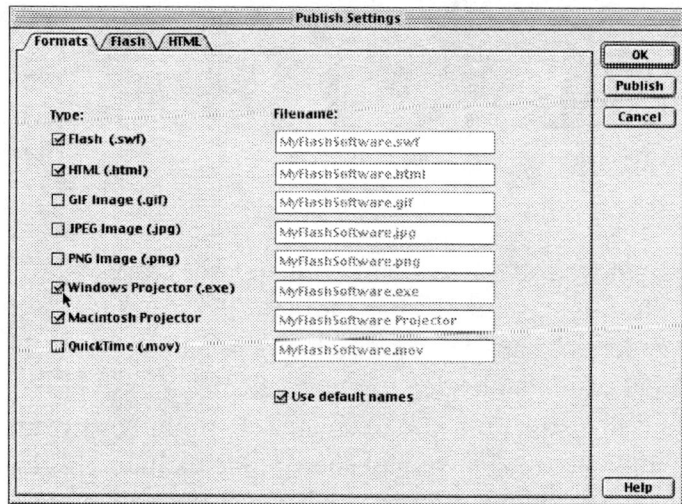

Publish Settings

Formats \ Flash \ HTML \

OK
Publish
Cancel

Type: | Filename:
☑ Flash (.swf) | MyFlashSoftware.swf
☑ HTML (.html) | MyFlashSoftware.html
☐ GIF Image (.gif) | MyFlashSoftware.gif
☐ JPEG Image (.jpg) | MyFlashSoftware.jpg
☐ PNG Image (.png) | MyFlashSoftware.png
☑ Windows Projector (.exe) | MyFlashSoftware.exe
☑ Macintosh Projector | MyFlashSoftware Projector
☐ QuickTime (.mov) | MyFlashSoftware.mov

☑ Use default names

Help

Looks intimidating but it is actually an easy to use tool. Click on the items you want to create. By default Flash will create a SWF (Flash web movie file) and an HTML web page to access the SWF file.

Note that you can create a image file, QT movie, or a projector, in case you want to display the animation locally on your computer.

❏ Make sure Flash SWF and HTML are selected. Make sure the other options are turned off.

❏ Click on the Flash tab to view additional Flash movie settings.

FLASH PUBLISH DIALOG

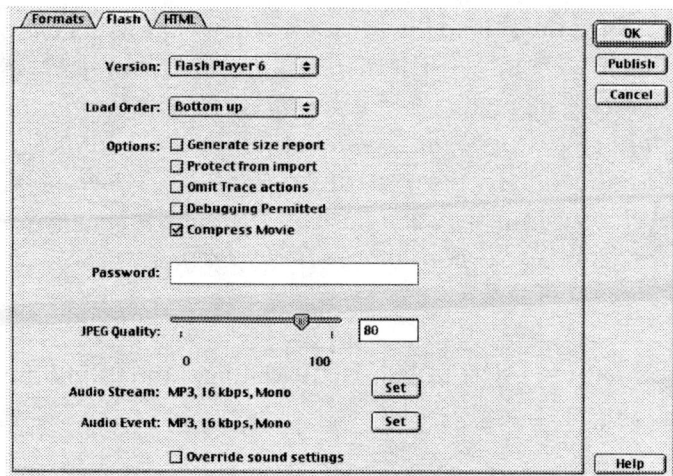

Formats \ Flash \ HTML \

OK
Publish
Cancel

Version: Flash Player 6
Load Order: Bottom up

Options: ☐ Generate size report
☐ Protect from import
☐ Omit Trace actions
☐ Debugging Permitted
☑ Compress Movie

Password:

JPEG Quality: ———————▭——— 80
0   100

Audio Stream: MP3, 16 kbps, Mono   Set
Audio Event: MP3, 16 kbps, Mono   Set

☐ Override sound settings

Help

Version is a useful feature but beware if you save to an older version you may loose some of the ActionScript features and capabilities that you created in your animation.

Load Order sets which layer will be loaded and viewed first. Since we most often create from the bottom this is the default, but if your timeline starts at an upper layer you may want to choose Top down.

Generate size report is a great feature because it generates a text file that tells you frame-by-frame how much information is being downloaded. Great information to know if you need to revise your animation to better accommodate modem users.

Protect from Import prevents others from importing your Flash movie from the web and converting it back into an editable Flash file.

❑ Turn on the Protect from Import option.

Omit Trace Actions prevents the output window from displaying comments that would be used to debug ActionScript. Trace is an ActionScript command.

Debugging Permitted turns on the debugger to allow debugging a Flash movie over the internet.

Password if debugging is permitted then you should password-protect your movie file.

Compress Movie is on by deafualt and is a great new addition to Flash MX. In addition to all of the other methods and techniques used to make Flash fast on the web this feature compresses ActionScript text and text heavy documents.

JPEG quality will compress imported bitmapped images. It does not effect vector graphics.

Flash also includes **MP3** which is wonderful compression for your audio files. Unless you are familiar with audio and the advantages of MP3, I suggest using the default settings.

The last tab is for the HTML document that Flash will generate. If you plan on importing your Flash file into DreamWeaver then these settings are irrelevant.

HTML PUBLISH SETTINGS

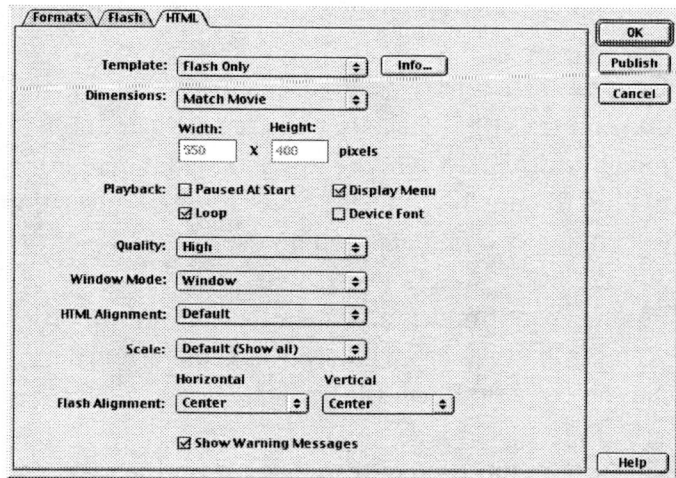

❏ Click on the template menu and work your way through the list of options. Once an option is selected click on the Info button to see how it will display in the browser. After you have reviewed the options, select the Flash Only (Default).

Template: Flash Only (Default) ▼

Dimensions: The default is Match Movie, but you can also set movie dimensions in pixels or percent.
❏ Set Dimensions to Match Movie.

CREATING A FLASH ONLY WEB SITE

NOTE: *Flash is not a web standard, it is a plug-in. Flash does not exist (on the web) without an HTML document to carry it. You can build a Flash Only web site that fills the entire web page but it stilll relies on HTML to present it to the web browser.*

Want your Flash movie to fill your entire web page? Set the Dimensions to Percent and set the width and height to 100%. This not only makes your Flash movie fill the HTML document but also when the user resizes the web document it resizes your Flash Movie.

Display Menu displays a shortcut menu when users right-click (Windows) or Control-clicks (Macintosh) the movie when viewed on the web.

Click on the Help button to see some of the other features. Take a look at the quality settings. This is a really cool feature and something you will want to consider based on user playback speed.

❑ Set the quality setting to AutoHigh. *(This is a good option. It emphasizes image quality, but will drop the quality if the users playback speed is to slow or creating pauses in playback.)*
If you don't like the results on AutoHigh then try Auto Low which emphasizes fast playback at the expense of image quality, but improves appearance if the users computer can handle it.
Leave other settings at the Default unless you have read the help file.

❑ Click on the Publish button. This will save the HTML file and the SWF file to the same location that you saved your native Flash file.

Thats it as far as creation goes.

❑ Now that you have created the files, drop the HTML file onto a web browser to see the results.

Creating a Flash Only Web Site:
I often encounter students who want to create a web site completely with Flash. Hopefully this project demonstrates that Flash does not exist in a vacuum, even if HTML pages are used only as a container to convey your Flash content. Not only is Flash dependent on HTML for web display but the intelligent use of HTML, Javascript, and other web technologies can make your life easier as discussed below.

Flash VS HTML for a jump page:
If I were creating a jump page (a page of links to other important sites on the web) I would rather create those links in HTML then in Flash.
To illustrate if I had 20 links to other important sites and I created the links in Flash it becomes more difficult to manage and update.

HTML URL changes:

WHEN TO USE OTHER WEB TECHNOLOGIES

Making Changes in HTML

If you needed to update links in an HTML document you might go through the follwoing steps:

1. Download the HTML document from my site "Who cares if I lost the original."

2. Make the address changes or tweaks in HTML manually or by using my Web Publishing software,

3. Put the page back on my site.

4. Test the revised HTML page to make sure the new links are working

Making Changes in Flash

If you needed to update links in a Flash document you might go through the follwoing steps:

1. Find the original FLA file that you used to create the jump page links. *You cannot download and update the existing SWF, you need to find the original.*

"Now where did I put that source file—Ohh here it is—or at least I think this was the final source FLA!"

2. Find the correct frame or button script that contained the ActionScript to create the links and make the changes inside the ActionScript editor.

3. Create a new SWF.

4. Test the SWF to make sure the links and any other dynamic content is correct.

5. Make sure the SWF has the same name as the previous SWF.

6. Upload the new SWF

7. Test the existing web page with the NEW SWF to make sure it is working properly.

Conclusion: If you have an aesthetic reason to create a navigation bar or jump page in Flash then do it! Just make sure you keep track of the final FLA and note were the URL designators are located. On the other hand, capitalizing on other web technologies that are at your disposal (such as HTML) may be more time effective.

Flash has three types of symbols; graphics, buttons, and movieclips. While graphic symbols are pretty basic, buttons open the door to interactivity.

Flash Buttons can provide interactivity without programming. A HTML web button is something you click on, but a Flash button offers a doorway to exciting web interactivity. When you get to chapters on producing web games and dynamic photography you will see what I mean.

This chapter will show a simple rollover but later chapters will explore some of the power-user techniques and effects that you may have seen on the web. These were created using buttons inside movieclips, or movieclips inside buttons.

A rollover is pretty basic stuff, especially if you have been creating HTML-based web pages. A rollover is basically having a new image appear when you roll over an object that is defined as a button. If you have worked in either GoLive or DreamWeaver you had to make your rollover image the same size as the button in the "normal" state. This is not the case in Flash. Your rollover image can be as large or as small as you want it to be. When a user rolls over a button it could change the entire appearance of the stage. Rolling over a button can present text, sounds, music, images, or a combination of these. But even better than that, the button itself can be an animation and when the user rolls over it can change how the animation plays. A button can also be scripted to behave in a specified way and also make decisions based on what is happening in the movie.

In later chapters you will see how a button can be used as a game object.

BUTTON SYMBOLS NOT JUST BUTTONS

The next several chapters will explore the use of buttons. Controlling Flash animation, creating interactive web portfolios, offering users a choice about the content they wish to see, and providing users with control over sound for web playback to name a few.

This tutorial will take you through the basics of creating interactivity through the use of buttons in Flash. As you have already experienced in the previous lessons, the graphics and project are simpler in order to allow you to quickly gain the concepts. Your task is to take this basic information and apply your own imagination and creativity.

❏ Create a new Flash document and create a circle object on the stage that has no line and is filled with the color red.

❏ Select the object and choose Insert-Convert to Symbol.

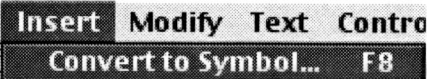

❏ In the Symbol Properties dialog name this object "button 1" and set the behavior to "Button".
(See diagram below)

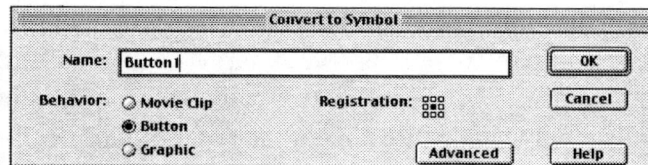

❏ Click OK to exit the Symbol Properties dialog box.

A button symbol is similar to a graphic symbol, in that you can reuse it many times during the animation. What makes a button symbol different is that when the user moves the cursor over the button it can change appearance, and when the user clicks on the button it can further change appearance. Of the three symbols (graphic, button, and movieclip) the button is the only symbol that can respond to a mouse event, such as a mouse click. This becomes important when you want to use ActionScript to respond to the users actions.

❏ To access the symbol editor for the button, display the Library palette (Window-Library) and double click on the icon for button1, as shown in the diagram.
Note: If you double click on the WORD "button 1", the Library palette will allow you to change the name of the symbol. If you double click on the button ICON in the Library palette, you will enter the symbol editor.

One way to be certain that you are in the symbol editor is by looking in the upper left corner of the Stage. In the example shown below Scene 1 is available but inactive. "button 1" is active and available for editing. If you wanted to return to editing the movie you could click on Scene 1, which would take you out of the symbol editor.

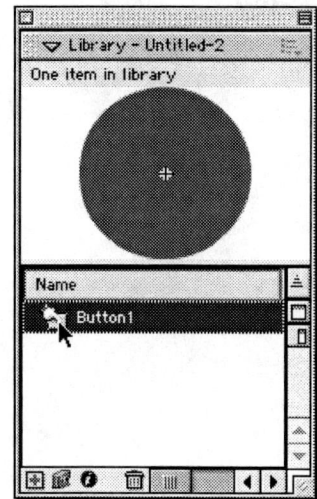

❏ Once you have accessed the symbol editor for "button 1" the timeline is replaced with "button states."

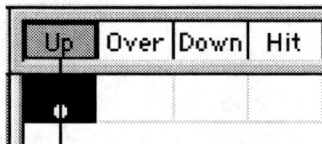

The **Up state** is what the button looks like when nothing is happening to it. The cursor is "not" over the button.
The **Over state** is how the button will appear when the cursor is moved "on top of" the button.
The **Down state** is how the button appears when the user "clicks" on the button.
The **Hit state** defines the "hot spot" area of the button and is discussed in more detail at the end of this chapter.

ADDING KEYFRAMES TO THE BUTTON STATES

By default Flash has a keyframe in the Up state but no keyframe in the other states.

❑ On your <u>Keyboard</u>: Push the F6 Key 3 times. This will insert a keyframe (copy of the image from the Up state) into the other three states. As shown.

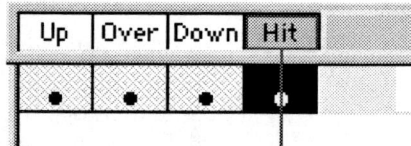

Up	Over	Down	Hit
●	●	●	◐

❑ Select the Over state and draw a large square over the existing circle.

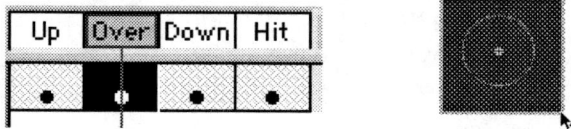

Up	Over	Down	Hit
●	◐	●	●

EXIT SYMBOL EDITOR

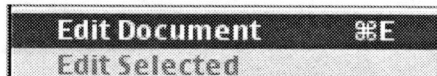

Edit Document   ⌘E
Edit Selected

Another way to exit the Symbol Editor is to choose Edit Document found under the Edit menu.

❑ Choose <u>Scene1</u> to exit the symbol editor and return to the movie. As shown.

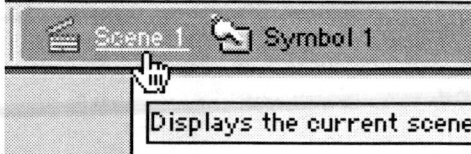

Scene 1   Symbol 1

Displays the current scene

❑ Choose Control-Test Movie to see if the Over state works. When you drag your cursor over the button object it should change from a circle to a square. Notice that when you click on the button the circle returns.

❑ Close the Test Movie window. Then using the Library palette double click on "button 1" to re-enter the button symbol editor..

❑ Once you are back in the symbol editor, click on the Down state.

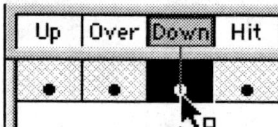

Up	Over	Down	Hit
●	●	◐	●

❏ Select the paint bucket from the tool palette, set the color to yellow, and fill the circle with the new color.

❏ Select the Scene1 button to exit the symbol editor.

❏ Choose Control-Test Movie to see if the Down state works.
When you drag your cursor over the button it changes into a square when you click on the button object it changes to a circle but in a different color.

❏ Save a copy of this Flash document. You may want to use it in the next project that discusses adding ActionScript to a Flash button.

Understanding the Hit State:
The hit state is not required in all buttons but is absolutely essential for some. For this reason I suggest you include a hit state in your buttons in order to avoid problems. The hit state is an invisible area that you create that defines the hot spot of the button. To put it in other words the Hit State defines the "Active area" of a button.
The following short experiment should help to illustrate what the hit state does and how it works.

❏ In the Library double click on the "button 1" to re-enter the button symbol editor.

❏ Once you are back in the symbol editor, click on the Hit state. You will notice the red circle.

❏ Delete the circle from the stage (in the Hit state), then draw a much smaller circle in its place. The color you use for this object is not important because **the user will never see the Hit state graphic**.

❏ Without exiting the symbol editor, choose Control-Test Movie. You should notice that when you touch the edge of the circle it does not change to the Over state, instead you have to be near the center in order to activate the button.

THE HIT STATE

The hit state defines the active area of a button. The graphic you use in the hit state will never be seen by the user because it only defines the "hot spot" of a button.

Up	Over	Down	Hit
●	●	●	○

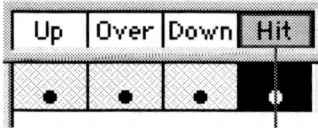

Further Exploration

If you are still not sure about the hit state then try the following.

❑ Close the Test Movie window.

❑ With the Hit state active draw a large graphic that covers half of the stage, then choose Control-Test Movie.

What you should see now is that the over state appears before you even get the cursor over the button. The shape drawn into the hit state never shows up on the stage, but now when the user drags the cursor into the Hot Spot area that was defined by the Hit state, the button changes.

Further Exploration:

To get more comfortable with Flash button states experiment with some of the following...

1. Create a face button that changes expressions when the user rolls over it.

2. Create a button that displays text information in the over state.

3. Add depth to your images. Import a greyscale and color copy of your image. Have the greyscale image display in the Up state and the Color image display in the Over state.

4. Create a type graphic for a button using an image editing application like Fireworks or Photoshop. Save a copy of the type image as a PNG file then apply a heavy blur to the type. Used the blurred type in the Up state and the clean type in the Over state, so the user has to roll over the button to read the type.

5. Create a new document where the object breaks apart when the user rolls over it, then comes back together in the Down state (make sure you include a hit state for this one).

The genius behind Flash ActionScript is the Actions window. The Actions window is designed to work for programmers but is especially designed to help non-programmers learn scripting. If you are a programer you can set the Actions window to allow you to type in pages of code unhindered. If you are not familiar with programming or if you are new to ActionScript you can set the Actions window to provide you with point and click button choices to create your code. Macromedia has made it so easy that with a bit of direction and a bit of practice anyone can learn ActionScript.

This book is developed with the visual artist in mind. Whether you have had previous scripting experience or never encountered a script before in your life, the remainder of this book will explore some of the key and basic commands of ActionScript. Telling an animation to stop on a particular frame is much easier in Flash than other scripting or programming languages. Being able to add commands to your visual creation and tell your animation what to do is incredibly rewarding. At first we will explore how to tell your creations to respond to your requests, later we will discuss how to allow your creations to respond to user requests. In Flash, being able to use scripted commands adds a new dimension to your creative capabilities. Interactive visual art is a new world for creative artists.

If you are a programmer you will note that ActionScript requires knowledge of Flash. The programming examples used in this book focus more on creating "smart objects" that know what they are and react accordingly rather than trying to control all objects with a single script.

USING ACTIONSCRIPT WITH BUTTONS

NOTE TO ARTISTS

NOTE TO PROGRAMMERS

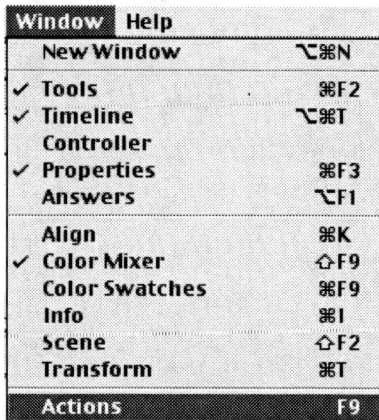

NORMAL MODE

This project uses a button to link to another web site. *To create a button symbol refer to the previous chapter.*

❑ Create a button symbol on the stage.
❑ Click once on the button to make it active.
❑ Choose Actions from the Window menu.

❑ Check to make sure that the actions are being applied to the button and <u>not</u> to a frame script.

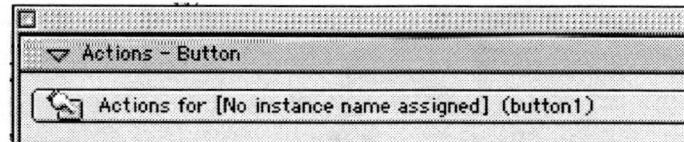

Note: If you see something like the following then the script will be applied to the frame and not to the button.

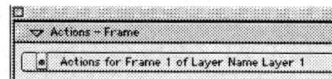

When first installed Flash should default to the Normal view for the Actions window.

❑ To make sure you are in the Normal Mode choose the pop-out menu from the upper right corner of the Actions window and make sure Normal Mode is selected, as shown below.

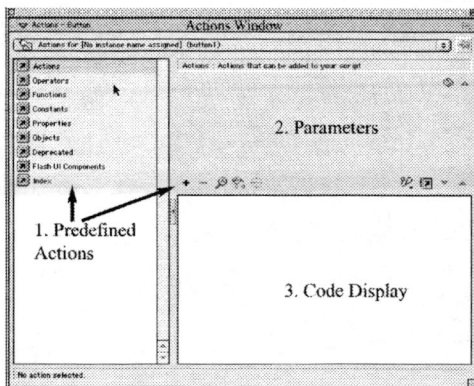

In the Normal Mode the Actions window is broken down into 3 primary areas:
1. Predefined Actions.
2. Parameters for those actions.
3. The code display area.

Predefined Actions make it easy to add ActionScript commands to your Flash document.

© BRADLEY KALDAHL 2003

Introduction to ActionScript

❏ Click once on the Predefined Actions book called Actions, as shown.

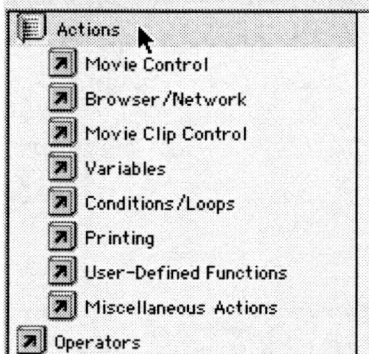

❏ Click once on the Browser/Network book in order to see the "getURL" command.

❏ You can drag the "getURL" command into the Code Display area or you can double click on the "getURL" command. Either way the result will be the same.

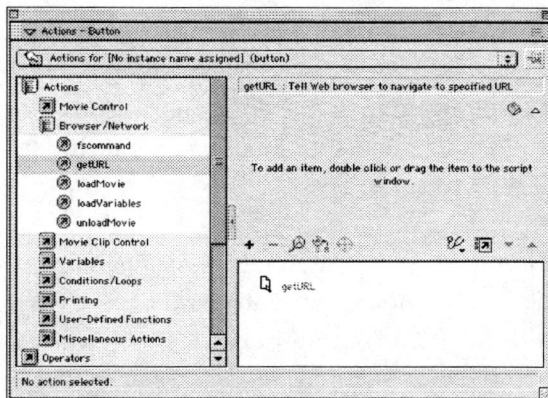

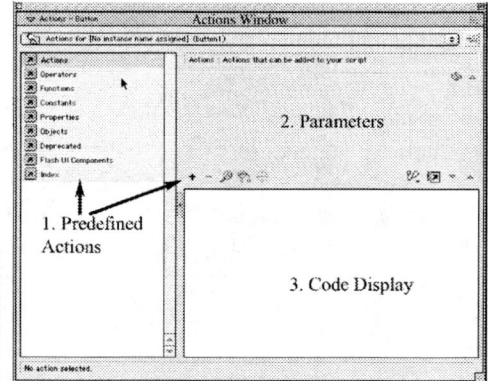

1. Predefined Actions

2. Parameters

3. Code Display

CONNECTING TO THE WEB

GET URL

```
on (release) {
    getURL("");
}
```

Click on line 2 "getURL("");" and note that the parameters displayed are specifically for this line of code.

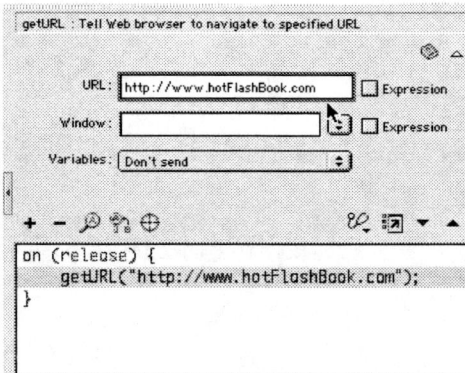

FRAME VS OBJECT SCRIPTS

ADDITIONAL EXPLORATION

Once you add the "getURL" command to the Code window Flash will automatically format the script for you, as shown.

❑ In the Parameters area, which is above the Code Display area, type in the URL address of the site you want to link to (http://www.hotflashbook.com).

NOTE: This example uses an absolute address but you could also use a relative address. (A relative address is the name of another document inside your site).

❑ Choose control-Test Movie.

If your computer is connected to the Internet the browser should launch. When your Flash project is published on the web it will jump to the URL you specified.

Frame scripts *are placed on a particular frame. Frame scripts produce a result when the playback head reaches that frame. If frame 20 has a script that says "stop();" the animation will stop at frame 20.*

Object scripts *are called when an event occurs. An event is something that occurs in the application or user does ie: "rolls over a button" or "clicks on the button." Object scripts or event scripts can respond to the users actions. Using the example above you could place on object script on a button that says stop(). When the user clicks on the button the animation stops. Code Example for a user event object stop script.*

```
on (user event) {
stop();
}
```

Additional Exploration:

❑ Create three more instances of your button symbol on the stage and set each instance to link to a different web page.

❑ Take a Photo of your face. Select the eyes and convert them into button symbols. Make the eyes change color during Over state. Have them link to another web page or site.

CHAPTER 17

Controlling Animation with ActionScript

Allowing the user an opportunity to control the animation not only involves the user in the viewing process but also makes the animation more entertaining.

For this project well place three buttons in an animation that allows the user to stop, start, and restart the animation as desired. This project provides additional experience with buttons and introduces some very basic, and easy-to-use ActionScript. In the further exploration section at the end of this project there is some code that can be used to create a rewind or step back button.

ABOUT THIS PROJECT

❑ Open an previously created animation that is at least 30 frames in length.
If you previously created the Solar Explosion then open a copy of that file.

❑ Choose Window-Panel Sets-Default Layout to reset the palettes.

SETUP

| Panel Sets | ▶ | Default Layout |
| Save Panel Layout... | | Designer [1024x768] |

❑ Create a new layer ⊞ (in your existing animation) and click on frame 1 in the new layer.

Insert Layer

By default the new layer will extend the full length of your existing animation timeline.
In the next few steps you will create a button symbol.

❑ Draw a red square on the stage. (Red for Stop).

CREATING A BUTTON SYMBOL

❑ Select the square, and choose Insert-Convert to Symbol.

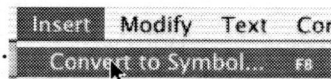

Insert   Modify   Text   Cor
Convert to Symbol...   F8

❑ Set the Behavior to button and call it "StopBttn."

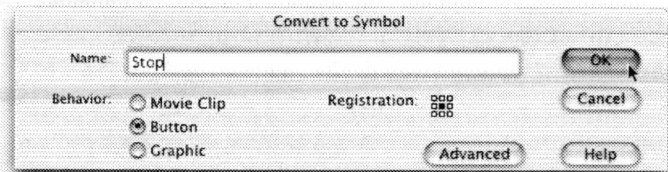

Convert to Symbol
Name: Stop   OK
Behavior: ○ Movie Clip   Registration: Cancel
           ⦿ Button
           ○ Graphic   Advanced   Help

ACCESSING ACTIONSCRIPT

❑ With the button still selected choose the menu Window-Actions.

Window

Actions   F9
Debugger   ⇧F4

SWITCH TO NORMAL MODE

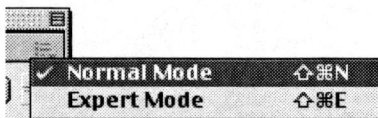

❑ Check to make sure you are in the Normal mode.

✓ Normal Mode   ⇧⌘N
  Expert Mode   ⇧⌘E

❑ In the Actions window the left side displays the ActionScript books with predefined commands and the right presents the ActionScript code area.

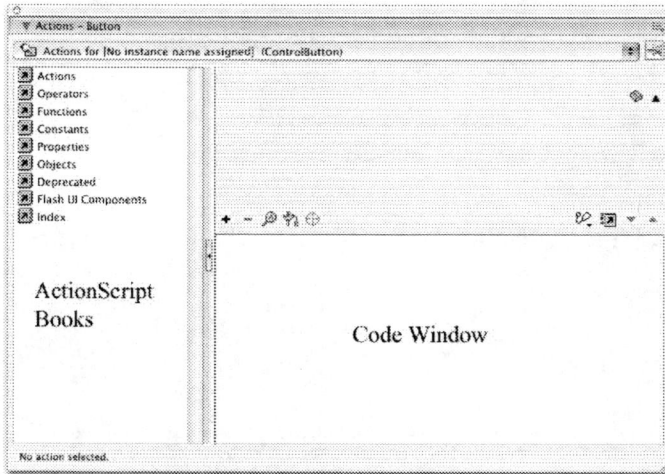

❑ Click once on the Actions book, then click once on the Movie Control book to display the Stop command as shown below.
Interface Note: A single click will open a book and a double click will apply a command.

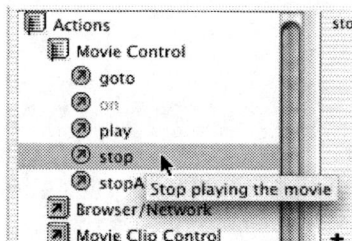

❑ Either drag the Stop command into the code window or double click on the Stop command to add this command to the code window.

❑ You should see the following code appear in the code window.

```
on (release) {
    stop();
}
```

❑ Close the Object Actions dialog.
❑ Choose Control-Test Movie to see how the button works. *The animation should stop.*

CREATING A STOP SCRIPT

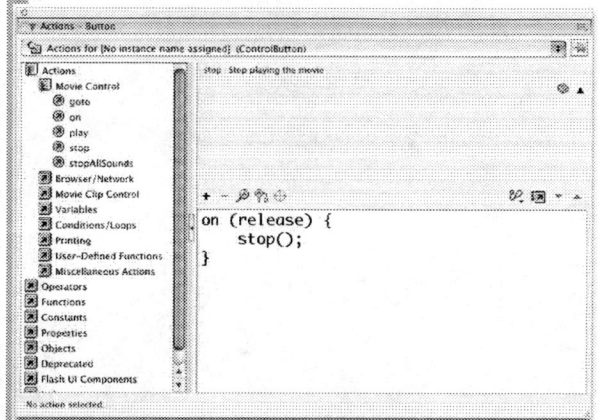

VIEWING THE SCRIPT

TESTING THE SCRIPT

CREATING A PLAY BUTTON

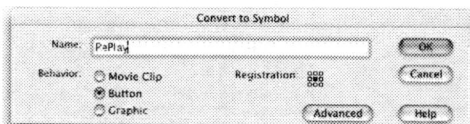

❑ Draw a Green square on the stage. (Green for go)

❑ Select the new square, and choose Insert-Convert to Symbol.

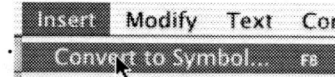

CREATING A PLAY SCRIPT

❑ Set the Behavior to Button and call it "GoBttn."

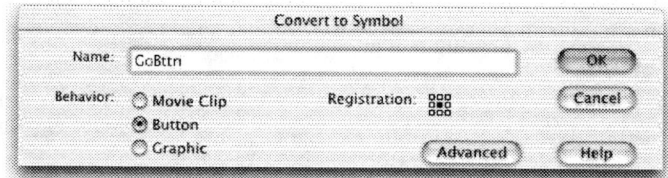

❑ With the button still selected choose the menu Window - Actions. Choose the **play** action and drag it into the code area, as shown below.

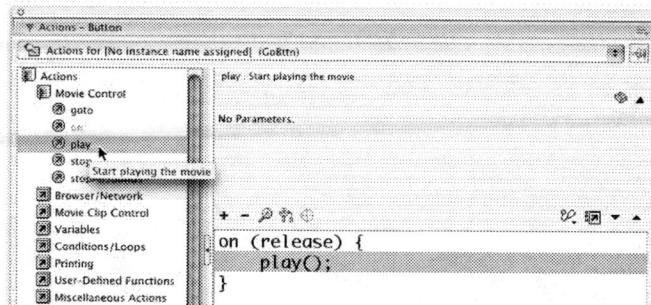

❑ Close the Actions Window.

❑ Draw a Blue square on the stage (Replay).

REPLAY BUTTON

❑ Select the new square, and choose Insert-Convert to Symbol and name the new button "Replay."

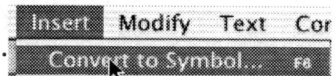

❑ With the button still selected, choose the menu Window-Actions. Choose the **GoTo** action and drag it into the code area.

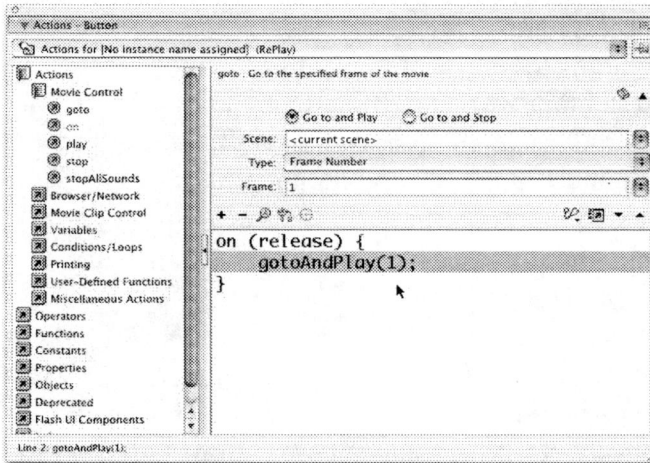

❑ Click on the goto line of code (as shown above) to see the parameters for this Action.

❑ The code window should display the following. *What the code says is that when the user releases the button, the movie will go to and play frame 1. This is the restart button.*

```
on (release) {
    gotoAndPlay(1);
}
```

❑ Close 🔲 the Object Actions dialog.

❑ Use Control-Test Movie to see if the buttons are working properly.

The stop, play, and goto actions are basic and used frequently.

ADDITIONAL EXPLORATION

Come up with creative buttons.

Additional Exploration:

1. Experiment with creating more eye catching and unique buttons. If you look on the web some of the coolest buttons do not use text but instead use symbols to represent the actions.

At the time of this writing the trend in web design is to produce small buttons, that are interesting, visually compelling and unobtrusive.

The goal is not to produce buttons for a single animation but to design buttons that can be used throughout your site.

2. Create a Step Back / Rewind button. For those of you who want to get more involved in the scripting aspects of Flash, create a new button and insert the following code. This code produces a simple rewind button. Each time the user clicks the movie steps back five frames.

```
on (press) {
  gotoAndPlay (_currentframe-5);
}
```

Ideally, we would want the rewind button to keep rewinding as long as the user holds the rewind button down but for now we will keep it simple.

LEARNING TIMELINE NAVIGATION

The concepts covered in this project open the door to a variety of topics. Your presentation could be a web portfolio, an interactive resume, a teaching tool, or any other type of content that might present the user with choices and allow them to respond.
We will explore basic navigation techniques using Flash and ActionScript.

While the visual content discussed, in this project, is simple this is an important project because it illustrates the differences between using timeline and object scripts and how they can compliment each other.

CHOOSING A TIMELINE OR OBJECT SCRIPT

Experience tells me that this project can be a bit frustrating because it requires several scripts to be placed strategically. With some projects you can shoot from the hip and design as you go. This project is not one of those times. For this type of project you need to plan what you want to happen before you begin.

To keep this chapter short while still presenting the technical information, I will use the concept of creating a child's learning game. The learning game will allow the child to choose between a Red circle and a Blue square. This project is very basic yet once you understand it you can easily extend the concepts into a much more elaborate Flash interactive, animated, presentation.

THREE VIEW WEB PRESENTATION

PROJECT

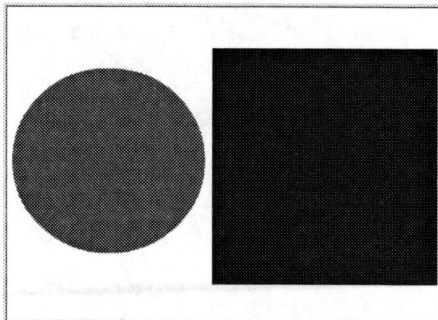

Red Circle
Button symbol

Blue Square
Button symbol

For this project we will create a 3 "view" presentation.

View 1. An opening Title page, we can also call it the "**Main Menu**". The main menu is used to provide the user with choices.

View 2. Responds to the first choice from the main menu and provide a return button to take the user back to the main menu.

View 3. Responds to the second choice from the main menu and provide a return button to take the user back to the main menu.

Project:

❏ Create a new Flash Document.
❏ Set the Panel Sets to Default Layout.

❏ Create a Red circle on the left side of the stage and convert it into a button.
❏ Create a Blue Square on the right side of the stage and convert it into a button.

Button Object Actions:

❏ Click once on the Red circle button and choose Window-Actions.

In the ActionScript Editor
❑ Click once on the Actions book, as shown.
❑ Click once on Movie Control (under Actions)
❑ Drag the "goto" command (under Movie Control) into the code window, as shown.

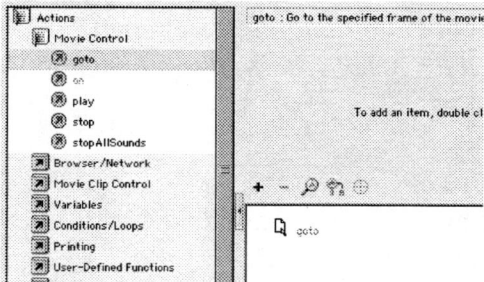

The goto command offers parameters to customize this command, as shown.

❑ Choose the gotoAndStop option. **⦿ Go to and Stop** as shown below.

❑ Change the script to got to and stop on frame 10.

Frame: 10

The red circle button is complete, now for the blue square.

❑ Move the Actions window so you can see the blue square, and click once on the blue square button to make it active.

❑ Drag the goto command into the code window as shown.

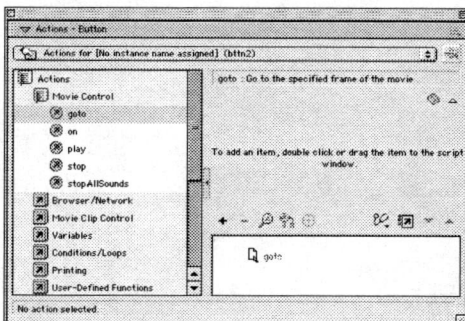

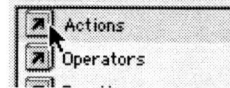

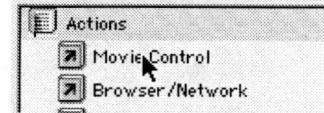

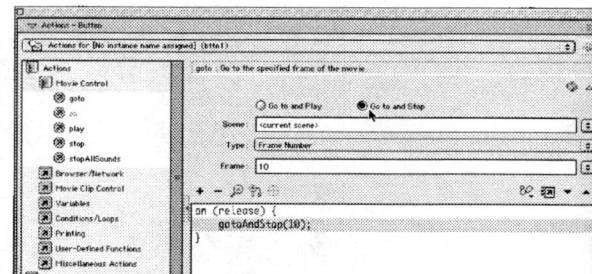

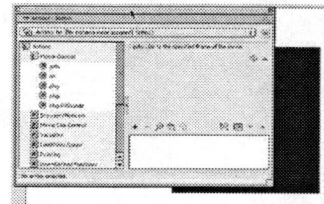

goto : Go to the specified frame of the movie

○ Go to and Play   ● Go to and Stop

Scene: <current scene>
Type: Frame Number
Frame: 20

```
on (release) {
    gotoAndStop(20);
}
```

❑ Change the parameters to Go to and Stop and this time have it stop on frame 20 as shown.

Now that the buttons are complete we can build the rest of this application. You might be wondering why place the scripts before building the animation? It is not required but it can help to avoid some minor mistakes.

On the timeline...
❑ Click on frame 9 and press the F6 key on the keyboard (insert keyframe).

❑ Then click on frame 10 and press the F7 key (insert blank keyframe), as shown.

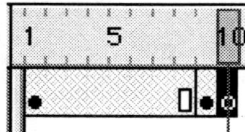

❑ With Frame 10 still active draw a red circle that fills the stage, and place the word RED on top of it.

❑ With the word RED still selected chose Modify-Break Apart, then choose Modify-Break Apart a second time to convert the type into raw vector information.
By breaking the type apart we do not need to worry if the user has the correct font installed on their computer.

❑ Select the circle and the word RED and convert this object into a button.

❑ With the button still selected choose Window-Actions and add the goto action to the code window. By default the code reads gotoAndPlay(1) which is exactly what you want.

Now for the Blue view.

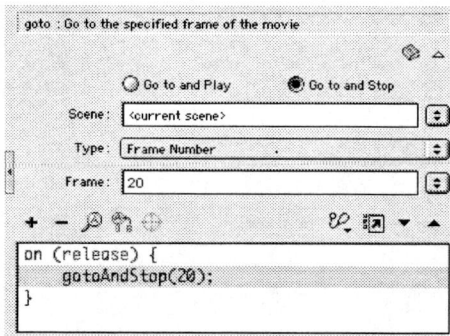

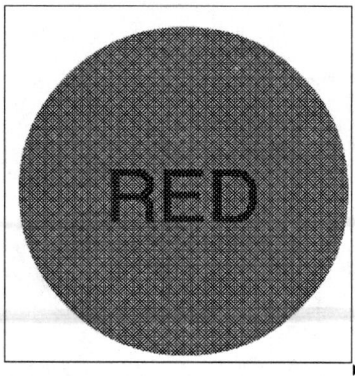

Choose Break Apart twice to convert text into a raw vestor graphic.

| Break Apart | ⌘B |
| Break Apart | ⌘B |

On the Timeline...

❑ Click on frame 19 and press the F6 key, then click on frame 20 and press the F7 key.

Reminder: F6 inserts a keyframe and F7 inserts a Blank keyframe.

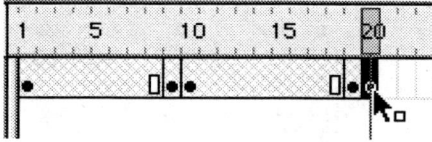

❑ With Frame 20 still selected, draw a large Blue square on the stage, place the text BLUE inside.

❑ Choose Modify-Break Apart twice to convert the type into a raw vector graphic.

❑ Convert the blue object into a button. (Insert-Convert to Symbol).

❑ With the BLUE Button still selected, open Actions from the window menu and add the goto command to the code window, as shown.

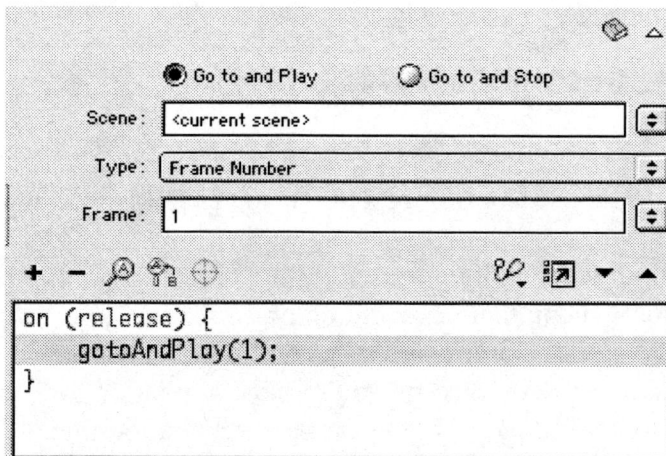

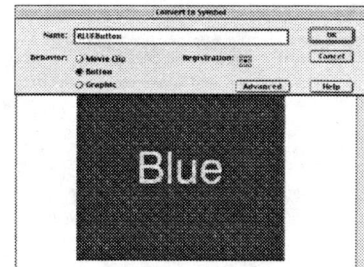

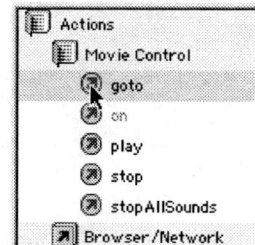

```
on (release) {
    gotoAndPlay(1);
}
```

❑ If you test the movie you will note that it plays through all three of the views without stopping. The last thing that need to be done is to add frame control to get the playback head to stop on the first view and wait for the user to interact.

TIMLINE SCRIPTS

❏ Add a new layer and click on frame 8, then press the F7 key 2 times..

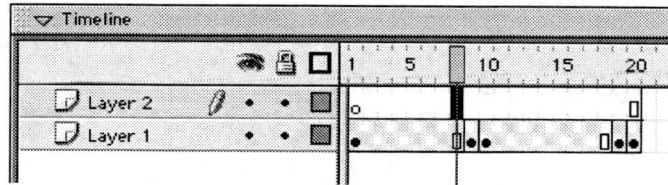

Timeline				1	5	10	15	20
Layer 2				o				
Layer 1								

❏ Click on frame 8 again and display the Actions palette.

❏ Drag the stop() command into the code window.

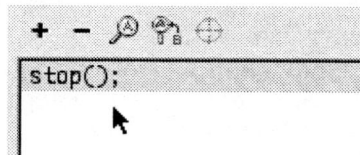

```
stop();
```

By putting a stop command onto frame 8 the movie opens and stops, waiting for user interaction.

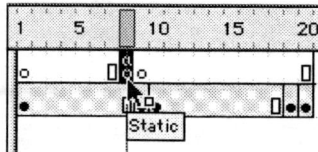

	1	5	10	15	20
	o		o		
			Static		

TESTING THE FINAL PRODUCT

❏ Choose Control-Test movie to see if it is working.

If all went well your user will be greeted with a main menu that has 2 button objects a circle and a square. The animation stops on frame 8 because we used a FRAME script and told the animation to stop(). If the user clicks on the circle button they will be taken to frame 10, "gotoAndStop(10)" The button script allows the user to choose because it can respond to a user evens such as Press and Release.. On frame 10 the user is presented with a large red circle button. If they click on this button they will be taken back to frame 1, the main menu. If the user clicks on the square they will be taken to Frame 20. and from there can return to the main menu.

As mentioned at the beginning this project is simplistic in the final results but provides the key to creating user interactivity and timeline control. Important concepts:

You should now see that there is a difference between timeline scripts and button object scripts. Each serves a particular purpose.

Timeline scripts are called when the playback head reaches the designated frame. Using this example when the playback head hits a stop command the animation stops and the timeline provides no opportunity for the user to restart the animation.

Button Object scripts: provide enormous potential for user interactivity. The ability to respond to user events such as press, drag, and rollover are the cornerstone of interactivity.

Additional exploration:

1. Adding Animation to the presentation:
• When the user goes to view 2 provide an animation instead of a static image. The key to doing this is the change the main menu button script from
gotoAndStop(Frame #); to
gotoAndPlay(Frame #):

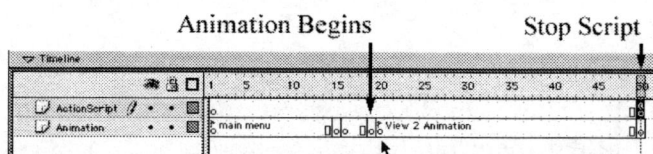

In the diagram above the play script will send the playback head to frame 20. A stop script placed on frame 50 will stop the animation once it is done. You would then need buttons to appear of frame 50 to allow the user to return to the main menu.

2. You could also use this project to create an interactive web portfolio:

• Create a new document and use Thumbnails of art images on the main menu as buttons.
For each "view" provide a full screen image of the final art.

3. Create an interactive Resume.
On the main menu, create buttons that lead into key areas of your resume such as Education, Work Experience and so on. Provide a return button on each view to allow the user to get back to the main menu.

4. Developing Customized Learning Software:

You could further this simple framework to teach a child colors, numbers, shapes, letters, words, sign language, and basic math as well as help the child learn computer skills. This also works as disability software in that it could be used with a touch screen computer.

Converting your games into CD software:

Flash productions can be converted into Windows or Macintosh software applications. Your software could be burned onto a CD. Because its Flash your software tends to be small and fast running. You can easily develop software applications for children that can run on that "old computer" that is collecting dust.

Start simple:

After you have developed several smaller applications and tested them on children you will have a much better idea of what works and what does not. Once you know what works then you may want to consider that complex commercial software.

CHAPTER 19

Button Sounds

TRIGGERING SOUNDS WITH BUTTONS

USING BUTTON STATES TO PRESENT A SOUND

Flash can utilize sound in a couple of different ways. A sound can be set to play or loop on the timeline. With Flash we can give users an opportunity to turn the sound off, lower the volume or even provide the user with a couple of different sounds and allow them to create their own mix! Sound can also be triggered when a particular frame is encountered. This project will demonstrate how sound can be triggered by an event such as a mouse-over or mouse-down on a button.

In this project you'll add a sound to the Over state and to the Down sate of a button.

❑ Create a new document, with a button symbol on the stage. *You may want you might create an Over and a Down state graphic for the button.*

❑ Use Control-Test Movie to make sure the button works.

❑ Import two short sound files into the movie by choosing File-Import to Library. Select a sound that represents a "mouse click" and a sound to be used when the mouse is over the button.
If you do not have sound files you can find there are a few sample sounds in the Flash Common Library. Choose Window-Common Library - Sounds.

For this project you will need two basic sound files. A mousedown "click" sound and a mouse over "wrrr" sound, saved in either the "AIF", "WAVE" or MP3 formats. If you do not have sound files you can use the samples sounds provided in the Flash Common Library.

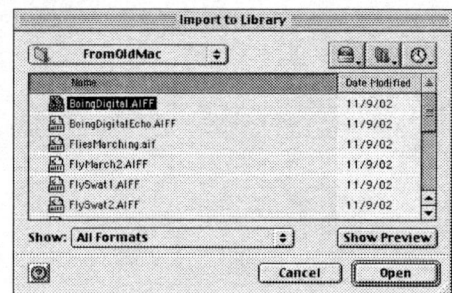

Import dialog box with sound selected.

Sound Import Problems

Play Button

Testing Sounds in Flash

Adding Sound to the Over State

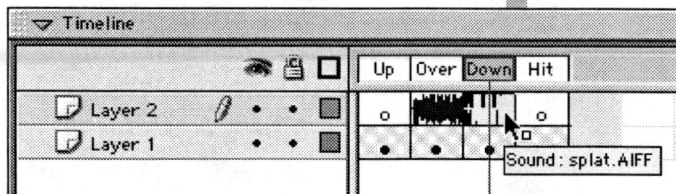

Adding Sound to the Down State

Note: *It is a good idea to have a sound editing utility, such as Peak. Flash is fussy and if the sound has any type of compression applied, Flash will refuse to import the file. If Flash refuses to import your sound file you can open it in Peak (or some other sound editing application) and to save it uncompressed in either the AIF or WAVE file format. This fixes the problem ninety nine percent of the time. If it cannot be opened in a sound editor the sound file may be corrupted.*

❑ Open the Library palette to see the imported sounds.
You can preview/listen to the sounds by clicking on the play button in the library palette.

Adding the sound to the button:
❑ Double click on the "button" in the Library palette, to enter the symbol editor for the button.

❑ Add a new layer to the button symbol.

❑ Add a keyframe to the Over and Down states on the new layer, as shown.

❑ With the Over state selected, in layer 2, drag the "over sound" file from the library onto the stage.

❑ With the Down state selected, in layer 2, drag the "down sound" file onto the stage, as shown

❑ Use Control-Test Movie to test the movie to see how it works.

If it works properly the over sound should play when you move the cursor over the button. When you click on the button, the down sound should play.

Adding sound to Flash buttons is easy. The real key is finding copyright free sounds (or creating your own) and saving them in an uncompressed format that Flash will accept.

CHAPTER 20

Controlling Timeline Sound

This short project provides a simple tool for controlling a sound loop on the timeline. Chapter 22 will provide a better tool for controlling sound using the ActionScript sound object.

The project:
❑ Launch Flash and create a new document.

❑ Choose Window-Panel Sets-Default Layout to rearrange the palettes.

❑ Import a background sound loop into the library.

❑ Display the Library palette, Window-Library.

❑ Drag the sound onto the stage.

❑ Click on Frame 15 and insert a keyframe (F6).

❑ Click on frame 1 on the timeline.

❑ In the properties palette set sound Sync to start, and the Loop to 50.

Theoretically, setting the Sync to start should mean that the sound will only start when the movie starts and will never start again, but if you use the ActionScript command "StopAllSounds" the sound will start again when the playback head hits frame 1. To understand this minor problem work through the next few steps.

❑ Create a button graphic on the stage called Stop sound.

THE PROJECT

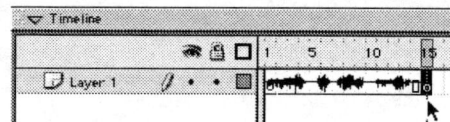

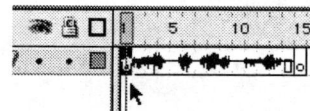

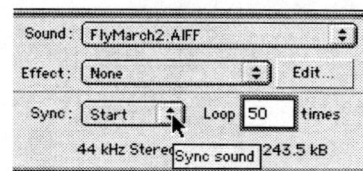

STOP ALL SOUNDS BUTTON

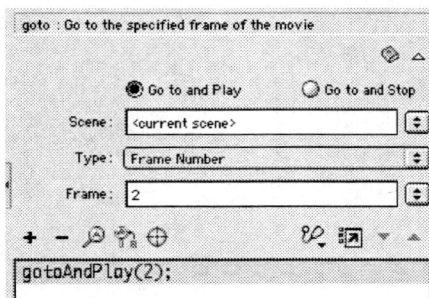

START SOUND BUTTON

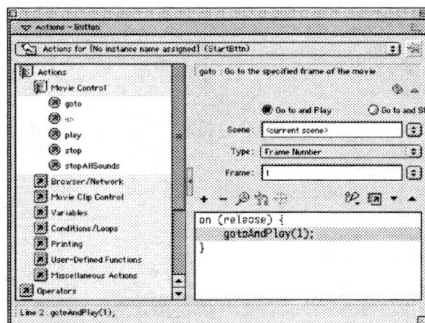

```
on (release) {
    gotoAndPlay(1);
}
```

❏ With the button graphic selected, open the Actions palette and choose Actions-Movie Control-stopAllSounds, as shown.

```
on (release) {
    stopAllSounds();
}
```

❏ Choose control Test-Movie, to see the effect.

Note: the button stops the sound temporarily, but then the sound starts again. To stop looping timeline sounds we need to prevent the playback head from going back to frame 1.

❏ Add a new layer to the timeline.

❏ On frame 15 insert a blank keyframe (F7).

❏ Open the Actions Palette and place the following script on frame 15.

```
gotoAndPlay(2);
```

❏ Choose control Test-Movie, to see the effect.

What changed? You are now sending the playback head to frame 2 which means the sound never starts again.

To get the timeline sound playing again you only need to send the playback head to frame 1.

❏ Create a new button symbol on the stage, to start the sound.

❏ Open the Actions Palette and insert a script to tell the playback head to go to and play frame one.

Note: You might be saying, "OK, this works but it is messing up my animation." In a few chapters we will discuss how to create movieClip objects that run independently. This means we could create a separate sound player application, convert it into a movieClip object and it will run on its own independent timeline.

Controlling Timeline Sound

CHAPTER 21

Dynamic Text Fields

This chapter explores ActionScript and some basic scripting concepts. If you are familiar with programming you may want to jump over this discussion and move directly to the project. If you are not familiar with programming then understand that the jargon might at first seem a bit confusing but hopefully by the end of this chapter, and as you continue on in the book, the concepts discussed will make more sense.

IMPORTANT TERMINOLOGY
BASICS

What is a variable? A variable is programming jargon for a container that can hold information. Generally variables are hidden inside the computer code and are never seen, but Flash has this cool feature that allows you to create a dynamic text field that acts as a variable. Part of the advantage of this is that we can see the variable. This can be helpful if you need to troubleshoot a problem script, or create a score counter for a game. Additionally this means you can use ActionScript to display and change text information directly on the stage or you can use ActionScript to capture user input, manipulate it and store it for later use.

VARIABLES

Creating variables in Flash is relatively easy. In the following example the variable **addStuff** is created and given a numeric value of 10.

```
addStuff = 10;
```

In this next example the variable myText is created and holds the text "Hello."

```
myText = "Hello";
```

Variables can be given almost any name you choose, with the exception of reserved words used by flash such as "go to", "call", or "play". On the

Numeric Variables

Text Variables

Button 1

```
1  on (press) {
2      mytxt = "ABCD";
3  }
4  |
```

Button 2

```
1  on (press) {
2      mytxt = mytxt + "EFG";
3  }
```

other hand you could use myPlay as a variable name without problem. It is also a good idea to give variables a name that helps you to remember what they do.

Numbers:
To provide a short example in Flash we could create a variable called addStuff and give it a starting value of 10.

```
addStuff = 10;
```

If we asked for the value of addStuff it of course would be 10. If later in our animation, we created the statement:

```
addStuff = 1+4;
```

addStuff would now have the value of 5. Note that 1+4 was NOT added to the value of 10 but instead replaced it. What if we wanted to add 4+1 to the existing value of addstuff. The script might look like the following:

```
addStuff = addStuff + 1+4;
```

Note: there are no quotes around numbers.

Text:
Variables can also contain letters or words. Most programming languages will refer to individual letters as **char** (short for character). A bunch of letters strung together are referred to as a **string**.

```
textStuff = "a string of letters";
```

In Flash a char or string will be enclosed in "quotes".

To combine letters to create a word or to combine words to create a sentence or paragraph is referred to as **concatenate** which means to combine or to join together.

In Flash the concatenate operator is + symbol. In the example on the left, when Button 1 is pressed, it places the chars "ABCD" into the variable called mytxt. When Button 2 is pressed it adds the chars "EFG" to form a final string of "ABCDEFG".

Dynamic Text Fields

If a programming statement is used to join several different words and put them into a variable called **greeting**, it could look like the following...

```
+  🔍 🔁 ⊕ ✔ ☰ 💬                          🏷 ✂
1 on (press) {
2     greeting = "Hi, " + "how " + "are " + "you? "
3 }
```

The result would look like the following...
```
Hi, how are you?
```

To use programming jargon you would say that the first **char** of the first **string** in the **concatenation** above is a capital H.
It would be silly to concatenate each individual word when instead you could simply create the variable called greeting using the following.
```
greeting="Hi, how are you?";
```

On the other hand you may have captured the user's name and stored it in a variable called userName. In order to concatenate the user name with the string, you might do something like the following.

```
1 on (press) {
2     greeting = "Hi, " + userName + " how are you?"
3 }
```

Note that in the above statement the strings are enclosed by quotation marks but the variable that contains the user's name is not in quotes.

If the information provided so far does not make sense at first reading, then take some time to reread it. It will help with understanding the following project.

One of the things that is enjoyable about applications like Flash is that it offers easy entry into the world of computer programming. The concepts you learn here will be applicable to other programming languages and by gaining some basic programming skills you can dramatically expand the range of what is possible with Flash.

THE LOOP COUNTER PROJECT:

For this project we will create a variable that counts the number of times our animation loops and we will use the dynamic text feature to display this information on the stage.

❏ Create a new Flash document and make sure the background color is white.

❏ Using the text tool [A] draw a text box in the center of the stage.

CREATING DYNAMIC TEXT

❏ While the text field is still active use the Properties palette to set the text field to "Dynamic Text".

❏ Set the text options as shown.
1. Turn word wrap on
2. Turn selectable off.
3. Most importantly name the variable **"count."**

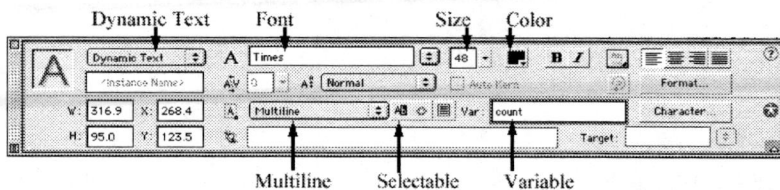

The variable name does not have to be the word count and can be any word you want. The key is to choose something that is both easy to remember and that helps to remind you what this variable does. Since this variable will be used to count the number of times our animation loops "count" is a good name.

Dynamic Text   Font   Size   Color

Multiline   Selectable   Variable

IMBEDDING FONTS

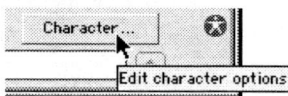

Note: The text field uses the fonts in the user's computer. If you choose an unusual font, it will most likely revert to the user's default of Times or Ariel. The text options palette does provide the option of imbedding font outlines. To imbed font outlines select Character on the Properties Palette. Use this feature sparingly in order to avoid excessively large Flash animations.

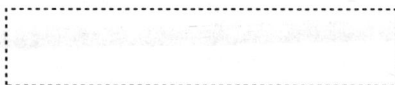

Now that the text field is defined as Dynamic Text, the text field will appear on the stage as a dotted outline (or a blue outline when selected). The dotted outline will vanish when viewed in a browser.

❏ Click on frame 12 of the timeline.

❑ Choose Insert-Frame (F5). Insert Frame will extend the timeline without adding a new keyframe.

❑ Add a new layer.

Layer 1 contains the text field so we will add a new layer to use for ActionScript code.

❑ Insert a keyframe on frame 12 of the layer 2.

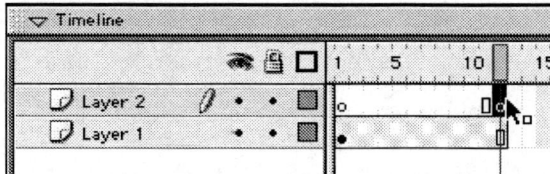

❑ With Frame 12 of layer 2 still selected choose Windows-Actions. Make sure you are in the Normal Mode.

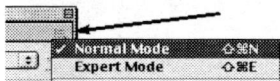

❑ From the Actions books choose Actions-Variables-set variable, and drag this command into the actions window as shown.

❑ In the "Variable:" field, enter the name of the text field variable: "count".

❑ In the "Value:" area select the Expression button, then type in the Value: "count + 1".

❑ The script window should display the following

```
count = count+1;
```

❑ Test the movie to make sure it works.

If all is working properly you should see the text field increment by one for every loop the animation makes.

One way you might use this simple script is as a timer in an interactive web game. You would provide the user with a specific amount of time to complete the game and once the time is expired the game is over. If you look at the additional explora-

ADDING A ACTIONSCRIPT LAYER

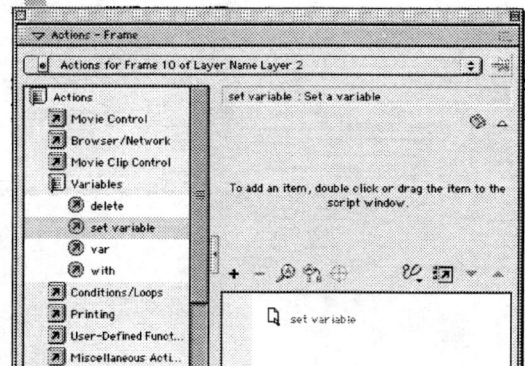

Set Variable command

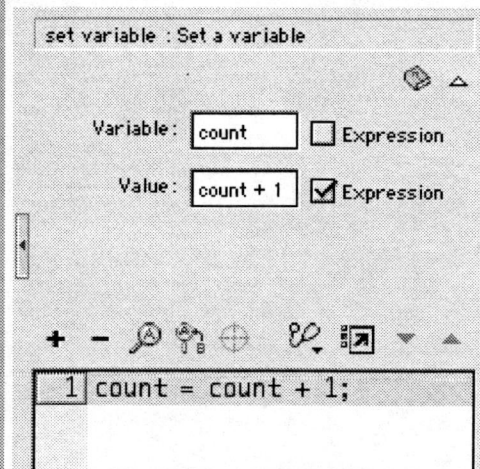

GAME TIMER

tion you will see how this can be accomplished using an "if" statement.

Note to programmers: Since the default playback speed is 12 frames per second the timer would "theoretically" increment once every second. If you test the timer with a stopwatch you will note that it is not technically accurate. Computer processor speed, RAM, the type and amount of animation and other factors will alter Flash playback speed and the "real" frames per second. My upcoming book "ActionScript for Artists" discusses how to access the computer's clock in order to create a technically accurate timer.

ADDITIONAL EXPLORATION

Additional Exploration:

1. Create a futuristic animation with animated counting numbers.

USING IF STATEMENTS

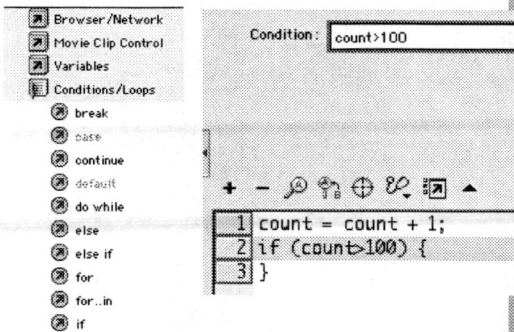

2. You can add an "If" statement to this script, to check the number of loops.

❑ Double-click on frame 10 of layer 2, to display your ActionScript.

❑ Select the "If" statement from the Actions Book, as shown.

❑ In the ActionScript palette, type in the Condition: count>100.

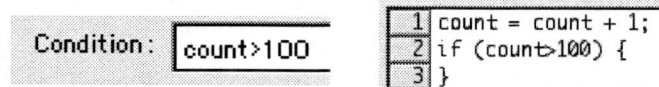

```
Condition: count>100
```

```
1  count = count + 1;
2  if (count>100) {
3  }
```

Pop Quiz Question: How could you create a timer that counts down rather than counting up?

❑ With the IF statement still selected, choose the Stop command from Basic Actions. Your script should look like the following:

```
1  count = count + 1;
2  if (count>100) {
3      stop();
4  }
5
```

❑ Test the movie to see if the "If" statement is working.

Note: that you could have easily dropped in a "goto" statement in place of the "Stop" command in order to have the movie go to a game over animation.

When ActionScript is used to take control of the sound the results can be exciting. Not only can you control the start and stop of the sound but you can also control sound volume and speaker balance. You can access and load MP3 sound files that are not currently imbedded in your SWF. This means that the user does not need to wait for a sound heavy SWF to download, they will download the player application you created and only wait to load individual sounds. In addition this means that you can create a sound player and upload new sound files without rewriting the SWF. You can also use ActionScript to check to see if the sound has been loaded and is ready to play.

Before you begin this project you will want to create a sound-off and a sound-on button images. Each button should be no bigger than 50x50 pixels. If you choose to work in Photoshop, remember to Save-For-The-Web using the PNG-24 file format.

Set-up

❑ Launch Flash and create a new document.

❑ Choose Window-Panel Sets-Default Layout.

Panel Sets	▶	Default Layout

❑ Create graphics that will represent the sound-off and a sound-on-button. Remember each should be no larger than 50 x 50 pixels.
If you created the button in any application other than Flash choose File-Import to import them.

Wow!! Total Sound Control

This chapter explores creating an ActionScript "object". What is an object? The simplest explanation is that objects have a variety of commands that can be used to modify the object. But first we need to tell Flash what the object is and give the object a name before we can apply the commands.. Being able to control sound offers a wealth of creative opportunities. For example, as you become more knowledgeable you could create a graphic that, as the cursor moves closer the sound becomes louder.

The buttons shown below were created in Flash.

Project Set-up

❑ If the buttons are not on the stage, drag them from the library onto the stage.

❑ Convert the button graphics into button symbols. Name the sound-off-button "SoundOff". Name the sound-on-button "SoundOn".

❑ If you have time you can experiment with adding an over and a down state for the buttons.

❑ Import a small sound loop into Flash.

The Project

Rather than placing the sound in the Flash movie, we will leave it in the library. In order to control a sound that is in the library we need to set its "Linkage", which basically means to give it a name and to tell Flash that it can be used from the library.

❑ Select the sound in the Library palette, then choose the Options pop-out menu and select Linkages.

The Identifier is how ActionScript will refer to the sound, so choose a name that you will be able to remember later.

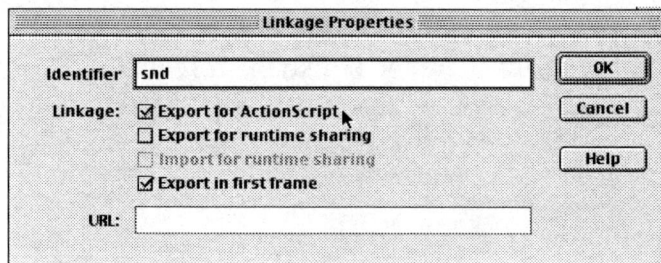

❏ Use the Identifier "snd" for this sound, as shown. Set the Linkage to "Export for ActionScript", and Export in first frame" then close this dialog.

Adding the ActionScript:
❏ Click once on the off-button on the stage, to select it, then choose Window-Actions (or F9 on the keyboard), to display the Actions Window.

❏ Choose Actions—Movie Control—Stop All Sounds command and drag it into the Actions window as shown..

ActionScript to Stop Sounds

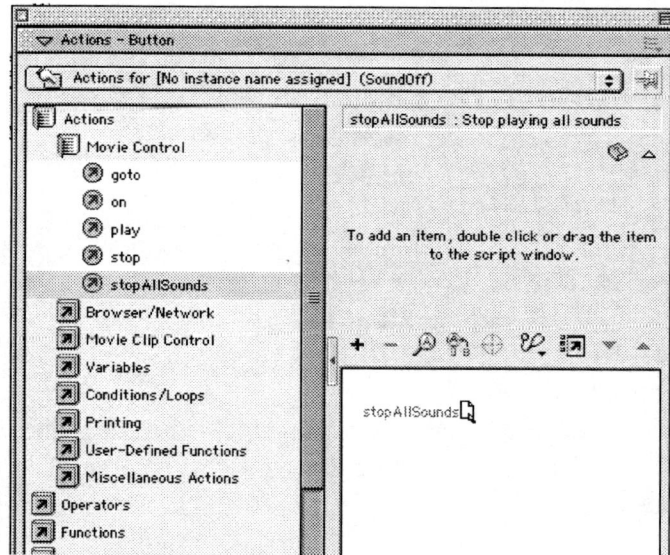

The script should look like the following.

```
on (release) {
    stopAllSounds ();
}
```

❏ Close the Object Actions dialog. The sound-off-button is now complete.

For the on-button the scripting is a little more involved.

❏ Click once on the on-button on the stage, to select it, then choose Window-Actions (or F9 on the keyboard), to display the Actions window.

❏ On the right side of the Actions window is a pop-out menu. Use it to switch to Expert Mode. This will allow you to type code directly into Flash.

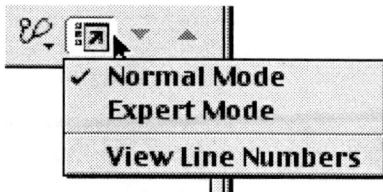

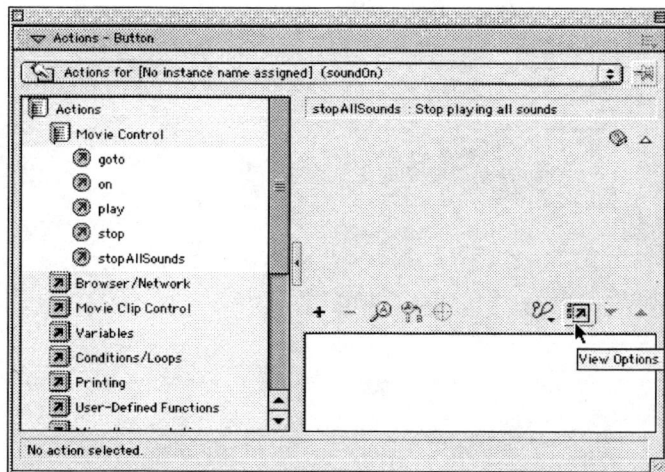

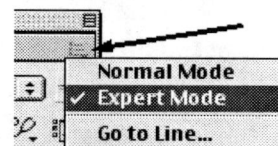

OR

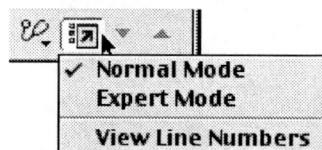

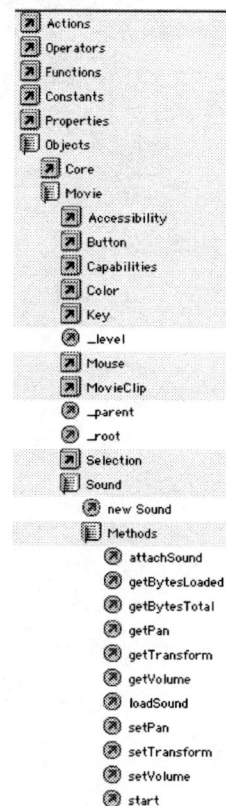

❑ Type in the following code exactly as shown.

```
on (release) {
    mysnd=new Sound();
    mysnd.attachSound("snd");
    mysnd.start(0,50);
}
```

Explantation of the code:
On release is the event that triggers the following actions.

`mysnd= newSound();` creates a variable mySound as a container that can hold sound.

`mysnd.attachSound("snd");`
attaches the linked library file to the variable mySound.
Note: that the name we used in the Symbol Linkage properties (for the library sound) must exactly match the name used in the attachSound command.

`mysnd.start(0,50);` starts the sound playing and uses the loop parameter to repeat it for 50 times.

Checking for Errors:
❏ Click on the Check Syntax button as shown in the diagram.

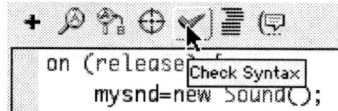

```
on (release
        mysnd=new Sound();
```

If there is an easily identifiable problem with the code you will receive and alert message.

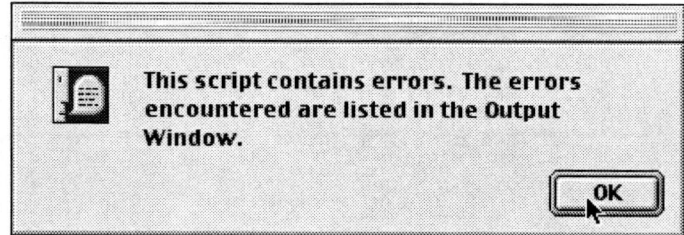

This script contains errors. The errors encountered are listed in the Output Window.

OK

Flash will also display the Output dialog which will inform you what the problem is. At first the error message in the Output window may not make much sense, but as you become more familiar with Flash and ActionScript you will find the message save a lot of problem solving time. In the example below the message indicates that the event handler on(release) needs a closing curly brace at the end. This is a common script error. The output window says that line 1 has an opening curly brace. It also says that line 5 should have had a closing curly brace.

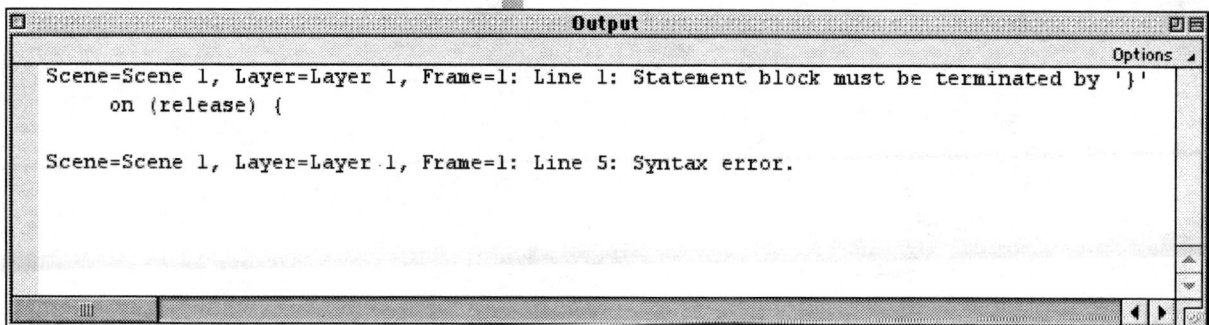

Output

```
Scene=Scene 1, Layer=Layer 1, Frame=1: Line 1: Statement block must be terminated by '}'
        on (release) {

Scene=Scene 1, Layer=Layer 1, Frame=1: Line 5: Syntax error.
```

Options

❑ Once you have corrected any major errors close the Actions window and test the movie. Note the sound will not start until you click on the start button.

Additional Exploration.

1. See if you can find a way to get the sound to start when the movie starts.

2. See if you can import another sound and use the same movie with a new sound.

Adding sound volume buttons:

3. ❑ Create three small buttons that fit onto the stage and allow the user to choose different sound volume of either, loud, medium and quiet. The key to having these buttons work is using the same variable (mysnd).

setVolume allows you to set the volume from 1 to 100.
Once you get the buttons to work create simple graphic symbols that allow the user to visually understand the purpose of these sound volume buttons. Try to create the symbols without using text.

```
//Loud button
On (release) {
mysnd.setVolume(100);
}
```

```
//Medium button
On (release) {
mysnd.setVolume(75);
}
```

```
//Quiet button
On (release) {
mysnd.setVolume(40);
}
```

Speaker Balance buttons:

4. ❏ Create three new buttons to allow the user to switch from left to right speaker.
Note: These button will not be very useful if the user does not have stereo speakers.

setPan allows you to set the sound from the left (-100) to the right (100) speaker.

Once you get the buttons to work create simple graphic symbols that allow the user to visually understand the purpose of these sound volume buttons. Try to create the symbols without using text.

```
//Left Speaker
On (release) {
mysnd.setPan(-100);
}
```

```
//Both Speakers
On (release) {
mysnd.setPan(0);
}
```

```
//Right Speaker
On (release) {
mysnd.setVolume(100);
}
```

This is where the real fun begins. Now that you know how to create an animation, a button symbol, and use basic ActionScript, the movieclip feature opens the door to power-user web creation.

You have already seen how movieClips can help to build your animation. What this and several following projects will demonstrate is how we can use ActionScript inside a movie clip to create smart animated objects. Flash is the only commercial animation application that has this capability. Even Macromedia Director does not provide this powerful feature. The examples provided in this chapter and book are only the beginning of what you can do when you begin creating smart animated objects.

For this project you will first create a simple animated button that stops when the user rolls over it, and starts when the user rolls off. The animated button will then be converted into a movieclip that can be used repeatedly in other animations. In the next chapter we will use the same concept to create an interactive Web game.

As you continue to work with Flash you'll want to refer to this chapter to review the steps on "converting an animation into a movieclip".

❑ Create a new Flash Document and reset the palettes to Default.

❑ Create a circle on the stage and convert it into a button symbol called "ballButton." Add a simple over and down state to the button.

PROJECT

CREATE A BUTTON SYMBOL ON THE STAGE

Putting Actions into an Animated Button

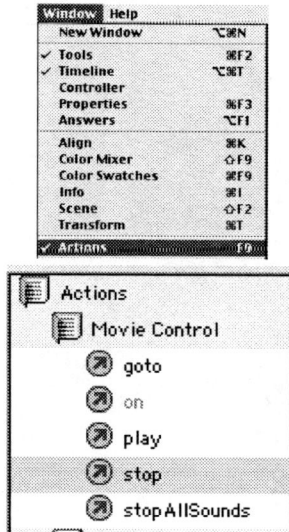

on (rollOver) {
    stop ();
}

The Final Button Script

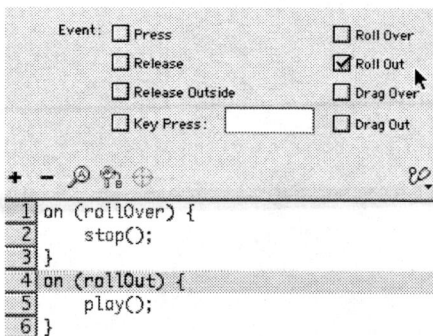

For this project we will add our scripts before we animate the object.

❏ Click once on the button object on the stage and choose Window-Actions.

Make sure you are in Normal Mode in the Actions window.

✓ **Normal Mode**　　　　⇧⌘N

❏ Choose Actions-MovieControl and drag the stop() action into the script.

❏ Select the first line of the script on(Release) and change the event to on(Rollover) as shown.

```
on (rollOver) {
  stop ();
}
```

The script you just created tells the player that when you roll over the button the movie should stop.

❏ Select the last line in the script then drag the play command below the last line, as shown in the diagrams

```
1 on (rollOver) {
2     stop();
3 }
      play
```

❏ Click on line 4 and change the "on(Release)" event to on(rollOut) as shown in the diagram.

Your Script should now look like the following...

```
on (rollOver) {
    stop();
}
on (rollOut) {
    play();
}
```

❑ In the upper right corner of the stage, set view to 50%.

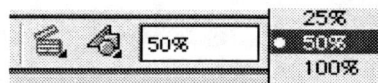

❑ Place the button beyond the far left edge of the stage, as shown below.

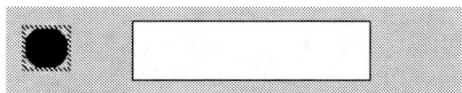

❑ Insert a keyframe on frame 50, and then position the button beyond the far right edge of the stage.

❑ Click on frame 1 and use the properties palette to create a motion tween so the button moves from the far left slowly beyond the right edge of the stage. See diagram.

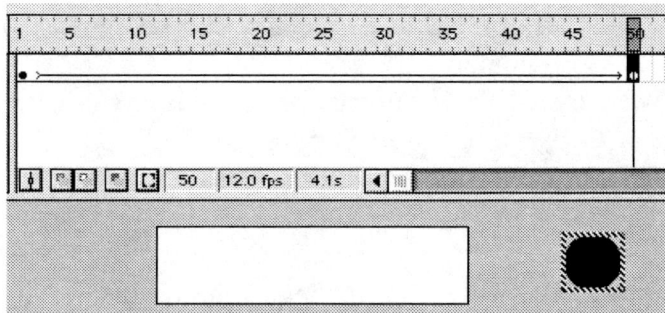

❑ Test this movie using the Control-TestMovie command. If all went well the button should move across the stage. When you roll the mouse over it should stop and when you roll the cursor it should start moving again. But Wait!!, it gets better.

❑ Save this movie as "buttonStop.fla".

Note: A button can be placed in a movieclip and the button will still act according to its script.

MAKING THE MOVIECLIP

STEP 1- SELECT ALL FRAMES

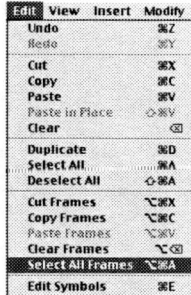

In the previous few pages you created a button symbol and added ActionScript to stop the movie when the mouse is over the button, and resume playing when the mouse was moved off the button.

Creating the Movieclip.

❏ Click on any frame on the timeline and choose Edit-**Select All Frames.**
*Note: there is a major difference between Edit-Select All and Edit-***Select All Frames***.*

You should now see all of the frames on the timline highlighted.

STEP 2- COPY ALL FRAMES

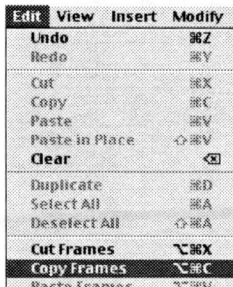

❏ With all of the frames selected, choose Edit-**CopyFrames.**
*Note: there is a difference between Edit-Copy and Edit-***CopyFrames***. Edit-CopyFrames will copy all of the selected frames in your animation.*

❏ With all of the frames copied, choose Insert-New Symbol.

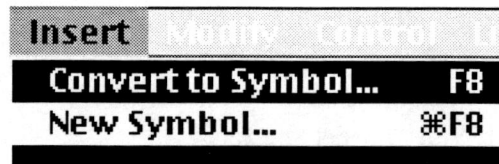

STEP 3 CREATE THE MOVIECLIP SYMBOL

❏ Set the behavior to **Movie Clip** and name it "BallClip".

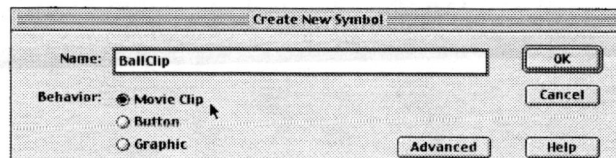

❑ When you choose OK you will enter the movieclip symbol editor. Look at the timeline and the stage, you will notice that both are empty.

❑ In the symbol editor, click on frame 1 to highlight it, then choose Edit-**Paste Frames**.

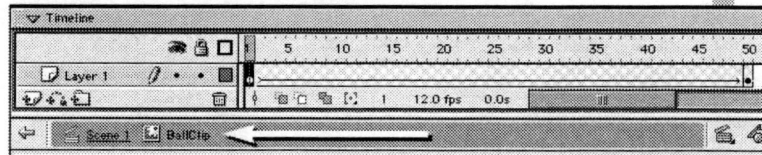

| Paste Frames | ⌥⌘V |

Note: Below the timeline that you are in the BallClip symbol editor.

❑ Choose Window Library to display the Library palette.

| ✓ **Library** | F11 |

Make sure the Library palette is displayed, and that you can see the "BallClip" displayed in the Library palette before continuing.

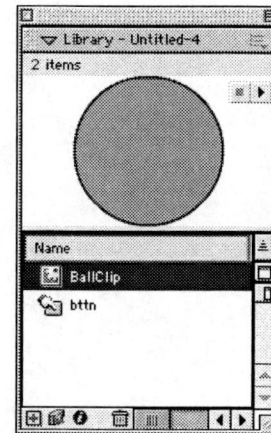

❑ Create a new document.

I suggest that it is always better to use a movieclip symbol in a NEW document because it helps to avoid confusion. This suggestion is based on classroom experience.

CREATE A NEW DOCUMENT

❑ In the new document, drag several instances of the "BallClip" beyond the left edge of the stage. Place them at various locations, on the left edge.
(See diagram.)
They can all be placed in frame 1 of layer 1.

❑ Test the new movie using Control-TestMovie.

Is this great or what? Each object moves independently. When you roll over an object it only stops the individual movieclip while the rest continue to play.

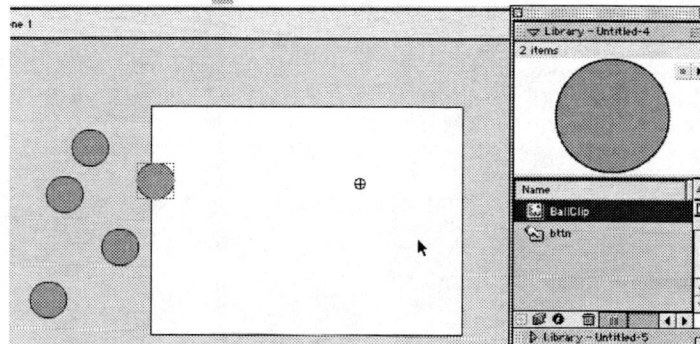

Important: If you had problems with this project, I encourage you to walk back through the steps and try again. This is one of those concepts that can take a while but once you get it, you will be amazed at what you can do.

ADDITIONAL EXPLORATION

Additional Exploration:

1. Have each object appear in a different color or transparency. Select one instance of the BallClip on the stage, then experiment with the effects available in the Effect palette.

2. If you have not already done so, change the Over and Down states of the buttons inside the movieclip. Note how the changes are reflected in all instances of the movieclip.

3. See if you can create an animation where several animated movieclips link to a different web sites. See if you can figure out how to create a different over and down state for each separate movieclip.

CHAPTER 24

Creating a Web Game

This is a simple Arcade style web game that will extend your familiarity with movieclips. With a little imagination you will come up with a variety of objects that would lend themselves to the Arcade style game format. This project can also be used to create a variety of other interactive games. "Underwater Bursting Bubbles" is one example of a children's game that is described at the end of this chapter in Further Exploration.

There are several components that make up a good Arcade game. These are just a few.

1. A Compelling Idea. Something unusual, fun or creative. Zombies, frogs, flies, and ducks are always fun, but instead let your imagination go wild. Come up with something amazing or bizarre.

2. Challenge. The objects need to move and they should not be too easy to hit. Other challenge elements that are beyond the scope of this project are scoring and a timer. Both can be added, and will be discussed in a later chapter.

3. Sounds. If your game is to swat flies then a good squashy splat sound can make it much more fun.

In this project I am going to assume that you have read and understood the information in the previous chapters.

GAMES

WHAT YOU SHOULD KNOW

To produce this project you should know:

• How to create and tween an object.
• How to create a button, and how to set its Over, Down and Hit states.
• How to add sound to a button when the user clicks.
• How to access the ActionScript editor.

❑ Create a new document and set the palettes to default.

START WITH A BUTTON

❑ Create a simple graphic on the stage and convert it into a Button Symbol.

❑ Open the library palette, and double click on the button symbol. *If you cannot tell which object is the button symbol, expand the palette to see the labels.*

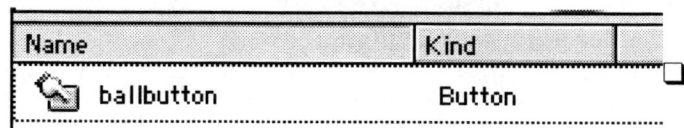

Name	Kind	
🖐 ballbutton	Button	

Add a keyframe to each of the states (if they are not already there).

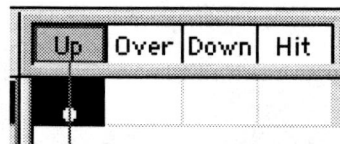

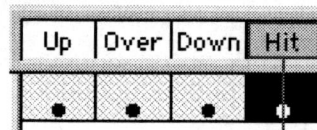

Up	Over	Down	Hit
●			

Up	Over	Down	Hit
●	●	●	●

When the user drags over our button, we want to make it look like the button is targeted in our arcade game. *This can be accomplished by changing the buttons color in the Over state.*

MODIFY THE OVER STATE

❑ To change the balls color: Open the button in the symbol editor, select the Over state, select the paint bucket tool from the tool palette, set the color to amber or orange and click on the button object to change its color.

❑ Adding the cross-hairs: With the fill turned off, and the line thickness set to one pixel, draw a circle around the object. Then draw the cross-hairs.

Now when the user rolls the cursor over the button, the user has the impression that the arcade object is being targeted.

❑ Select the button Down state. Use the lasso tool to select and break the button apart. The goal is to present the illusion that the object was shot. If you want you can add in a bit of smoke and fire. See diagram.

Note: You may find it fun and exciting to create your button states in either FireWorks or Photoshop. If you know Bryce or a 3D application you could come up with some very cool arcade game objects for your button states. Even though FireWorks or Photoshop bitmapped images can take up extra file size, this button object is pretty small and the impact on your file size should be minimal.

❑ To make the game more challenging you could make the Hit state smaller.
The Hit state does not show up in the animation but it does affect where the cursor must be placed in order to select the button.

CHANGE THE DOWN STATE

ADD THE BUTTON SOUND

Now to add a "Bang" sound. If you have a bang sound lying around, then do the following. If you do not have a bang sound choose Window-Common Libraries-Sounds and use the "Bucket Hit" sound. The "Smack" sound will also work.

❑ Add a new layer to the button states.

❑ Click on frame 1 of the new layer and hit the F7 key 3 times. (To create a blank keyframe in each of the states.)

❑ Select the Down state on the new layer.

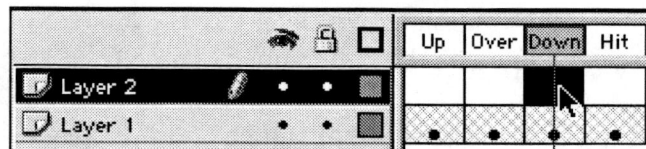

❑ Import a sound file. AIF or .WAV. (or use the Bucket Hit sound from common libraries).

❑ With the down state selected, drag the sound onto the stage.

❑ Return to Scene 1.

❑ Choose Control-Test Movie to see how it works so far. When you roll over the button it appears in the cross-hairs. When you successfully click on the moving button, the "bang" sound occurs.

This game object needs a bit of code to make it complete. After it explodes it should vanish.

MAKE IT VANISH

❑ Click once on the button on the stage, then choose Window-Actions (F9) to display the Actions window.

❑ *Make sure you are in the Normal Mode.*
The script we are going to use will make the object invisible. Whether an object is visible or not is an ActionScript Property.

Creating a Web Game

❏ In the Actions books, select Properties and drag _visible property into the script area.

Above the script area you will note that visible is an expression that can be edited.

❏ Change the expression to _visible = 0.

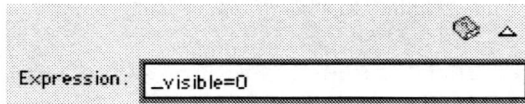

Expression: | _visible=0 |

Your script should look like the following.

```
on (release) {
    _visible=0;
}
```

This script says that when the button is clicked it will vanish, or is no longer visible.

❏ Close Object Actions and save this movie as "GameSource.fla"

This is not the final game. It is the source file that will be used for the final game.

❏ Choose Control-Test Movie to see if the script is working properly. When the user rolls over the button it should change in appearance. When the user successfully clicks on the button it should make a bang sound, explode, and vanish.

Kind of a boring game at this point. What is missing? Challenge!! A moving object is more exciting than a static object.

❏ Move the object far off the left edge of the stage.

❏ Click on Frame 1 of the timeline and apply a motion tween using the Properties palette.

❏ Click on frame 30 and insert a keyframe (F6) and move the object far off the right side of the stage.

ANIMATE THE GAME OBJECT

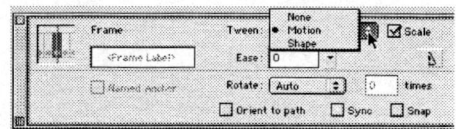

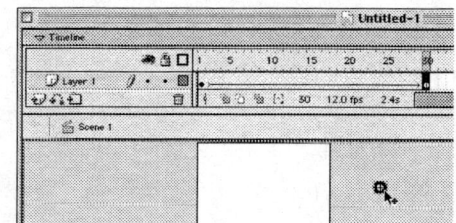

❑ Choose Control-Test Movie to see if the object is working.

Note: You may notice that the object does not always disappear. This is because, in our actionScript we set the visibility to 0 when the users "releases". We could change the script to on(press) but then the down state of the button exploding will not appear. Later chapters will discuss how to address this.

Now to create the final game. In order to have a truly exciting game we will need to have several instances of this object. A game with only one target gets old quick. With Flash and movieclips creating several instances is easy. In the next few steps you will convert this animation into a movieclip and then we can place several instances on the stage of a new movie.

❑ Select all of the frames for this movie.
Click on a frame in the time line, and choose Edit-Select all frames.

❑ Choose Edit-Copy**Frames**.

❑ With all of the frames copied choose Insert-New Symbol.

MAKE THE GAME OBJECT REUSABLE

CONVERT TO MOVIECLIP

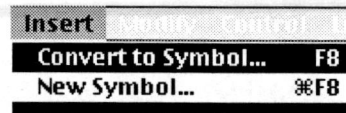

❑ Select the movieclip option and name it "ArcadeBall".

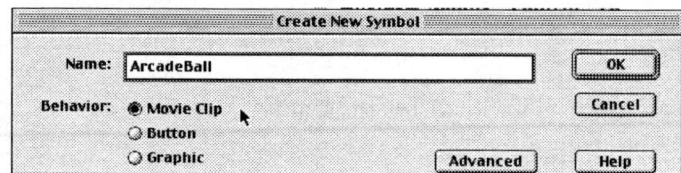

❑ In the symbol editor, click on frame 1 to select it, then choose Edit-Paste **Frames**.

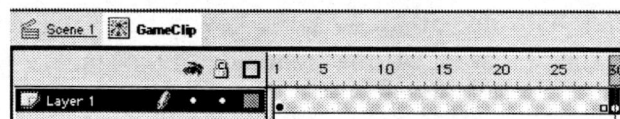

❑ Open the Library palette.
Make sure the Library palette is displayed, and that you can see the GameClip before you continue on.

❑ Create a new document.

❑ In the new movie, drag 10-20 copies of the GameClip to the far left side off the stage. Stagger the placement. *They can all be placed in frame 1 of layer 1.*

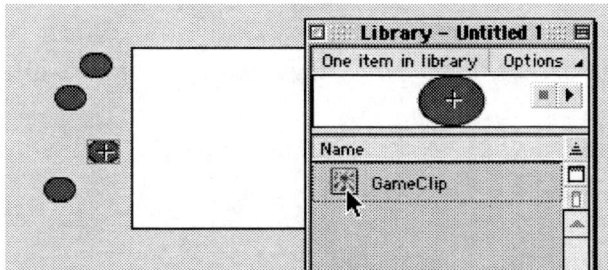

Project Notes:
This project makes a great preloader for content heavy web sites. It downloads fast and offers the user something interesting to do while they are waiting.
A really attractive sci-fi variation on this project is to set the background to black. Then revise the buttons with a gradient fill, where the inside is a color and the outer edge is set to black. It will look like floating stars.
In the final movie, you can use the effects palette to change the color of each object and also resize each object to add variation.
If you duplicate the movieclip, in the destination movie, and open it from the library palette, you can shorten the timeline. Add several copies of the duplicate clip in order to have different objects moving at different speeds.

❑ Test the movie using Control-TestMovie.

❑ Save this document as FlashGame1. FLA

Great Stuff!! In upcoming chapters we will discuss how you can make the hit more interesting and how you can display the user's score.
This is just the beginning of what can be produced using Flash movieclips to create "smart objects."

Further Exploration:

1. Come up with an interesting concept for an arcade style game. Create the graphics, then follow the steps in this project to develop something new, unique and interesting.

2. Underwater Bursting Bubbles.
The following is an example of how you can use the same project to create an interesting children's game that is nonviolent but still utilizes the point and shoot techniques discussed here.
Create a graphic of a bubble using either Photoshop, Fireworks, Freehand, Illustrator or Flash. Create a new document. Add a graphic to the down state of the bubblebutton that makes it appear to pop. Add a "pop"

Further Exploration

3. Making the Game More Challenging

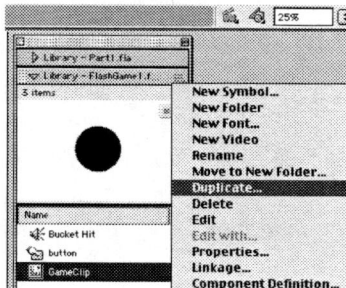

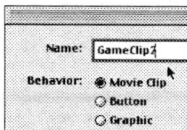

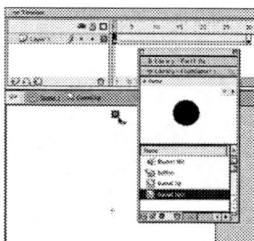

sound to the down state of the bubblebutton. Script the button to vanish when the user releases the mouse. Convert the single bubble animation into a movieclip. Create a new movie with a background image of an underwater scene. Place 10-20 instances of the bubblePop clip at the bottom of the stage.

3. Open the library palette and click on the "GameClip" symbol. In the upper right corner of the library palette choose the pop-out menu and Duplicate, as shown.

❏ Change the name to "GameClip2" and choose OK.

❏ Double click to open "GameClip2" to access the "GameClip2" symbol.

❏ Reduce the stage size to 25%.

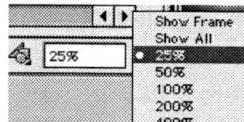

❏ Click on frame 1 of "GameClip2" and move the object to the top of the stage, as shown.

❏ Click on frame 30 of "GameClip2" and move the object to the bottom of the stage.

❏ Choose Scene 1 and place several new instances of "GameClip2" at the top of the stage.

❏ Test the movie.

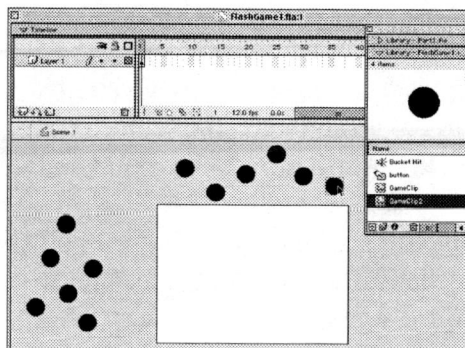

Creating a Web Game

CHAPTER 25

Smart Object WOW Effects

This is another example of using movieclips to encapsulate simple animation to create a "smart object." To see an example of this project go to http://hotflashbook.com/mactech/MacTech.html then choose "Visual 2 Circle fade".

By the completion of this project you should begin to get a feel for using smart objects. The screen shots do not do justice to the experience of revealing a picture beneath. Please look at the web based example.

When I ask programmers how they would accomplish this effect the first thing they mention is an array to track cursor location and complex equations to perform the effect. With smart objects this effect is easier than most imagine.

In a previous chapter, you produced an animated interactive web game using movieclips. What if the movieclips did not move but instead waited for the user to click or, roll over them? Then let's say that you create a new movie with an interesting photograph in the background. Rather than immediately presenting the photograph, you cover it with these animated movie-clip-buttons and, as the user drags over them, they explode or vanish slowly revealing the image behind.

SCREEN SHOT EXAMPLE

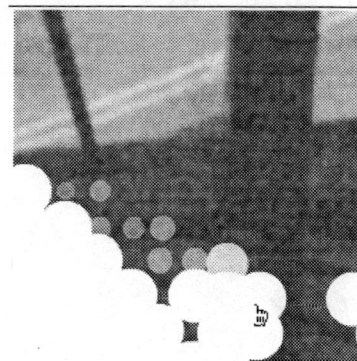

RELATED PROJECTS

As you explore the wealth of artistic Flash web sites, you will see that this concept is used repeatedly in a variety of interesting and unusual ways. As I mentioned in first chapter of this book, this is the power user stuff that Flash offers. No other web publishing application that I know of, including Director, can provide this type of graphically fascinating effect as easily. If you are a design artist, you will be absolutely amazed by the wealth of opportunities you have with this concept.

After a lecture on this topic a student approached me and asked if the same effect could be produced using the image of worms (or some such thing) as opposed to simple white objects? The answer is "yes" but I still wonder, to this day, what creation that student came up with. I imagine one day encountering a web page that is covered with slithering worms and as you drag over them the image behind is revealed.

PROJECT OVERVIEW

Just as in the previous project, you will create a movieclip and place several instances of it into a new final movie. The final destination movie will have two layers. Layer one for the background image and layer two for the movieclips which will cover the image until the user rolls over them.

The movieclip will start out as opaque white and respond to a rollover event by getting both smaller and more transparent until it has vanished. This project will take you step-by-step through the process of creating this animation but if you can figure out a Flash solution without using the step by step instructions, it will be to your benefit.

Here is the movieclip timeline.

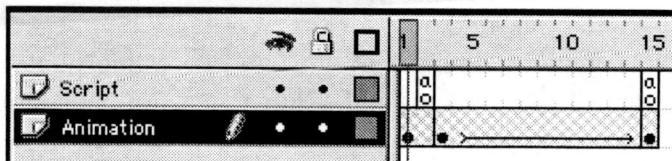

Smart Object WOW Effects

The animation layer has a white button that starts as opaque and stops on frame 2. Frame 3 - 15 tweens to transparent while getting smaller. The button instance on frames 1-2 has a control script.

```
on (rollOver) {
 gotoAndPlay (3);
}
```

The script layer has only two scripts. Frame 2 tells the movie to "stop" and frame 15 also tells the movie to stop.

Quick quiz: If frame 2 tells the movie to stop, then how is the user able to view the rest of this short movie?

Project setup:

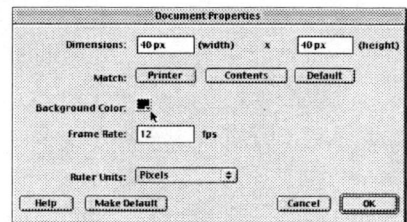

❑ Create a new movie, and set the Document size to 40x40 pixels. Set the background to black as this will help you to better see the white circle button you will create in the next step.

Creating the white button:

❑ Create a white circle that fits inside the stage.
❑ Convert the white circle into a button symbol.

Creating the shrink and fade tween:

❑ Insert a keyframe at frame 3 on the timeline.
❑ Insert a keyframe at frame 15 on the timeline.

❑ With frame 15 selected, choose the resize button on the tool palette and make the "white-circle-button" as small as possible.
Note: keep the circle positioned in the center of the stage. To help with centering, use the View-Grid-Edit Grid option and set the grid to 20 px x 20 px.

❑ With frame 15 still selected, click on the button on the stage and use the Properties palette to set the Alpha to 0%.

PROJECT SETUP

CREATE THE BUTTON

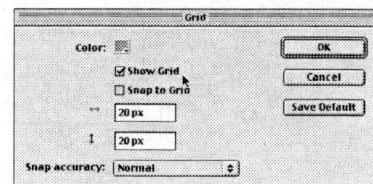

©BRADLEY KALDAHL 2003

CREATE THE TWEEN

❑ Select frame 3 and create a motion tween between frame 3 and frame 15.

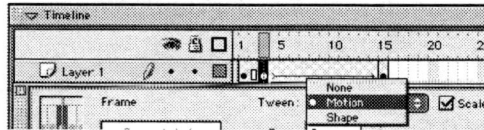

❑ Test the movie to see how it works.

The button should start as bright white then shrink and fade into nothing by the end of the animation. The next step is to add frame control to get it to stop while it is still white, and also to get it to stop at the end of the animation and prevent it from looping.

CREATE FRAME CONTROL

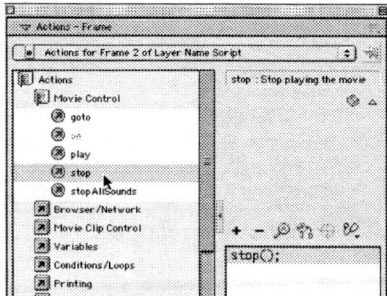

Adding Frame Control

❑ Add a new layer to your animation and label it Script.

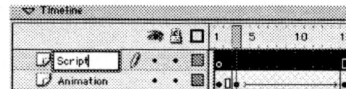

❑ Select frame 2 and insert a Blank keyframe (F7).
❑ Select frame 3 and insert a Blank keyframe (F7).
❑ Select frame 2 and select Window Actions

Actions .

❑ Create a "stop" script.

`stop ();`

❑ Select frame 15 (on the ActionScript layer) and insert a Blank keyframe, then open the ActionScript dialog box and insert a "stop" script.

`stop ();`

The timeline should now look like the example shown on the left.

The frame scripts will stop the movie at frame 2, where the button is still large and opaque, and wait for user input. The stop script on frame 15 will stop the animation so the button is transparent to reveal the image behind.

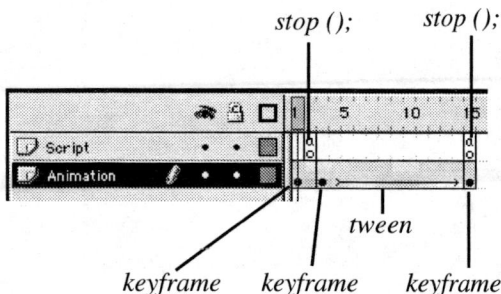

stop ();   *stop ();*

keyframe   *keyframe*   *keyframe*
tween

Adding Button Control

❑ Select **frame 1** of layer 1, then click once on the white-circle-button on the stage to select it.

❑ Choose Window-Actions

Actions   **F9**

❑ In the ActionScript dialog box make sure you are in Normal Mode and drag the "goto" action into the script window.

```
📋 Actions
   📋 Movie Control
      🔾 goto
      🔾 go
```

❑ Change the script to "gotoAndPlay(3)", as shown in the diagram.

❑ Select the "on (release)" line of code and change the event to "on (rollover)". Your script should look like the example shown below.

```
on (rollOver) {
  gotoAndPlay (3);
}
```

❑ Test the movie to see how it works.
At start-up the white button appears unchanged, when the mouse rolls over the white button it begins to shrink and fade. If it does not respond in this way, then go back to the step on "Adding Frame Control" and walk through the steps to see if you can spot the error.

Troubleshooting tip: *If the button does not respond, the most likely cause is that the GoTo and play ActionScript was **not** applied to the button on frame 1. If this is the case, make sure you apply this action correctly then also find the mistaken location that this script was applied and delete it.*

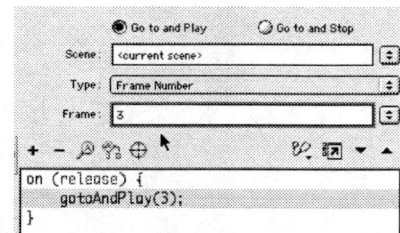

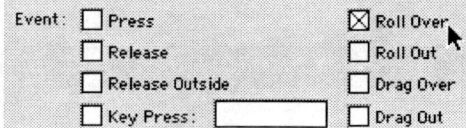

Go to and Play   ○ Go to and Stop

Scene: `<current scene>`

Type: `Frame Number`

Frame: `3`

```
on (release) {
    gotoAndPlay(3);
}
```

Event: ☐ Press   ☒ Roll Over
       ☐ Release   ☐ Roll Out
       ☐ Release Outside ☐ Drag Over
       ☐ Key Press: ☐ Drag Out

CREATING THE MOVIECLIP

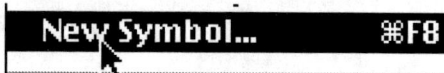

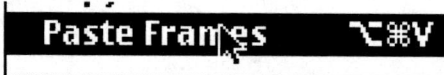

Cut Frames ⌥⌘X
Copy Frames ⌥⌘C

New Symbol... ⌘F8

Paste Frames ⌥⌘V

CREATING THE FINAL ANIMATION

File Edit View
New

Creating the Movieclip

❏ Select all of the frames of the animation.
Click on any frame in the timeline then choose Edit-Select-Frames.

❏ Choose Edit-Copy Frames.

❏ Choose Insert-New Symbol.

❏ Set the symbol type to movieclip and name this clip "ButtonFade".

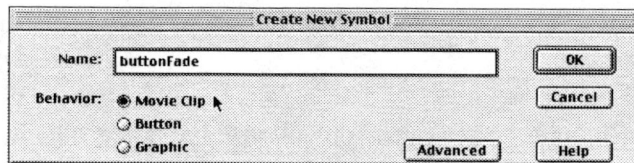

❏ Click on the first frame of the timeline in the movieclip symbol editor, and choose Edit-Paste Frames.

❏ Save this movie as "ButtonFadeSource.fla" just in case you experience problems.

You have now created a movieclip of this button and its actions. This clip can be used repeatedly on a variety of images in the future without repeating all of the previous steps. To use this clip continue with the few remaining steps.

Creating the final animation

❏ Choose Window-Library (F11) to display the library palette. Make sure that you can see the ButtonFade clip.

❏ Create a new movie that is 640 pixels by 480 pixels.

❏ In the new movie import a background image. *Flash prefers the PNG format but JPEG and GIF will also work. For this project do not worry about the image.*

Smart Object WOW Effects

❑ Make sure the image is placed on layer one.
You do not need to add frames to this movie because the movieclip already has its own independent timeline with all of the frames, actions, and animation required to make this effect work.

❑ In the new movie, add [icon] a new layer.

❑ With frame 1 of the new layer selected drag a instance of the movieclip "buttonFade" onto the upper left corner of the new movie.

Note: When you drag the movieclip onto the new movie, Flash copies both the clip and the associated button into the library of the final project.

❑ Continue to drag new instances of the movieclip "buttonFade" onto the stage and place them side by side.
Trouble Shooting Note: If you are dragging instances of the movieclip and see small white dots, it means that there is a problem with the movieclip. Empty movieclips will show up as small dots. Walk back through the steps on "creating movieclips" to correct the problem.

❑ Once you have ten or more instances of the movieclip in the final document you may want to choose Control-Test Movie to make sure it is working.

❑ After several instances have been positioned you may want to use the Copy and Paste commands to reduce some of the tedious work of placing individual clips.

❑ Save and test.
I just love this effect!

Remember, you can use this clip repeatedly on a variety of different images. In addition, you can also open the symbol editor for the button and change its shape or replace it with an image to create a variety of effects. You can also open the movieclip and

ADDING THE MOVIECLIPS

Empty movieclip

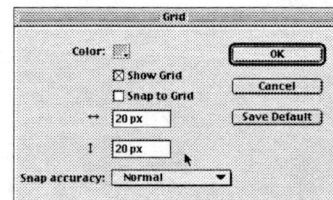

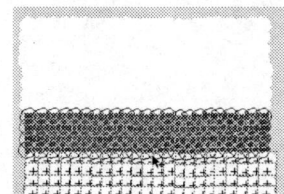

Copy & Paste multiple clips

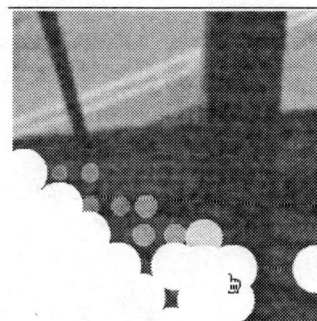

modify the rotation of the tween or the way it fades to add even more variation.

FURTHER EXPLORATION

Further exploration:
Open the Library palette in you final project, and try the following to add more interest or diversity.

1. Double click on the white button symbol, in the library of the final project. Change the object from a circle to a square.

2. Double click on the movieclip symbol and edit the tween (from frame 3-15) to spin while shrinking and fading.

3. Import a PNG-24 image to replace the button.
If you use a PNG image you will want to try to use an image that looks like it belongs. Worms, Rocks, grass, or anything that you might need to move to reveal what is underneath.

4. Edit the movieclip so instead of a motion tweened shrink and fade, you are using a shape tween from frames 3-15.
Remember a shape tween requires two objects that are not symbols.

5. What if the buttons faded in before becoming solid? This would give the viewer a glimpse of the image beneath before they had a chance to drag over the buttons.

6. What if each button was a short animation that the user would drag over?

Smart Object WOW Effects

This chapter deals with variables and explores the effect created by dropping individual characters into a dynamic text field one frame at a time. The effect produced is analogous to a typist keying in letters one at a time. Because I have kept the ActionScript basic the typing will gradually slow down over time. If you are a programmer you should be able to easily see why this animation slows and figure out a way to prevent it. If you are not a programmer, don't worry, the fact that this animation slows down is not a big deal and might even enhance the experience.

As you explore this project I'm sure you will come up with a variety of interesting and unique uses. One option, discussed in the further exploration section, is to use this project to create random falling letters, similar to the effect seen in the movie The Matrix.

THE PROJECT

❑ Create a new Flash document.

❑ Using the text tool 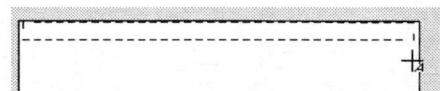 draw a text box that begins at the left edge and goes to the right edge of the stage.

SETTING UP THE TEXT FIELD

❑ While the text field is still active, choose the Properties palette and set the text to dynamic text, multiline, with selectable turned off [AB].

❑ In the Var: area type in "txt", as shown.

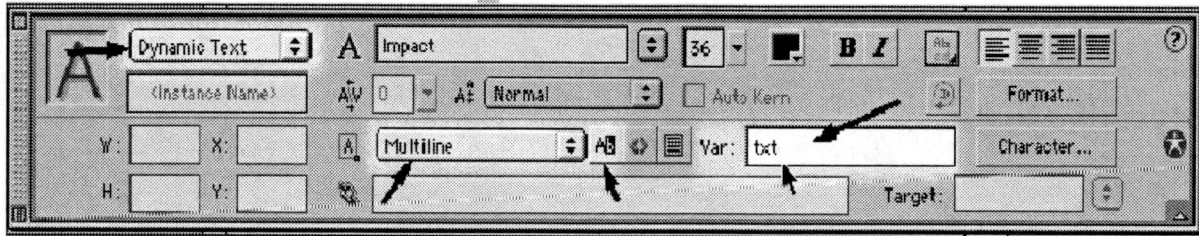

❑ Now that the text is defined as dynamic, with the text tool active, stretch the text field so it covers the stage. Make sure the top of the text field does not go beyond the upper edge of the stage.

❑ With the text field still selected set the font to Ariel, 48 point, and set the type color to bright green using the Properties palette.

❑ Choose Insert-Frame (F5) on frame 6 of the timeline.

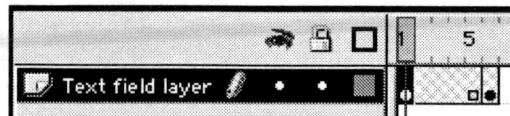

ADDING THE SCRIPTING LAYER

Adding an ActionScript layer:

❑ Create a new layer.

❑ Click on frame 1 of layer 2.

❑ Choose Window-Actions.

❑ In the Actions Window switch from normal to expert mode as shown.

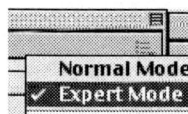

❑ In the script type in the following exactly as shown.

```
txt = txt + "H";
```

What this line of code says is that the variable txt will now have the letter H added to it. Flash knows it is a letter because you put quotation marks around the letter.

The code window should look like the following...

```
+ 🔎 🐾 ⊕ ✔ ▤ 🗨
  txt = txt + "h";
```

❑ Test the animation using Control-Test Movie.

Save some time by copying and pasting the frame.

❑ Click on frame 1 and choose Edit-Copy Frames.

Copy Frames ⌥⌘C

The keyboard shortcut for copy frames on the Mac is Command-Option-C and Control-Alt-C on the PC.

❑ Click on frame 2 and choose Edit-Paste Frames.

Paste Frames ⌥⌘V

The keyboard shortcut for copy frames on the Mac is Command-Option-V and Control-Alt-V on the PC.

❑ Click on frame 3 and "Paste Frames", then continue on from frame 4-6 pasting frames one frame at a time. Your timeline should now resemble the diagram.

Editing the Scripts:

❑ Click on Frame 2 and edit the script, by changing the letter "H" to "E".

❑ Click on frame 3 and edit the letter "H" to "L".

❑ Click on frame 4 and change the letter "H" to "P".

❑ Click on frame 5, then replace the letter "H" with the "!".

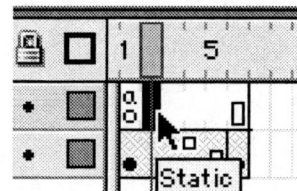

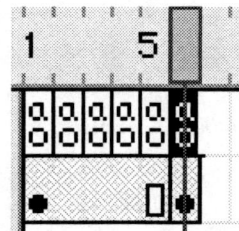

Not working? Check to make sure the text field variable name and the variable name you used in the ActionScript are identical.

FURTHER EXPLORATION

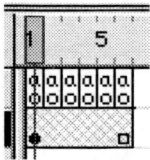

Understanding the Script:

```
x = random(2);
text = x add "\n" add  text;
```

x=random(2); x is the variable, and random(2) will produce the random number of either 0 or 1.

text = x add "\n" add text; - In this line we are setting the text field so the new number will appear at the top of the field pushing all of the other numbers lower to create the letter falling effect. The "\n" forces Flash to add a hard return or "newline" after each letter.

Note: The Matrix effect described here does not always work. I find I have to experiment and play and sometimes start from scratch. If you cannot get this effect to work do not be overly bogged down trying to create the effect. You can always search Flashkit.com for alternative examples and methods to create the effect.

❏ Click on frame 6 and replace the letter "H" with an empty space " ". Note that the blank space must be enclosed by quotes.

❏ Test the movie to see if it works.
You should see the letters H, then E, then L, P, !, space, then repeat over.

Further Exploration:
Convert this movie into movieclip, call it TypingTextClip.

1. Use the TypingTextClip in a new animation. Have it start small, then slowly expand in size. It will continue to type while it grows in size.

The Matrix:
The following example uses the same technique discussed in this chapter to create the Falling Letters.
The trick to creating a Matrix effect is to get the letters to appear to fall or cascade down.
Create a text field that is about 2 characters wide.
The width will be based on the font and point size that you use.

Your timeline should look like the diagram shown at the left, frames 1-5 have the following script.

```
x = random(2);
text = x add "\n" add  text;
```

Frame 6 says go to frame 1 and play.
Once you get the letters falling, save this animation as a movieclip and place several of them in a new movie. NOTE: Too many copies of the movieclip placed onto a page will make the effect run slow.

Dynamic Typing Letters

In this project you will create a game object (a bug) that will flip over and vanish when the user clicks on it and keep score. The project combines timeline animation with simple scripts and uses encapsulation in order to create smart reusable objects. In order to keep this chapter brief the steps will be shorter and assume you know how to perform the actions. For this reason you may want to check off steps as you go because each step is important. Test often to see if it is working along the way. You may need to refer to previous chapters to obtain specific steps.

Before you begin, you should be familiar with the following:
How to place a script in a button.
How to convert a timeline animation into a movieclip.
How to add a sound to a specific frame of the timeline.
How to move symbols from an existing documents library to a new document.
How to create a dynamic text field.

❏ Create a new document and reset palettes.
❏ Create a 2 frame animation of a walking bug. Test to make sure it is working.

❏ Convert the BugWalk into a movieclip, call it BugWalk1.
Select all and Copy all Frames. Insert-New Symbol. Paste frames into the new movieclip.

❏ Save this document as source1.fla.

WHAT YOU SHOULD KNOW BEFORE YOU BEGIN

THE PROJECT

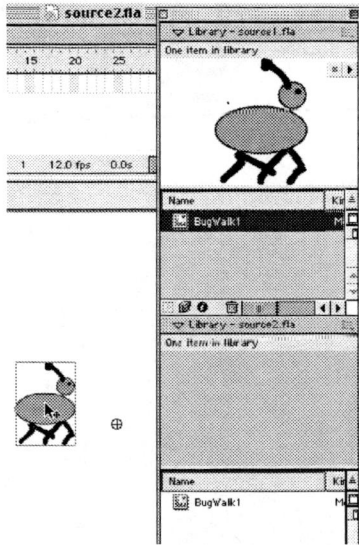

PUTTING A MOVIECLIP IN A BUTTON

❑ Open the Library palette (Window-Library).

❑ Create a new document, and save it as Source2.fla.

❑ Drag the BugWalk1 Clip from the Source1 library into the Source2 document.

❑ In the Source2 document test the movie to make sure the bug animation is still working.

❑ Click on frame 5 and insert a keyframe (F6).

❑ Click on <u>frame 1</u> then <u>click once on the bug on the stage</u> then choose Insert Convert to symbol.

❑ In the Convert to symbol dialog name it BugButton2 and choose the Behavior of Button.

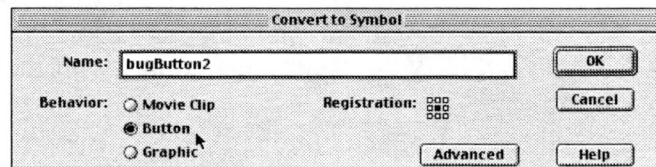

You have just placed a movieclip inside a button. Alternatively you could have create the button first and then replaced the normal state with a movieclip, the over state with a different movieclip, and the down state with yet another movieclip. Flash is COOL!!

Note: If you click on frame 1 and click on the bug on the stage and look at the Properties palette you will see it is a button symbol. If you click on frame 5 and click the bug you will see it is a movieclip. This is intentional.

❑ Click on frame 1 then click once on the bugButton on the stage and open the Actions window (F9).

❑ Switch to normal mode. Use Actions-Movie Control - and drag the goto command into the script window.

❑ Set the goto command to go to an play frame 6.

❑ Change the event to Press.

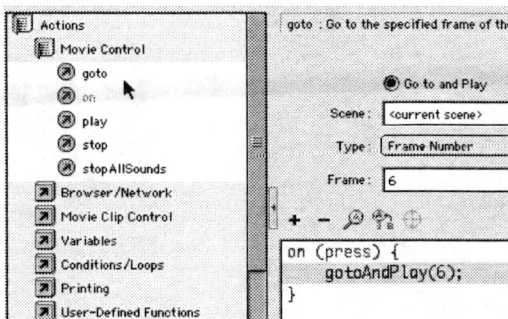

❑ Your code should look like the following...

```
on (press) {
        gotoAndPlay(6);
}
```

Now to add in the animation that will occur when the game object is hit. To do this we will use some frame by frame animation.

❑ Click on frame 6 and insert a keyframe.

❑ Use the free transform tool to rotate the bug slightly.

❑ Click on frame 7 and insert a keyframe.

❑ Use the free transform tool to rotate the bug a little more.

❑ Repeat this process until the bug has flipped over onto its back.

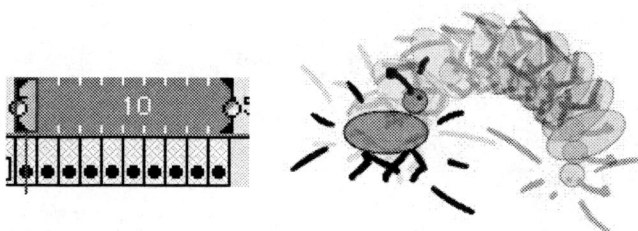

CREATING AN ANIMATED HIT

In this example I have a 10 frame animation of the bug flipping over and drew some motion lines directly onto the stage. You could also use the original raw vector graphic of the bug to have break apart or flatten and squash.

❑ Test to see how the animation looks.

❑ Click on the very last frame of the animation and insert a Blank keyframe.

Now that the object scripts and animation are complete we need to add some frame control.

❑ Insert a new layer on the timeline and call it Scripts.

❑ Click on frame 4 of the scripts layer and insert 2 blank keyframes.

❑ Click on frame 4 and display the actions window. (F9) and place a stop(); script.

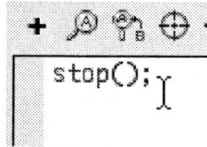

❑ Click on the last frame of the Script layer and place the following script. You may need to switch to expert mode in order to insert this script.

```
_root.score = _root.score +1;
stop();
```

Your timeline should look like the following.

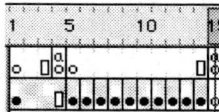

This script says that on the final or root movie we will have a dynamic text field called score and when the bug hit animation ends the user will get 1 point. In addition it tells this bug animation to stop on an empty frame so the bug does not return.

❑ Test the animation.
If all went well your bug should be walking and when you click on it flips over, crashes, and disappears. Do not worry about the score part yet. The dynamic text field called "score" will only be placed on the final movie when we assemble all of the pieces.

Adding sounds:
❑ Add a new layer to your timeline and call it sound.

❑ Click on frame 6 of the sound layer and insert a Blank keyframe (F7).

❑ With frame 6 still selected find a good "bang" or "swat" sound and place it on the stage.

❑ Click on the 3rd to last frame of your sound layer, insert a Blank keyframe (F7), and insert a good "Whump" or "Boing" sound when the bug hits the ground. Your timeline should look like the following.

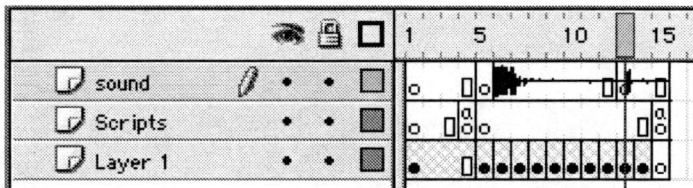

Note: for this demo I am using basic sounds from Window-Common libraries-sounds.fla. I placed "Bucket Hit" on frame 6 and "Book Drop" on frame 13 but odd, silly, unexpected, or unusual sounds can really make the final game interesting.

This smart object is ready to go.
❑ Choose File-Save.

❑ Convert this animation into a movieclip called "bugclip3". *Select all and Copy all Frames. Insert-New Symbol. Paste frames into the new movieclip.*

❑ Display the library palette, and make sure you can see the source2 library. You may need to minimize some of the unused libraries such as the source1.fla.

❑ Create a new document, and save it as source3.fla.

❑ Drag an instance of the bug3Clip far off the left side of the stage in the source3 document.
NOTE: You may want to use the Free Transform tool to make this object smaller as you will be using many of them in the final game.

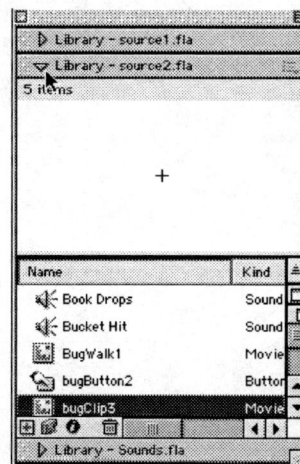

Click the triangle to minimize a library.

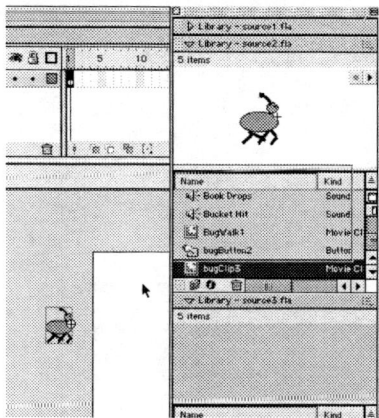

❑ Click on frame 1 of the source3 document and then set the Tween to Motion on the properties palette.

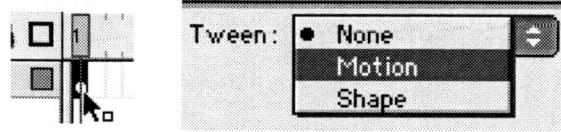

❑ Click on Frame 50 of the timeline and drag the bug far off the right edge of the stage.

❑ Test to see if it is working. The bug should walk across the stage and when you click it a hit sound occurs, it flips over, and a "whump" sound occurs.
❑ If everything is OK choose File Save.

Note: You could create additional new documents with bug moving faster or slower, diagonally, or from the top to bottom or from right to left. For that reason in the following step we will call this "finalGameClip1" because you may decide to create variations.

❑ Convert this animation into a movieclip and call it "FinalGameClip1". *Select all and Copy all Frames. Insert-New Symbol. Paste frames into the new movieclip.*

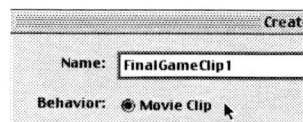

❑ Make sure the Library palette is visible and that you can see the "finalGameClip1" in library source3.

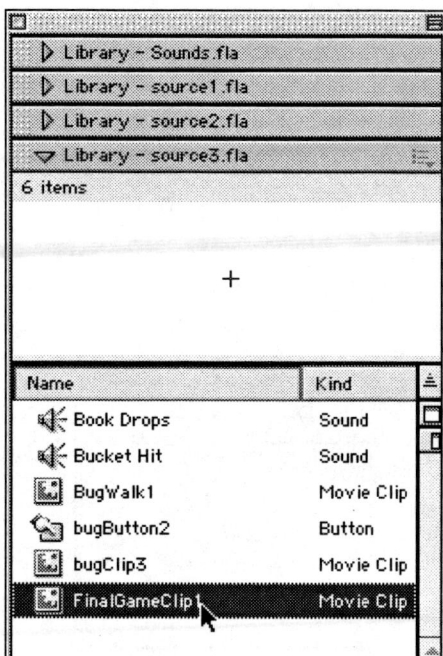

❑ Create a new document and save it as "FinalGame.fla".

❑ Drag one instance of the "finalgameclip" to the left side of the stage and test it to see if it is working.

NOTE: CHANGING THE ANIMATION DIRECTION

❑ If so then go crazy and drag several instances of the "finalgameclip" onto the final stage.

❑ On the final stage create a Dynamic text field and give it the variable name score.
Make sure that you use a font and color that will show up on your stage.

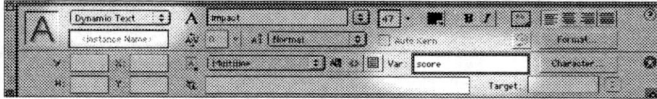

This has been an involved project. It is possible that some things may have gone wrong along the way. Do not get discouraged. If you encountered problems you may want to repeat the project. The second time through will go much faster and will make more sense. By breaking development down into 3 source documents hopefully you found it easier to discover and fix problems along the way.

Additional Exploration:

1. Adding variety in the game.
❑ Open source3.fla and save it as source3b.fla.
❑ Click on frame 50 and shorten the timeline to 30 frames to make some faster moving bugs.
❑ Convert this object into a new movieclip and call it FastGameClip2.
❑ Add several instances of this new clip to your FinalGame.fla.

2. Creating more variety in the game.
❑ Open source3.fla and save it as source3b.fla.
❑ Click on frame 1 and move the bug to the top of the stage.
❑ Click on frame 50 and move the bug to the bottom of the stage.
❑ Convert this object into a new movieclip and call it topDownGameClip3.
❑ Add some top down clips to your FinalGame.fla.

ADDING A SCORE FIELD

Project Summary:

Step 1: *Create a simple or complex animation and convert it into a movieclip.*

Step 2: *A: Convert the movieclip into a button and animate it to behave however you wish when it is clicked on.*
B1: Add frame control scripts to get it to stop and wait to be clicked on.
B2: Add a script to increase the _root score.
C: Add an object control script (only to the first instance) so when the object is clicked the animation will play.
D: Add in complimentary sounds to create a bit of additional interest.
E: Finally convert that into a new movieclip.

Step 3: *Animate the movieclip in whatever direction you want it to move in the final game.*

Step 4: *A: Place multiple instances onto the final stage.*
B: place a dynamic text field called score to increase when the user gets a hit.

3. Capturing user misses.

What if the user clicks and misses the object, maybe they should lose points. Here is an easy way to do it.

❑ Create a new document and use Flash to Draw/ Paint an interesting background for your final game. Make the image large enough to cover the entire stage.
❑ Convert this large graphic into a button symbol.
❑ Open that actions window for this button and place the script as shown.

```
on (press) {
    _root.score = _root.score -1;
}
```

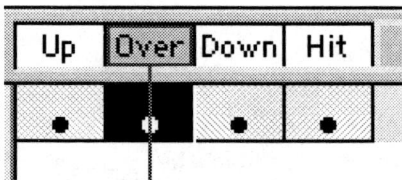

Note you could also use the sound object discussed in previous chapters so your miss will still make a "bang" sound.
❑ Convert this large button into a movieclip.
❑ Open the "FinalGame.Fla" and save as FinalGame2.fla, just in case you make a mistake.
❑ Add a new layer to the FinalGame2 and drag your background clip into the new layer.
❑ Move the background layer behind the game layer.

4. Wild animated Buttons.
❑ Create 3 small movieclips that are all about the same size.
❑ Create a new document and create a button on the stage that is about the same size as your 3 small movieclips.
❑ Open the buttons symbol editor and place one animation in the normal state, a different animation in the Over state and a different animation into the Down state.

```
on (press) {
    _root.score = _root.score - 1;
}
```

This project will discuss creating a layer mask and also demonstrate how the mask can be controlled with ActionScript. The ability to control a mask with ActionScript is new to Flash MX and will not work with older versions of Flash.

In conventional terms a mask covers areas that we do not want to see, much like a Halloween mask might cover the face. In Flash a mask is actually a window to allow us to see through to what is behind. Regardless of how Macromedia uses the term mask we can create some cool effects.

Note: A mask does not need to be a symbol, it can be a raw vector graphic, which is fun because you can use a shape tween on the mask object to create unusual effects.

❑ Import an image and place it on the stage in layer 1.

❑ Lock layer 1.

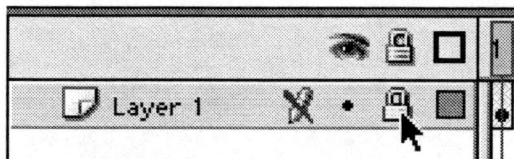

❑ Create a new layer, (layer 2).

❑ On layer 2 draw a circle, square, (or other shape) remembering the filled area will become transparent and allow us to see through to the layer beneath.

❑ Select the object on layer 2, and choose Insert-Convert to Symbol.

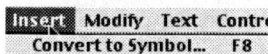

INTERACTIVE LAYER MASK

In Flash a mask is an object that allows user to see through one layer into the layer underneath. It also restricts us from seeing anything outside of the mask.

PROJECT

❏ Call it "MaskClip" and make sure it is a movieclip.

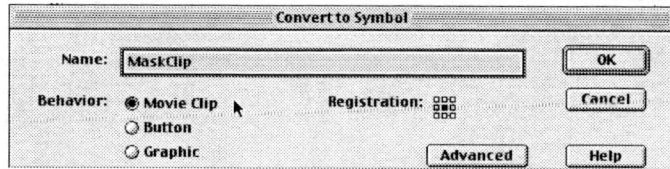

Convert to Symbol

Name: MaskClip

Behavior: ● Movie Clip
○ Button
○ Graphic

Registration:

OK
Cancel
Advanced
Help

❏ Click on Layer 2 and choose Modify-Layer.

Modify Text
Layer...

❏ Change the Layer properties from Normal to Mask as shown.

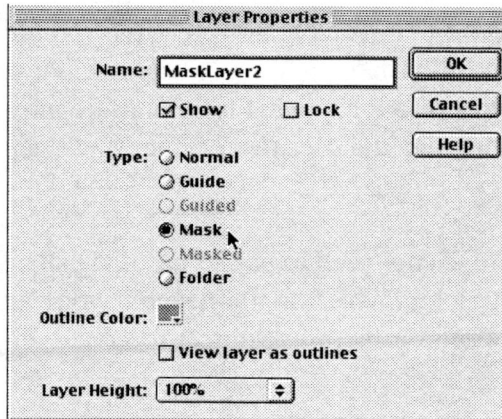

Layer Properties

Name: MaskLayer2

☑ Show   ☐ Lock

OK
Cancel
Help

Type: ○ Normal
○ Guide
○ Guided
● Mask
○ Masked
○ Folder

Outline Color:

☐ View layer as outlines

Layer Height: 100%

CONVERTING A LAYER INTO MASK

❏ The last step is a bit hard to describe but click and push Layer1 halfway into Layer2.

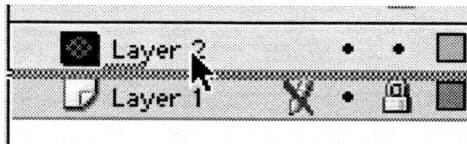

Layer 2   •   •   ▢
Layer 1   ✗   •   🔒 ▢

❏ If you did it properly layer 1 should be indented under layer 2 as shown,

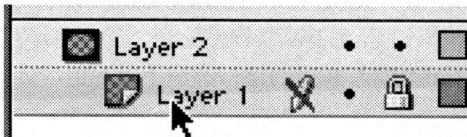

Layer 2   •   •   ▢
Layer 1   ✗   •   🔒 ▢

❏ Choose control test movie to see if the mask is working.

ActionScript Layer Mask

If all went well you should be able to see through the mask object on layer 2 to the image on layer 1.

In previous versions of Flash you could not script the mask object, but as of Flash MX you can apply a variety of scripts to the mask object as demonstrated below.

❏ On the stage click once on the mask object then choose Window-Actions.

❏ Set the Mode to Expert.

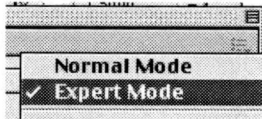

```
     Normal Mode
  ✓  Expert Mode
```

❏ Choose Actions-Movie Control and drag the ON command into the actions window.

❏ When prompted choose press as shown.

❏ Click in between the curly braces to set the insertion point.

```
1 on (press) {
2    |
3 }
```

❏ Under Actions-Movie Clip Control drag the startDrag command into the Actions window.

```
  removeMovieClip        1 on (press) {
  setProperty            2    startDrag
  startDrag              3 }
                         4
```

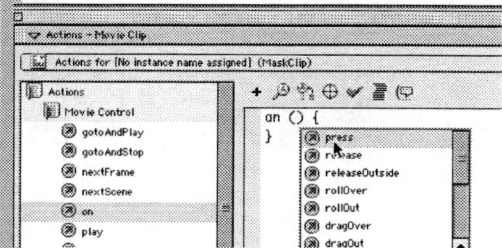

```
on (press) {
startDrag();|
}
```

❏ Type in the word "this" as shown below.

```
on (press) {
    startDrag(this);
}
```
`startDrag( target, lockcenter, l, t, r, b );`

MAKING MOVIECLIPS DRAGGABLE

❑ Click below the lower curly brace, and drag the on

[⿰ on] command into the actions window, below the lower curly brace.

```
1 on (press) {
2 startDrag();
3 }
4 |  I
5
```

```
1 on (press) {
2 startDrag();
3 }
4  ▯ on
5
```

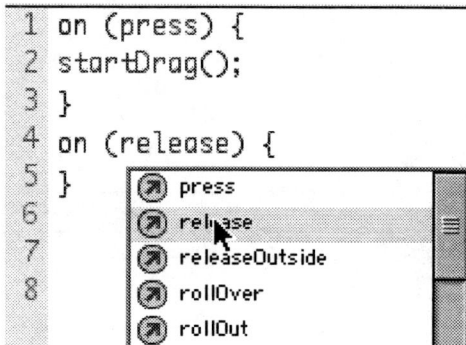

❑ This time choose the release option.

❑ Place the insertion point between the curly braces and place the stopDrag command.

```
1 on (press) {
2 startDrag();
3 }
4 on (release) {
5 }  press
6    release
7    releaseOutside
8    rollOver
     rollOut
```

```
  removeMovieClip
  setProperty
  startDrag
  stopDrag
  updateAfterEvent
  Variables
```

```
1 on (press) {
2 startDrag();
3 }
4 on (release) {
5    ▯ stopDrag
6 }
7
```

THIS

The startDrag command needs to know which object is going to be draggable. The word "this" tells the startDrag command that the object that has the script (in other words this object) is the one that can be moved. Note that the stopDrag command does not require a target.

❑ The final code should look like the following...

```
on (press) {
    startDrag(this);
}
on (release) {
    stopDrag();
}
```

❑ Test the movie to see if it is working.
When the user clicks and drags on the mask it should move around and follows the cursor. When the user releases the mask should stop moving.

Flash provides streaming capabilities, which means that while your user is watching the first part of your Flash animation, the second part may be still downloading in the background. This is obviously a better solution than to make the user wait until all of your movie is downloaded before starting. If your Flash project is well designed, even users with a slow modem can begin to see animation while the rest of your content downloads.

What is a preloader?
In order to avoid long waits with content heavy movies, the author creates a small movie that plays and loops while the rest of the movie files are being downloaded. Of course the preloader should be as visually stimulating as possible, and it should be a prelude to the larger movie file that is being downloaded.

This project will demonstrate a simple preloader script that will allow the opening scene to continue to loop while larger files continue to download.

What to include in a preloader: Simple vector graphics used as symbols, simple type used as symbols. Use only a few symbols to keep the file size small or introduce new symbols at later frames rather than on the first frame.
What you should not include: Large sound files, scanned or bitmapped images, and by all means avoid using the word "wait" as in please wait, or "loading". Telling the user that they are waiting defeats the purpose of streaming content. If I know I am waiting then by nature I feel impatient, and annoyed that I have to wait. Rather than asking the user to wait, entertain them.

STREAMING MEDIA

WHAT IS A PRELOAD MOVIE

WHAT TO INCLUDE IN A PRELOADER

THE PROJECT

PRELOADER ANIMATION

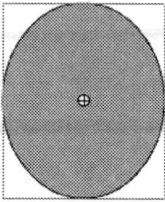

I used a simple shape tween of a green ball that shrinks.

Project:

This chapter will be more explanation and instructions than a project. The following steps are provided to give you an overview of the process.

Create a new Flash animation.

Import a large movieclip, sound file, or scanned bitmapped image and place it into a new blank keyframe on frame 70. The large files on frame 70 will take a while to download. In the example shown at the bottom of this page I used a raw vector graphic of a square, then cut and moved bits and pieces using frame by frame animation from frame 30-70. I did this to demonstrate that even simple raw vector graphics that are not used as symbols dramatically slow download time.

Create an animation from frames 1-30. This will represent our preloader so it should not contain any large bitmapped images, sound files, or video clips. If it is an animation, it should be designed to look acceptable when it loops back to frame 1.

In addition to a simple looping animation, you could also use the Interactive Web Game, Dynamic Text Fields or the Animated Typist as a preloader. The advantage with these three projects is that they require little or no download time, so your users get visual information right away. Of course, what you use as a preloader will depend on the audience you expect to see on your site.

The example below shows how the timeline might look.

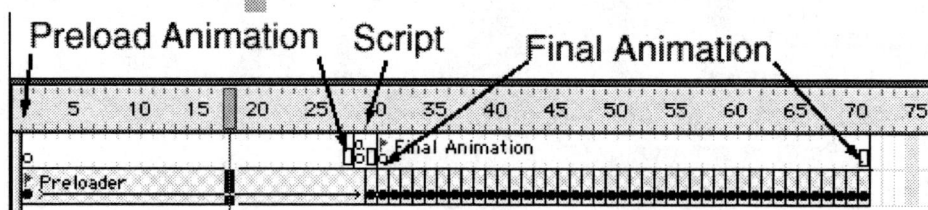

Preload Animation   Script   Final Animation

Flash MX

Create a new layer for ActionScript commands.

In frame 30 of the ActionScript layer, insert the code shown below.

```
-------------------------------------------
if (_framesloaded >= _totalframes) {
        gotoAndPlay (31);
} else {
        gotoAndPlay (1);
}
-------------------------------------------
```

Some of you are pretty familiar with ActionScript and code and may want to enter expert mode to type the code. I always make typos so I will show you how to use the ActionSript books to enter the code.

Step by Step

❏ Click on frame 30 of the timeline and press the F7 key 2 times to insert blank keyframes.

❏ With frame 30 active choose Windows-Actions, and make sure you are in expert mode.

❏ In the Actions book open the Conditions/Loops, and find the "if" statement and drag it into the script window.

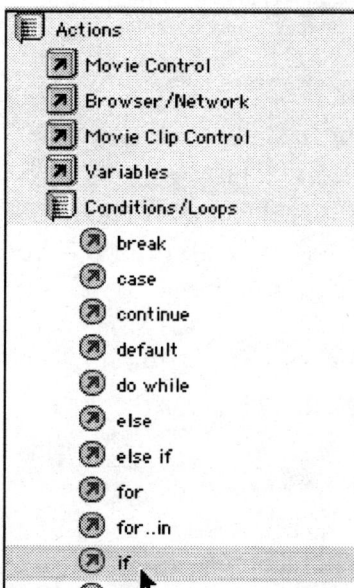

❑ Click in between the parens.

```
if (|) {
}
```

❑ Look for the Actions Book called properties and double click on the `_framesloaded` property.

```
Properties
  _alpha
  _currentframe
  _droptarget
  _focusrect
  _framesloaded
```

❑ Your code will now appear as follows.

```
if (_framesloaded) {
}
```

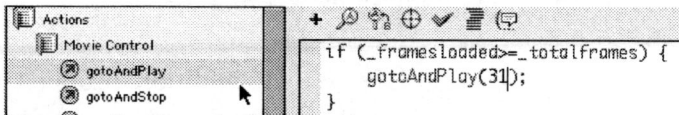

❑ With the Flashing insertion point still visible type in `>=` which means greater than or equal.

```
if (_framesloaded>=) {
}
```

❑ With the Flashing insertion point still visible, double click on the property `_totalframes.`

```
Properties
  _alpha
  _currentframe
  _droptarget
  _focusrect
  _framesloaded
  _height
  _name
  _quality
  _rotation
  _soundbuftime
  _target
  _totalframes
```

```
Actions                    + P 🔍 ⊕ ✔ ≣ ⊙
  Movie Control            if (_framesloaded>=_totalframes) {
    gotoAndPlay                gotoAndPlay(31);
    gotoAndStop            }
```

❑ Click behind the opening curly brace and press the return key on the keyboard.

```
if (_framesloaded>=_totalframes) {
}
```

❑ With the insertion point flashing choose Actions-Movie Control, and double click on the gotoAndPlay command. Enter the correct frame number to continue the movie once all frames have been downloaded. In this case it is frame 31.

❑ Click behind the closing curly brace } and type in the word "else { " as shown, then press the enter key.

```
if (_framesloaded>=_totalframes) {
    gotoAndPlay(31);
}else{
    |
```

❑ With the insertion point shown double click on Actions-Movie Control-gotoAndPlay.

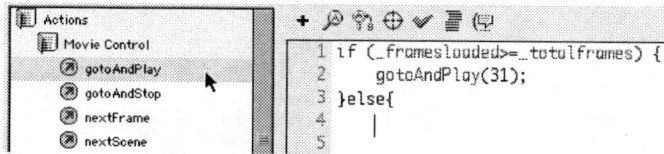

```
Actions
  Movie Control
    gotoAndPlay
    gotoAndStop
    nextFrame
    nextScene

1  if (_framesloaded>=_totalframes) {
2      gotoAndPlay(31);
3  }else{
4      |
5
```

❑ With the insertion point in between the parens type in the number 1.

```
}else{
    gotoAndPlay(1);
```

❑ Finally click behind the semicolon ; and press the enter key.

❑ Close the else statement by adding a closing curly brace }.

Your code should look like the example shown.

```
if (_framesloaded >= _totalframes) {
        gotoAndPlay (31);
} else {
        gotoAndPlay (1);
}
```

What the code is doing.

When the playback head hits frame 30 it checks to see if ALL (_totalframes) have been downloaded to the user's computer. If not then the else statement is read which says go to and play frame 1.
Every time the playback head hits frame 30 it checks again. When all of the frames have been downloaded (if (_framesloaded >= _totalframes){ gotoAndPlay (31);) then the animation jumps to frame 31 and continues to play.

The preloader will continue to play until the number of frames loaded is greater than or equal to the total number of frames on the timeline. If this still does not make a lot of sense the upcoming chapter on download testing visually illustrates how Flash is downloaded on the web and how your animation is effected by different download speeds.

The preloader is now ready. Even users with very slow connections will be greeted immediately with your preload movie which will continue to loop until all of the files have been downloaded.

The code could also be modified to selectively download portions of your movie while looping on selected portions. The following code would be placed on frame 30 and check to see if all of the content up to frame 50 has been downloaded before continuing on to frame 31.

```
if (_framesloaded >= 50) {
        gotoAndPlay (31);
} else {
        gotoAndPlay (1);
}
```

Users with fast connections will never know the loops are there, but users with slow connections will be impressed. Even if there are pauses in download the developer can selectively choose where the pause will occur.

I sometimes hear people complain about Flash sites because they "take so long to load." My response is that the problem is not with Flash but instead the developers who did not optimize the site. Taking the time to plan, structure, and test to make sure all users are accommodated should be considered an essential part of the development process.

The next chapter will discuss how to test your preload clip to make sure it is working.

CHAPTER 30

Flash offers built-in capabilities to check your movie download speed with different types of connections. Flash not only offers the ability to see how the movie will playback but also can display frame by frame problem areas or content heavy areas in your movie.

All of the testing takes place inside Flash by choosing Control-TestMovie.

This project is ideal for testing to see if your preloader is working and to determine how your users will experience your Flash site.

TESTING A FLASH MOVIE AT DIFFERENT CONNECTION SPEEDS

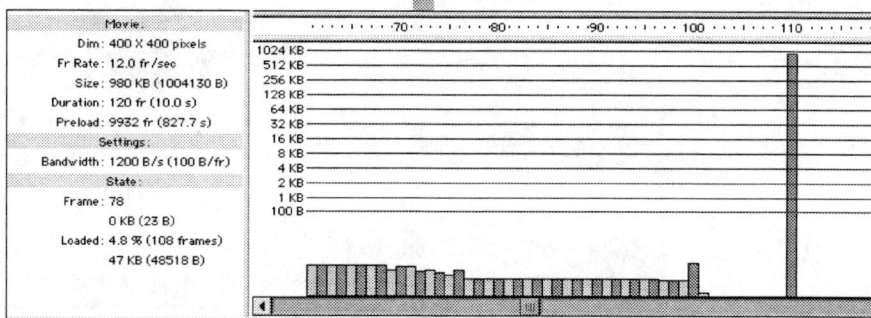

Movie:	
Dim: 400 X 400 pixels	
Fr Rate: 12.0 fr/sec	
Size: 980 KB (1004130 B)	
Duration: 120 fr (10.0 s)	
Preload: 9932 fr (827.7 s)	
Settings:	
Bandwidth: 1200 B/s (100 B/fr)	
State:	
Frame: 78	
0 KB (23 B)	
Loaded: 4.8 % (108 frames)	
47 KB (48518 B)	

❑ Open a large Flash movie and choose Control-Test Movie.

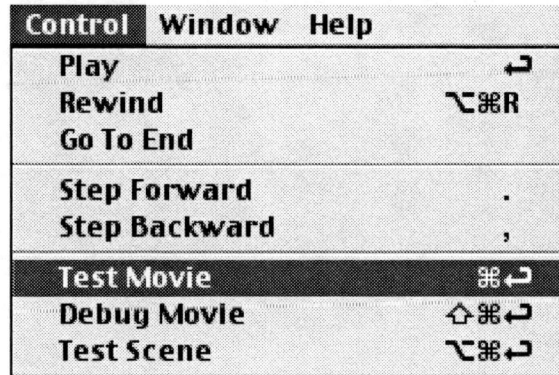

Control **Window** **Help**

Play	↵
Rewind	⌥⌘R
Go To End	
Step Forward	.
Step Backward	,
Test Movie	⌘↵
Debug Movie	⇧⌘↵
Test Scene	⌥⌘↵

❑ Once the Test Movie window finishes opening choose Control-Stop. Now that you are in the TEST MOVIE mode you can tinker with the different settings to see how your movie will play based on different connection types.

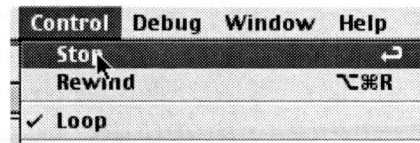

Control Debug Window Help

Stop	↵
Rewind	⌥⌘R
✓ **Loop**	

❑ Choose the Debug menu to select a download speed to test. Note that Flash allows you to create Custom-User Settings.

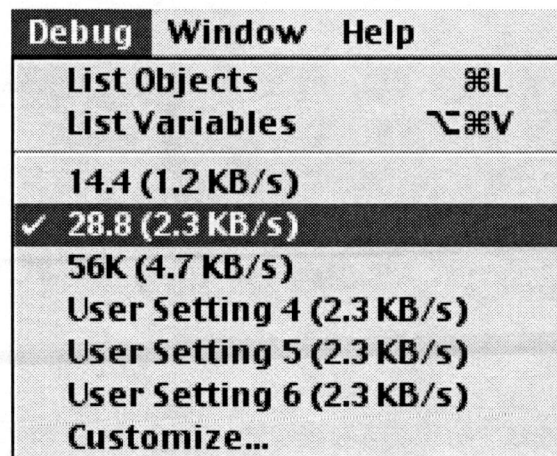

Debug **Window** **Help**

List Objects	⌘L
List Variables	⌥⌘V
14.4 (1.2 KB/s)	
✓ **28.8 (2.3 KB/s)**	
56K (4.7 KB/s)	
User Setting 4 (2.3 KB/s)	
User Setting 5 (2.3 KB/s)	
User Setting 6 (2.3 KB/s)	
Customize...	

**FLASH
MOVIE PLAYBACK OPTIONS**

❑ Under the View menu turn on the Bandwidth Profiler, and the Frame By Frame Graph, then select Show Streaming.

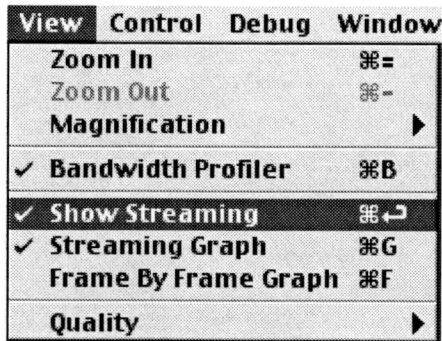

View	Control	Debug	Window
Zoom In			⌘=
Zoom Out			⌘-
Magnification			▶
✓ Bandwidth Profiler			⌘B
✓ Show Streaming			⌘↵
✓ Streaming Graph			⌘G
Frame By Frame Graph			⌘F
Quality			▶

At the top of the graph a green bar represents how much information has been downloaded and is ready for playback. Additionally you can see the position of the playback head.

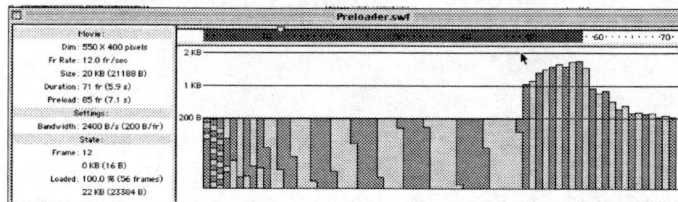

The Bandwidth Profiler, shown below, provides information about the movie. The area you are concerned with is at the bottom, which indicates how much of the movie has been loaded.

```
Movie:
         Dim: 400 X 400 pixels
     Fr Rate: 12.0 fr/sec
        Size: 980 KB (1004130 B)
    Duration: 120 fr (10.0 s)
     Preload: 9932 fr (827.7 s)
Settings:
   Bandwidth: 1200 B/s (100 B/fr)
State:
       Frame: 78
              0 KB (23 B)
      Loaded: 4.8 % (108 frames)
              47 KB (48518 B)
```

The Graph provides a frame-by-frame display of the download size of individual frames.

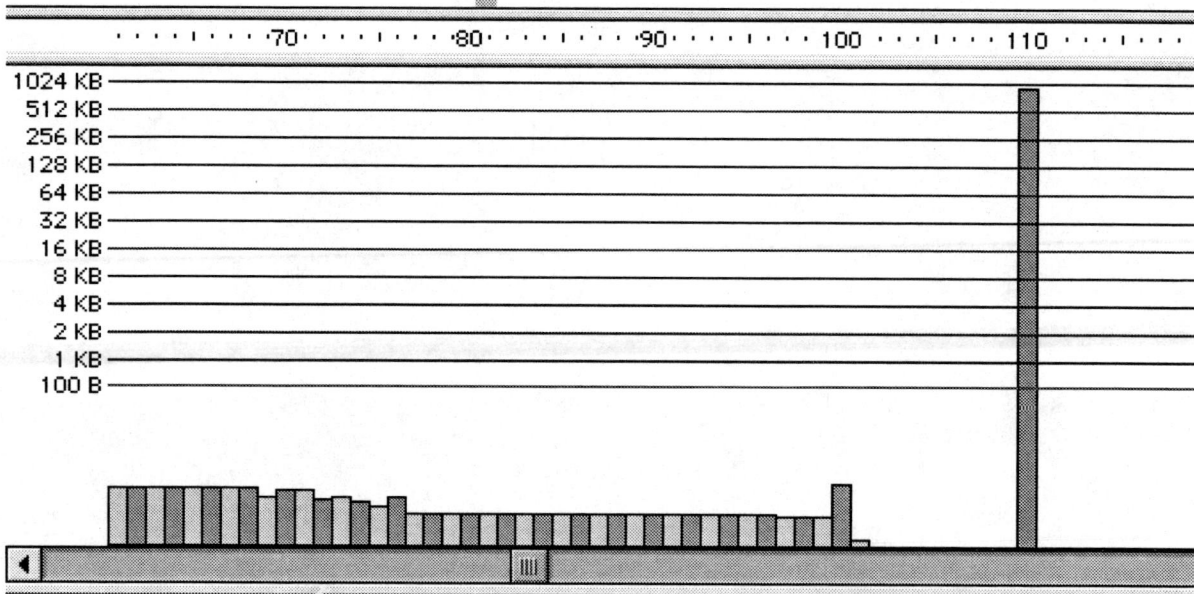

Download Testing

CHAPTER 31

Load Movie

The loadMovie command allows you to load an SWF file into a movieclip.

As an example, you might want to create an online portfolio to showcase your Flash animations (or other artwork) to potential employers. You could lump the animations together into one huge SWF file but even with a preloader the employer may be waiting longer than you prefer. You could link from one HTML document to another. On the other hand you could create a player document, like the image shown above, and allow the user to load the SWF files into your player. The loadMovie command in a player file allows users to only download the Flash files they want. The loadMovie command also provides the capability to overlay one animation on top of another.

In this project you will create a small animation and publish it as an SWF file, then create a player document in order to load the small SWF.

❏ Create a simple animation that is 200 x 200 pixels in size.

LOAD MOVIE COMMAND

❑ Save the simple animation as loadme.fla then choose Control-Test Movie to create an SWF file (which by default will be called loadme.swf).

❑ Create a new document (player document) and draw a square on the stage that is 200 x 200 pixels.

❑ Convert the square to a movieclip (call it loaderClip) and make sure to set the registration point to the upper left corner, as shown.

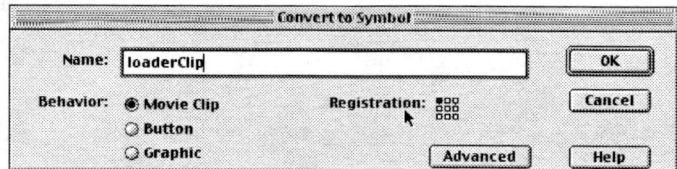

Convert to Symbol

Name: loaderClip   OK

Behavior: ● Movie Clip   Registration: ▓▢▢   Cancel
          ○ Button   ▢▢▢
          ○ Graphic   Advanced   Help

❑ With the loaderClip selected give it an instance name on the Properties palette. As shown in the digram below call it "load."

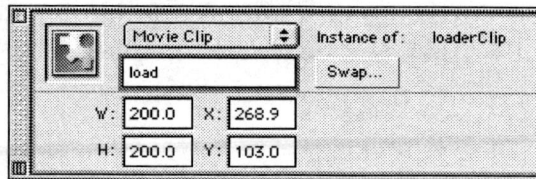

Movie Clip ⬍   Instance of: loaderClip
load   Swap...

W: 200.0   X: 268.9
H: 200.0   Y: 103.0

❑ Create a button symbol.

❑ Insert the following code into the button.

```
on (release) {
    loadMovie("loadme.swf", "load");
}
```

❑ Save this document in the same location as the loadme.swf.

❑ Test the player file to see if it loads the loadme.swf into the movieclip.

Actions
  Movie Control
  Browser/Network
    fscommand
    getURL
    loadMovie
    loadVariables
    unloadMovie

CHAPTER 32

Path Animation

This is a relatively simple concept and can produce some great results. I saved it for a later section in this book because it is a buggy feature. The tutorial, and steps, included with Flash do not always work, for whatever reason. The procedure provided may seem a little superstitious but it works almost all of the time. So if you have tried Flash path based animation in the past and had problems, then this technique is worth trying. If you have never tried path based animation, you will have a good experience from the start if you follow the steps in this project.

What is path based animation? Forcing the motion tweened object to follow a specific path that you create.

THE PROJECT

❏ Launch Flash and reset the palettes to the default layout.

❏ Create a ball in the center of the stage and convert it into a graphic symbol.

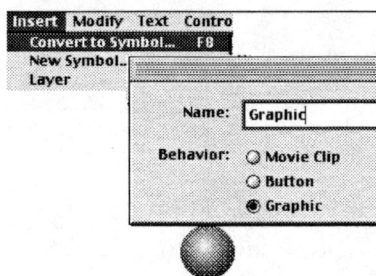

❏ Add a new keyframe at frame 30.

Path Animation

❑ Select Insert-Motion Guide from the menu. This will add a new layer to the timeline called the Guide layer.

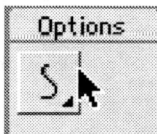

❑ Choose the pencil tool from the tool palette. You might wish to set the pencil tool options to "Smooth" but for this demo, it is not critical.

USE THE PENCIL TOOL ON FRAME 1 OF THE GUIDE LAYER

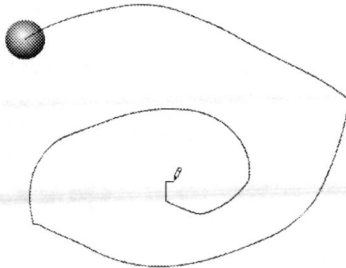

❑ Select frame 1 of the Guide layer.

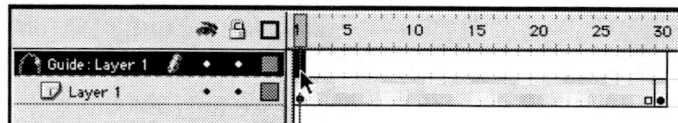

❑ With the pencil tool selected and frame 1 of the Guide layer selected, draw a path that represents the direction you want the ball to follow. Begin at the location of the ball and work outward. Try creating a spiral path as shown in the example. (Do not worry about making the path perfect, you can refine your technique later.)

❑ Select frame 1 of layer 1.

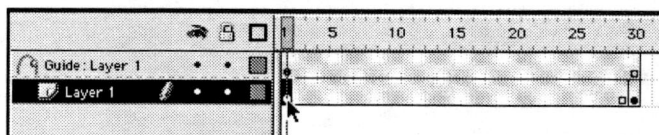

❑ With frame 1 selected, choose the Properties palette. Set the Tween to Motion and turn on the three options, Orient to path, Sync, and Snap.

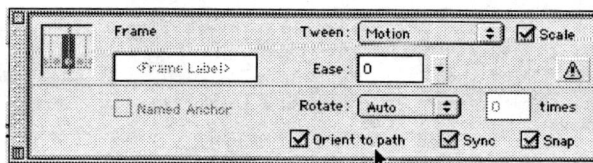

Path Animation

❏ Select the last frame of layer 1 (as shown).

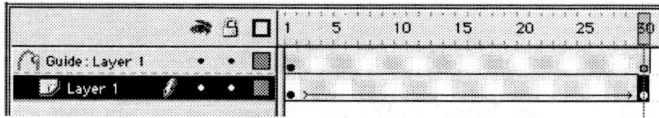

❏ With the last frame selected, move the ball so its center point is on top of the ending point of the guide path, as shown. If all went well you will see the object "snap to" the animation path.

ALIGN THE OBJECT TO THE MOTION PATH

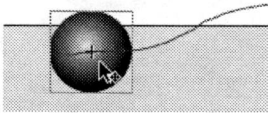

If the object did not snap to the animation path, or if you tested the animation and it did not follow the animation path then the following instructions should help.

❏ With the last keyframe of the object selected, set the Frame palette to motion tween, and turn on the snap option.

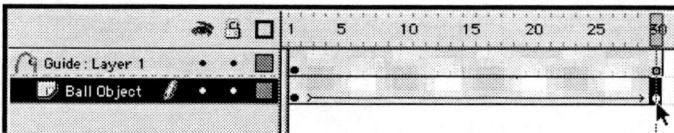

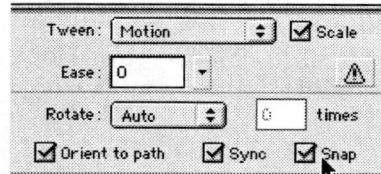

❏ Test the animation to make sure it works.

❏ Convert this animation into a MovieClip and call it "BallPathClip". It will be used in the next project, "Creating Onion Skin Trails". See examples below.

❏ Save this movie as "AnimationPath.fla".

APPLY THE TWEEN TO OBJECT LAYER

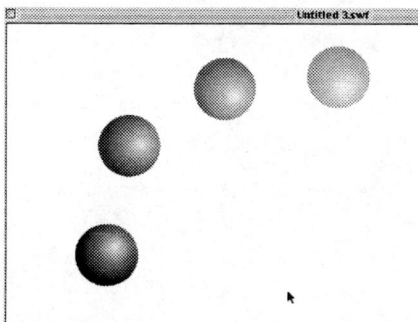

The following is a summary of the steps in this project.

1. Place or create a graphic symbol on the stage, using frame 1 of the timeline.
2. Add an ending keyframe.
3. Do not create the motion tween yet, instead choose Insert-Motion Guide from the menu.
4. Click on frame 1 of the **motion guide layer**, select the pencil tool, and draw the animation path.
5. Click on frame 1 of the object layer and create the motion tween. Use the tween options, orient to path, synchronize, and snap.
(You should see the object snap to the motion path.)
6. Click on the last keyframe, ending keyframe, of the object layer.
Align the object's center point to the end of the path or click on the last keyframe, select the motion tween and choose the snap option.

Additional Exploration:

1. Import an object from Illustrator or Photoshop and use path animation to move the object. The cool thing about path animation is that the object will rotate based on the path.

2. Create even more challenge with your web game. Open your web game Flash file and open the library. With the library displayed, create a new document. Follow the steps below to create a motion path for the animated ballClip. Remember, it is the center point crosshair that will follow the motion path. The center point crosshair for a movieclip may be in a much different location than the actual object that you see on the stage.

ADDITIONAL EXPLORATION

CHAPTER 33

Animated Motion Trails

MOTION TRAILS

If you have seen the movie The Matrix, there is a great trails effect. It appears that the actors are moving so fast that the camera can only capture the trails of their movement. When they stop, the trails catch up. This project is an attempt to create a similar effect.

One question I am frequently asked is...
"Is it possible to create the Onion Skin (trails) effect in a Flash web animation?"
The answer is yes and no.
There is not a button that can be turned on to create the Onion Skin trails during web playback, but there is a technique that can be used to create the effect. The technique is easier than creating each and every frame individually, but it is not as easy as simply clicking the Onion Skin button. One positive feature of the effect is that as the animated object moves faster the trails become more spread out and when the object stops the trails will catch up.

To create this technique requires a knowledge of movieclips, and an animation that moves in some direction other than a straight line. The animation path in the previous chapter makes a nice fit for this project.

Project overview: The simplest way to create the trails effect (without scripting) is to use multiple copies of a single movieclip. Have each successive copy of the movieclip start 1-3 frames later than the original, and set the alpha of each successive movieclip lighter than the previous. The diagram illustrates the concept.

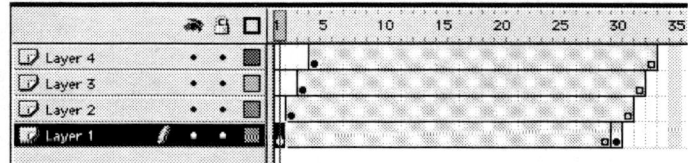

The step by step creation process is covered in the following short project.

PROJECT

❑ Create a new document and drop in an animated movieclip into frame 1, layer 1.
In the previous chapter you created the "BallPathClip" which will work well for this demo. Open the movie "AnimationPath" with the BallPathClip, and display the library palette. Create a new document. Drag a copy of the BallPathClip from the library palette onto the center of the stage of the new untitled movie.

❑ If you are using the "BallPathClip" from the previous chapter then the original animation was 30 frames long, so add a keyframe on frame 30.

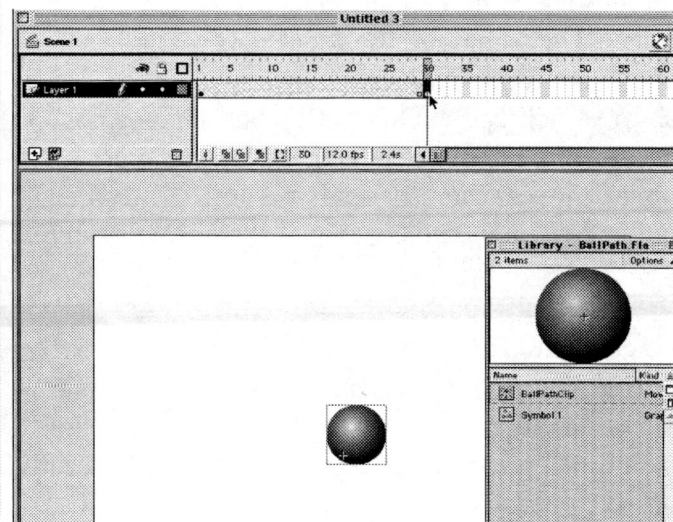

© BRADLEY KALDAHL 2003

❏ Add a new layer to the animation.

❏ Place a keyframe at frame **3** of the new layer.

❏ With frame 3 still selected drag another copy of the movieclip onto the stage and position it at exactly the same location as the first movieclip.

❏ Set the **alpha of this new layer to 80%**.

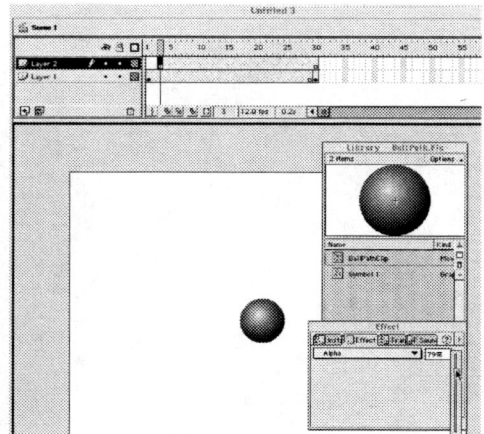

❏ Add a new layer to the animation.

❏ Place a keyframe at frame **5** of the new layer.

❏ With frame 5 still selected drag another copy of the movieclip onto the stage and position it at exactly the same location as the first movieclip.

❏ Set the **alpha of this new layer to 60%**.

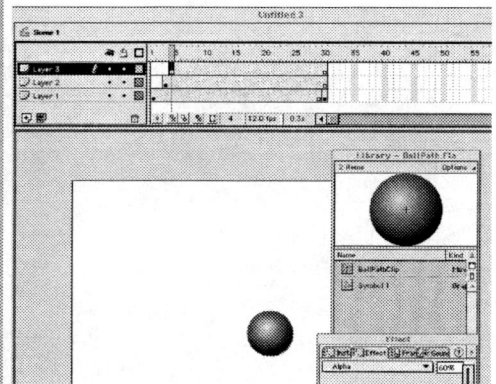

❏ Add a new layer to the animation.

❏ Place a keyframe at frame **7** of the new layer.

❏ With frame 7 still selected drag another copy of the movieclip onto the stage and position it at exactly the same location as the first movieclip.

❏ Set the **alpha of this new layer to 40%**.

❏ Test the movie to see the effect.

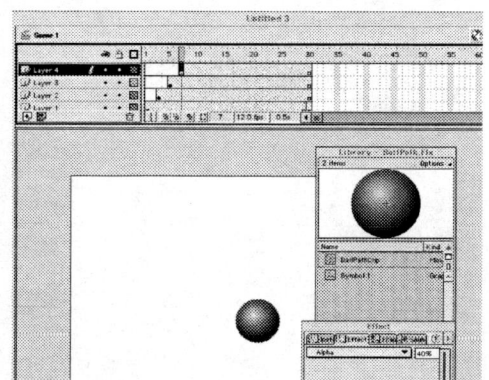

❏ To make the effect even more dramatic you could continue to add more layers, each with a lighter alpha than the previous layer.

Each movieclip runs on its own independent timeline. By starting each copy of the movieclip 1-3 frames later it produces a duplicate animation that is a fraction of a second slower than the previous animation. By setting the alpha of each successive movieclip a little lighter than the previous clip it produces the illusion of trails.

Pointers:
To make this effect really shine, each layer should have the same number of frames as the original movieclip. In the example shown, layers 2-4 are extended.

To make the effect look even better, the first layer should be on the top (in front of the other clips) and each successive layer should appear beneath.

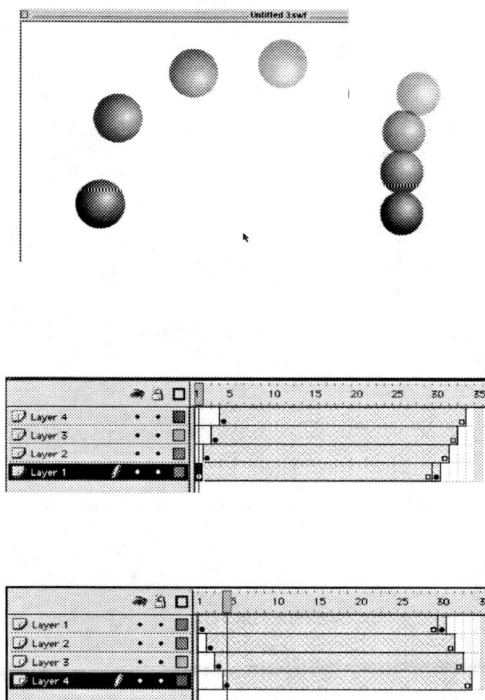

This effect is really fun with an animation that moves quickly then pauses for a few frames then resumes fast animation. If you are familiar with the movie "The Matrix", imagine an animation that moves at high speed (the trails slowly follow the high speed movement) then the animation pauses for a moment. The trails will catch up with the original animation, and appear to pause. Then the animation resumes rapid movement which again leaves the trails to slowly follow. The net result is a surrealistic illusion of slow and fast movement which appears to be captured in slow motion. You may also want to try this animation effect using, Chapter 8, Spinning Type, with the easing option turned on!!

Animated Motion Trails

This project will use a simple drag and drop game to cover three ActionScript issues. Making objects moveable, performing a hit test to see if one object strikes another and score keeping for a simple game. While the examples will be as simple as possible, these concepts are great for variety of interactive projects.

PROJECT

❑ Launch Flash and reset the palettes.

❑ Create a simple ball on the stage and convert it into a button symbol.

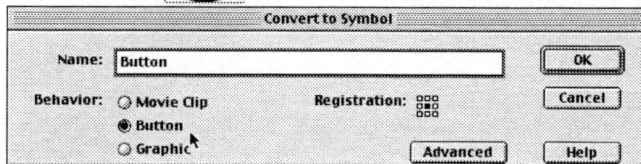

❑ Select the ball-button on the stage and choose Window-Actions to dispaly the ActionScript window.

❑ Set the Actions to Normal Mode.

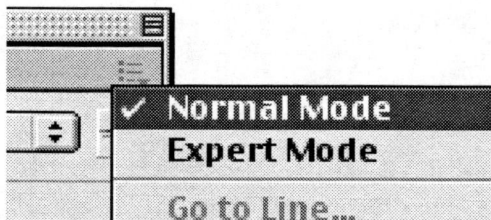

❏ Apply the startDrag action to the ball object, as shown. (Flash automatically adds the on release handler.)

STARTDRAG

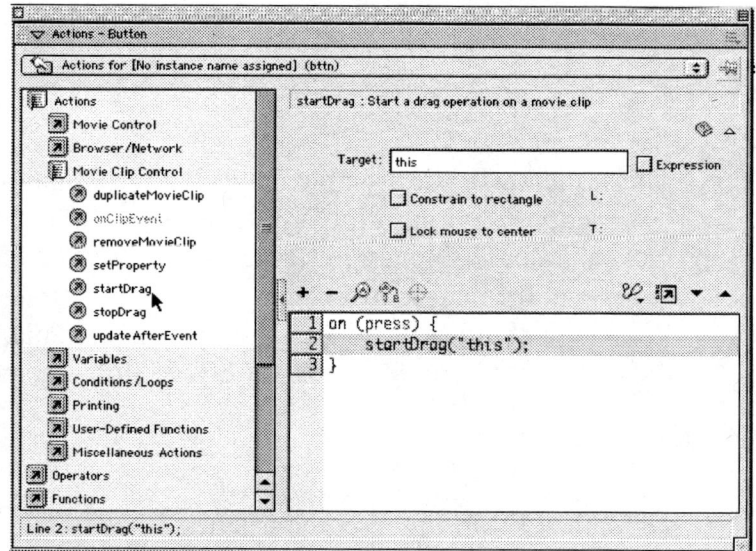

❏ Change on(release) to on(press).

❏ Click on the line of code "startDrag();" and in the parameters area enter the target this, as shown. Change the target to an expression which will remove the quotation marks.

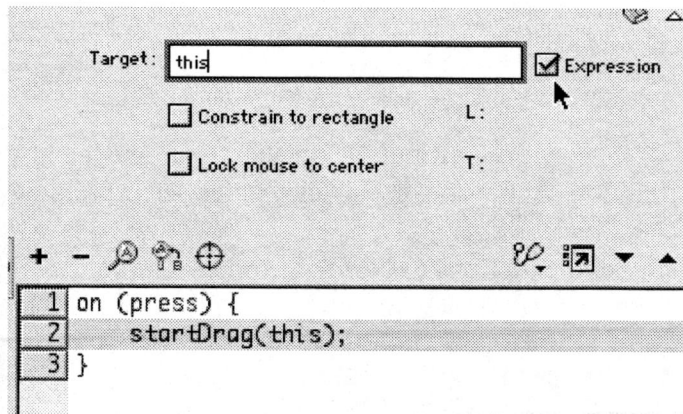

❏ Choose Control-Test Movie to see how it works. When you click and drag on the object, it follows the cursor, but it never stops following the cursor. You might use this technique if you wanted to hide the traditional cursor and replace it with an object that you created to represent the cursor.

The following steps will show how to release the object when the mouse is released.

❏ Click on line 3 of your code as shown.

```
1  on (press) {
2      startDrag(this);
3  }
```

❏ Add the StopDrag command to your ball-button object as shown. (Again by default Flash places it in the on release handler for you.)

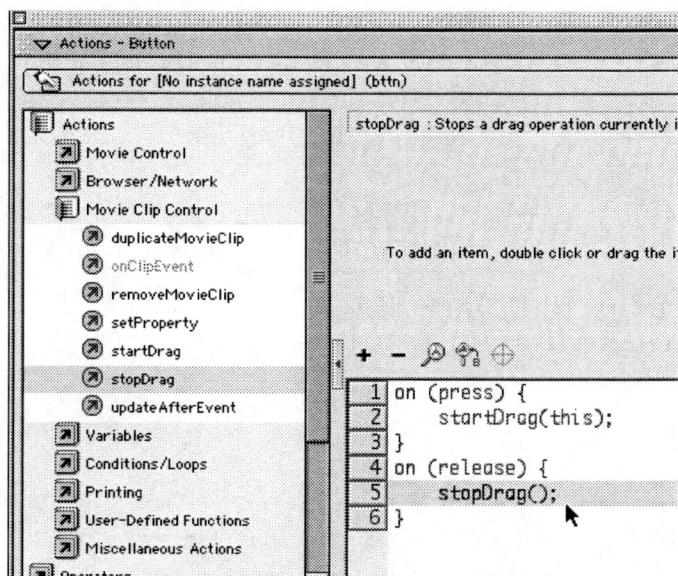

❏ Add releaseOutside to the event handler as shown.

The drag script should now look like the following.

```
on (press) {
    startDrag(this);
}
on (release, releaseOutside) {
    stopDrag();
}
```

❏ Choose Control-Test Movie to see how it works. *The nice thing about this little script is that it is completely contained in the ball object. You could save this object as a movieclip and place hundreds of them in a movie and each object still knows how it should act.*

One possible use for this script. Suppose your customer was a clothing retailer. Selling cloths on-line can be difficult because the customer wants to be able to try them on. One option would be to provide the user with a picture of a model and a variety of moveable shirts and pants.

Back to the project:
❏ To add interest, have the ball animate across the stage. To animate the ball, move the ball to the far left of the stage. Add a keyframe on frame 40. With frame 40 selected move the ball to the far right. Click on frame 1 and add a motion tween.

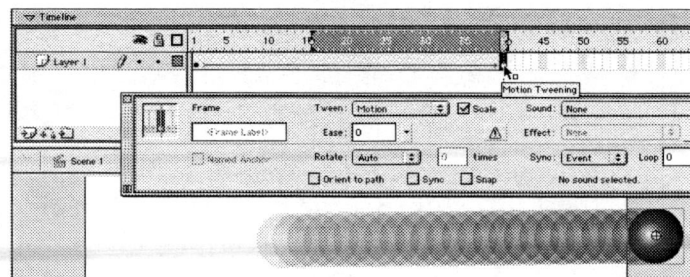

❏ Choose Control-Test Movie to see how it works. (It will not work as you might expect.)
If the ball is animated and you attempt to drag it will not follow the cursor, but instead will change its animation path based on how you move it.

While this may not be what you expected it does offer some possibilities for interesting game ideas. The first thing that comes to my mind is a virtual bowling game, where the ball appears at a random area and begins to roll towards the end of the bowling alley. The pins are in the center of the far end of the stage. The user must catch and align the ball in order to strike the pins.

TRYING TO DRAG AN ANIMATION

For this project, what we want is a ball that is both animated, and that the user can stop and drag around when they click on it.

Back to the ball-button script.
❏ Select frame 1 on the timeline, then click on the ball on the stage, then open the ActionScript dialog. (Make sure you are seeing Object Actions for the ball-button.)

❏ Add the following lines of code to the ball-button.

```
on(rollOver) {
stop(); }
```

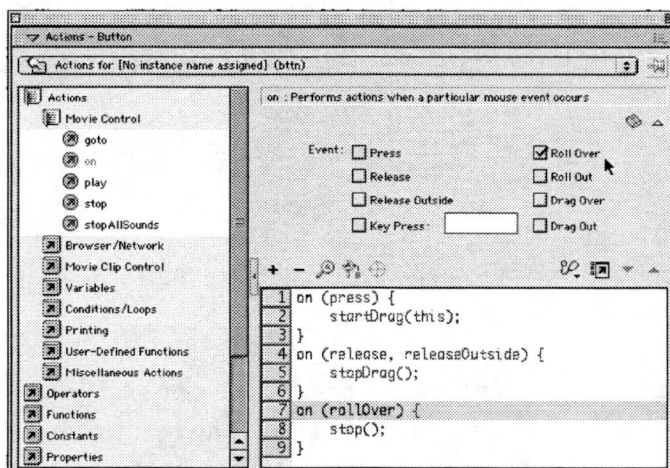

❏ Choose Control-Test Movie to see how it works.

❏ Save this movie as "balldrag.fla".

The next part of this project will discuss hit testing and score keeping.

To understand the scripts that will be added you will need to know what the final project will do.

The final project will have several instances of the dragBall animation that we just created, saved as

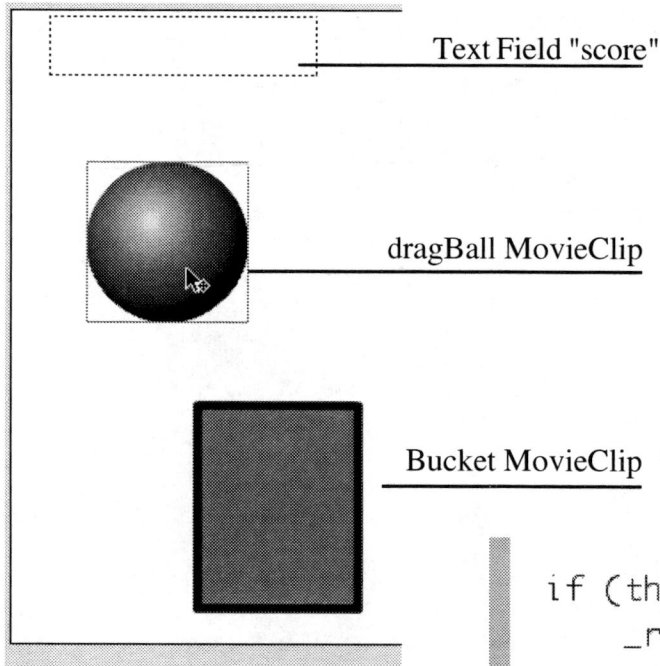

movieclip. It will also have a bucket that the user must drop the balls into. We will create a "hitTest" script to detect if the user was successful in dragging the ball into the bucket. Finally it will have a text field that will keep score of all of the balls the user drops into the bucket.

Explanation of the code:

The code that is placed inside the dragBall object.

HIT TEST

GAME SCORE

VISIBILITY

```
if (this.hitTest(_root.bucket)) {
    _root.score += 1;
    _visible = 0;
}
```

The hitTest begins with an *if* statement. **If** the statement in the parenthesis is TRUE then perform the actions in the curly brackets **{ }**.

`if(this.hitTest(_root.bucket))` compares to see if this. (the ballDrag object) hitTest (intersects with) the bucket in the main movie (_root.bucket).

If the if statement is true then the following line of code is executed.
    `_root.score += 1;`
Add 1 to the (root) movie variable called score.

    `_visible = 0;`
Make the dragBall object invisible.

Note: you could add a variety of additional actions to be executed when the ball hits the bucket. You could play a sound to indicate the object was hit. You could also have either the ball or the bucket play a short movie, such as the bucket could jiggle or expand to indicate it is full.

Here is an idea, after the ball disappears the bucket plays a short animation where it appears that the ball is grabbing onto the edge of the bucket struggling to stay out, before it finally drops down into the bucket!! Well, maybe not, but you get the idea.

❑ Click on frame 1 of the ballDrag movie then click on the ball object on the stage and open the ActionScript editor. (Set the ActionScript editor to expert mode.)

❑ Enter the following text after the on(release) handler. (See diagram)
```
if(this.hitTest(_root.bucket)){
    _root.score += 1;
    _visible = 0;
}
```

Make sure that there are two opening and two closing parentheses. Also, make sure there is an opening and closing Bracket { }for the if statement.

Your final dragBall script should look like the diagram shown on the right.

```
1  on (press) {
2      startDrag(this);
3  }
4  on (release, releaseOutside) {
5      if (this.hitTest(_root.bucket)) {
6          _root.score += 1;
7          _visible = 0;
8      }
9      stopDrag();
10 }
11 on (rollOver) {
12     stop();
13
14 }
```

❑ Convert the ballDrag movie into a movieclip *Select-All-Frames, Copy Frames, Insert-New-Symbol and name the movieclip "ballDragClip".*
Click on frame 1 then choose Edit-Paste-Frames.

❑ After creating the ballDrag movieclip, open the library palette.

❑ Choose File-New to create a new movie.

❑ Drag several instances of the ballDragClip to the far left edge of the stage.

❑ Test the new movie to make sure the movieClips are working.

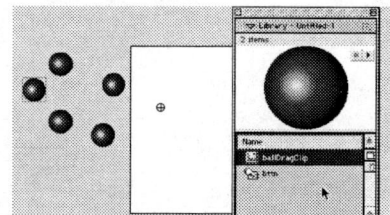

©BRADLEY KALDAHL 2003

Finally create the two objects that were referred to in our hitTest script. The hitTest script will look for an object, on the stage of the new movie, called "bucket". It will also need a text field variable called "score".

Creating and labeling the score text field.
❑ Create a new layer on the timeline.

❑ Select the text tool and create a text box in the new layer.

❑ With the text box still selected, choose the Properties palette set the text field to dynamic text and enter the word "score" into the Variable field, see diagram.

Creating and labeling the bucket clip.
❑ Add a new layer to the timeline.

❑ With the new layer selected draw a simple square object on the stage to represent the bucket.

❑ Select the bucket object with the pointer tool, then choose Insert-Convert-to-Symbol.
Name it "bucket", and be sure it is defined as a movieclip. See diagram.

❑ With the bucket-clip object still selected, choose the Properties palette and set it's Instance Name to "bucket"(all lower case). See the diagram.

❑ Choose Control-Test Movie to see how it works.

Based on this simple project you have additional tools for a variety of different interactive games.

DYNAMIC TEXT VARIABLE

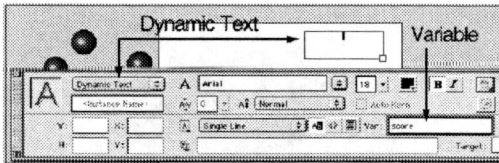

INSTANCE NAME

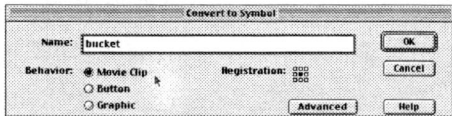

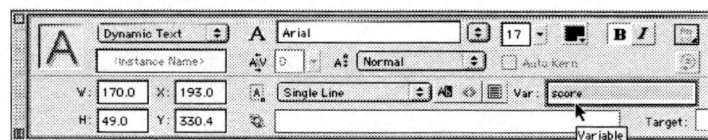

PROBLEMS?

If your score field is not working then check to see that you gave it a variable name and not an instance name.

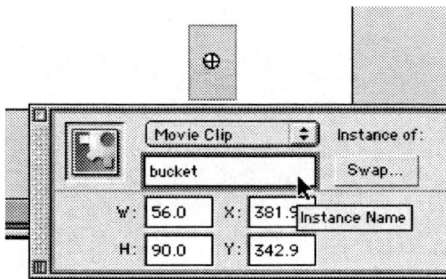

CHAPTER 35

The tool I use and recommend for capturing video is a product called Dazzle Hollywood DV Bridge. It requires a FireWire 1394 connection and works like a charm. On the Mac it does not even require drivers. Using this product you can plug a VCR into your computer (or use a digital camcorder). Not only can you capture video, edit, and create cool effects but you can also record it back out to conventional VCR tape.

If you are working on a Macintosh you can capture video directly into I-Movie, create your clips, scenes, transitions, and titles and save the final video for use in Flash. If you are working on the PC Dazzle includes a software package called MovieStar5 for capture, editing, and effects.

Using Dazzle Hollywood DV-Bridge with a Mac:
1. Plug it into your FireWire port on your Mac.
2. Plug your VCR into the S-Video or standard RCA plugs on your VCR.
3. Launch I-Movie.

HOW TO DIGITIZE VIDEO

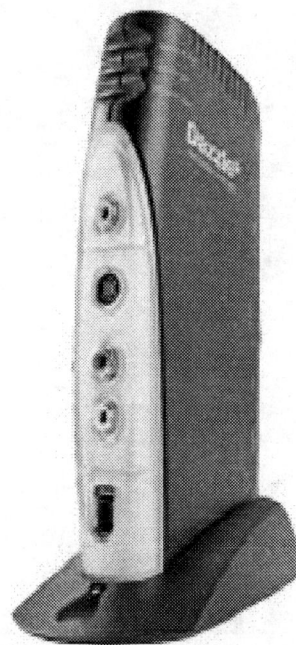

©BRADLEY KALDAHL 2003

In the Lower left corner of the Movie Window set the switch to DV.

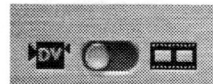

The Blue Screen will let you know that all of the connections are working.

Camera Connected

Turn on the camcorder or VCR and turn on the Play button inside I-Movie.

Preview the video onscreen and when you find a scene that you want to capture click the Import button. When the scene is finished click the import button again and the clip will now appear in the clips area.

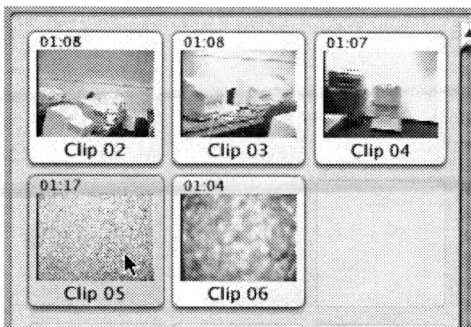

Once you have captured several clips from your video you can arrange the clips to the assembly area.

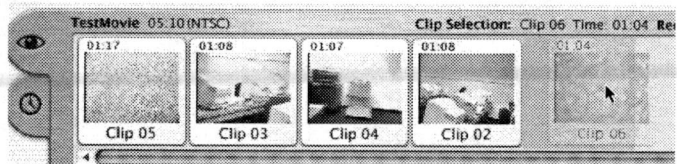

Adding a Transition:
Simply select the transition you want and drag it between the 2 clips in the clips assembly area.

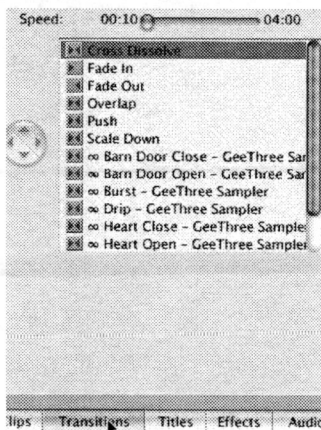

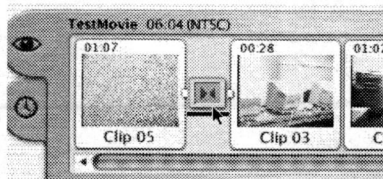

Titles and Effects are just as easy to add.

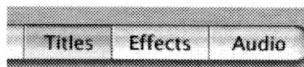

© BRADLEY KALDAHL 2003

Once you have created the movie choose File-Export. You can export the movie back out to your camera/VCR, for Quicktime which provides compression options or for DVD which produces the largest file sizes but also the highest quality.

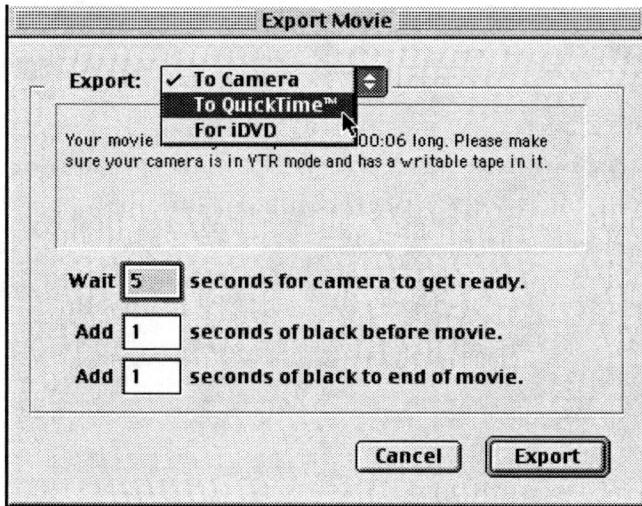

Export Movie

Export: ✓ To Camera
To QuickTime™
For iDVD

Your movie ... 00:06 long. Please make sure your camera is in VTR mode and has a writable tape in it.

Wait [5] seconds for camera to get ready.

Add [1] seconds of black before movie.

Add [1] seconds of black to end of movie.

Cancel   Export

Here are some of the Quicktime options:

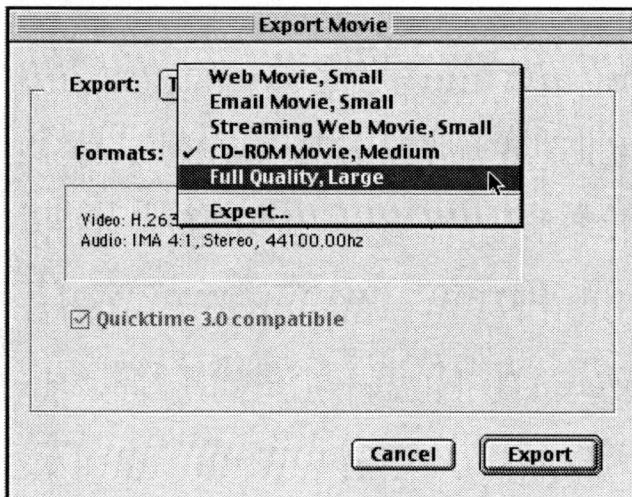

Export Movie

Export: [T

Web Movie, Small
Email Movie, Small
Streaming Web Movie, Small
✓ CD-ROM Movie, Medium
Full Quality, Large

Formats:

Expert...

Video: H.263
Audio: IMA 4:1, Stereo, 44100.00hz

☑ Quicktime 3.0 compatible

Cancel   Export

Note: Both DVD and Quicktime will import into Flash MX.

The Dazzle Hollywood DV-Bridge has made the video capture process addictively easy. The only area that I ran into troubles was trying to record back out to video tape. Turns out the problem was in the VCR and not with the DV-Bridge. If you use this product to edit for video tape the few words of advice I can offer are to use a video monitor attached to your VCR and toy with the Input and TV/VCR buttons on your video recorder.

Dazzle also offers a product called DVD complete that has won awards for ease of use and professional quality. http://www.dazzle.com

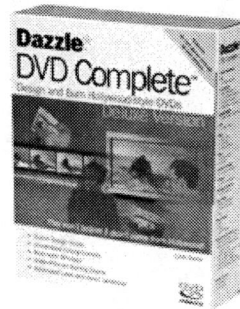

Dazzle DVD Complete
$99.99
DM-10000
Design and Burn Hollywood-Style DVDs
● All the DVD Design Features You Want
● Works with all Your Videos and Movies
● Add Chapters, Menus and Other Special Feature
● It's Easy. Just Click, Burn and Enjoy!

They won't believe it didn't come from Hollywood!

With DVD Complete™, it's easy to make DVDs like the ones designed in Hollywood movie studios. DVD Complete's project wizard guides you through the steps to go from camcorder to DVD. Capture video from a camcorder, add start-up overtures, interactive menus with multiple scenes, background audio, choose a graphical theme and then record to a DVD or CD. All you need to know is what you like, and DVD Complete™ will do the rest.

Once you have captured and edited your video the next issue for Flash is compressing the video in order to create a reasonable file size for the web. The next two chapters discuss different approaches for compressing and preparing video for Flash.

If you want to use video in Flash for the web the big issue is how to make the video file size small enough for web playback. If you are only using a few video clips or just starting out then using the Sorenson Spark Codec provided with Flash is one solution. The biggest advantage is that it is built into Flash so you do not need to buy additional software. If you are in a production environment where time is money then you may want to jump to the next chapter which discusses Sorenson Squeeze.

The import video settings built into Flash are not intuitive. This chapter will shed some light on the subject. If your video clips are large then you should wait until you are ready to leave your computer for a while before you import the video. The Sorenson Spark Codec can perform some amazing file size reduction to your raw video but it will also take a while to process. Finally if you choose to use flash to import your video, be prepared to spend some time experimenting. The difficulty with video is finding the smallest file size while obtaining usable quality. Determining what is usable quality may vary from customer to customer and project to project.

To write this chapter I used a raw video file that is referred to as "example." In the example the raw video was 1.24 seconds. The file size was 6.3 megabytes.

COMPRESSION BUILT-IN

When importing raw video Flash immediately presents the "Import Video settings Dialog". See diagram.

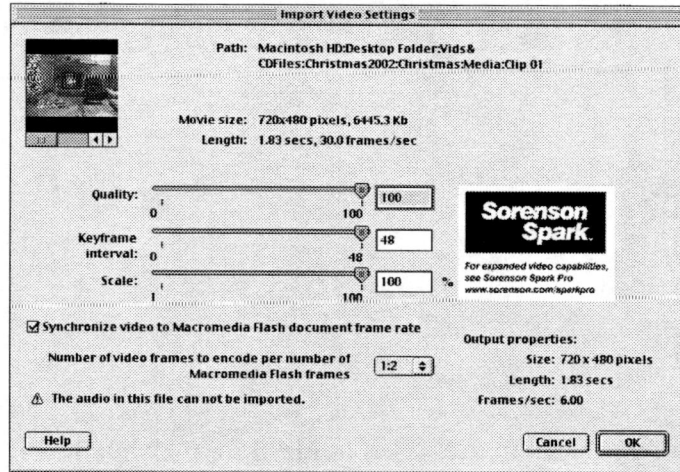

IMPORT VIDEO DIALOG

Understanding the Import Video Settings:

The Quality setting is pretty easy to understand. How good do you want the video clip to look?
Like the JPEG image file format a lower quality setting will degrade how well the video looks. Unlike JPEG, a quality setting below 50 is (in my opinion) not even worth looking at.

IMPORTANT:
KeyFrame Interval: In Flash a keyframe defines a critical point in movement. In the Sorenson Spark Codec a keyframe determines how many frames will display the complete data. In my tests, keeping the keyframe interval high will produce a smaller file size. Setting the keyframe interval low will dramatically increase file size without making significant improvements to your video quality.

The Scale setting is pretty straightforward. If your raw video is larger than the stage then scaling it will reduce file size. Unfortunately the Flash Video import dialog does not allow you to crop the video.

© BRADLEY KALDAHL 2003

Synchronize video to Macromedia Flash document frame rate: Turn this feature on.

This feature forces the raw video to match the frame rate of your Flash document. This will conserve file size and also make sure the audio matches the video. Your video may not play as smoothly but the goal here is to get the audio to synch and to keep file size realistic for web viewers.

Number of Frame per number of Frames of Flash: This is another file size reduction feature. 1:1 will match your video with Flash but 1:2 will reduce video file size. If you were playing the video on CD you would want 1:1, but to reduce file size for web a playback 1:2 might be acceptable. Test both options to see if you realize a notable difference on the web.

Import Audio: It is great that we can choose to eliminate audio. It takes extra file space and download time and may not be required for your video clip. Turn this feature off if you do not need the audio (to save file space). Leave it on if the audio is critical to your video clip.

Many of the raw video clips I capture import into Flash with an error message stating that the audio portion of the video clip cannot be used. Fortunately I often use video as a backdrop and do not want the audio.

⚠ **The audio in this file can not be imported.**

After you have set up the Flash Video import dialog choose OK.

In my example the video clip is only 1.5 seconds and only takes about 20 seconds to process. If the video clip is large then Flash can be tied up for minutes or longer while you wait for the video to be processed. This can be a major drawback for using Flash to compress video. Sorenson makes a product called Squeeze, which is discussed in the next chapter. The advantages with Squeeze are that it can run in the background, process multiple compression settings at the click of a button, and can batch process multiple files.

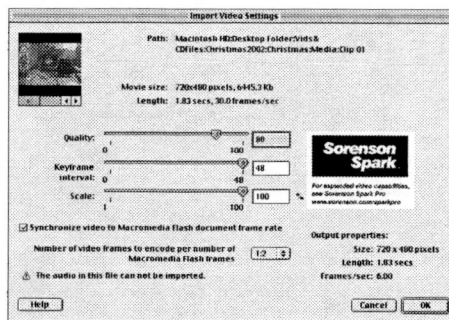

Once the video is processed Flash indicates that the video will require a particular number of frames. Choose yes. This will place the video onto timeline. Use Control-Test Movie to see if the video is acceptable. If not then you will want to repeat the process with different settings.

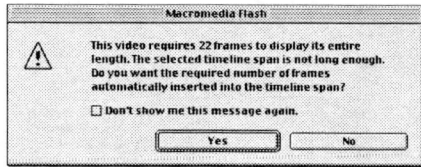

STREAMING VIDEO VS MOVIECLIPS

Streaming vs. Movieclips:
If you place the video on the root level timeline it will stream. On the other hand, if you convert the video into a movieclip then it will not stream but you can apply movieclip effects.

I originally thought that streaming would be the best for video but discovered that in Flash, streaming video tended to stop, start, and pause. It was not the smooth playback I had hoped for. (This was based on tests using Control-Test Movie, then using View-Show Streaming.) *Actual results on the web may be different.*

A video clip converted into a movieclip is kind of fun to toy with. Once it is a movieclip you can apply color settings. You can adjust the RGB values or the opacity to create the effect you seek for your video. As a movieclip it can be animated using a motion tween or the movieclip object can be controlled (to some extent) using ActionScript.

Making the video clip into a movieclip not only gave me more control over the effects I wanted to create but also using a preloader I could ensure that the entire video clip was downloaded before it started to play, which guaranteed smooth playback.

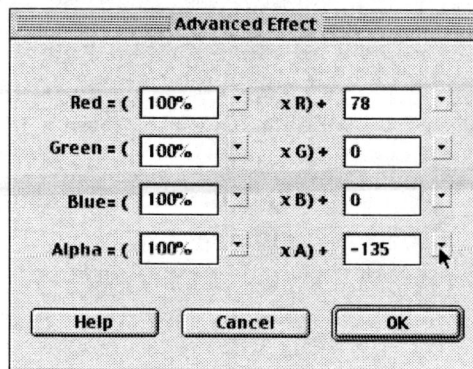

CHAPTER 37

Sorenson Squeeze

If you are doing a lot of video work then compressing video in Flash is not the best solution. Sorenson, the company that provided the compression codec for Flash, has a few different video compression products that are easier to use and also offer in-depth control for those who really want to fine tune the video.

Sorenson Squeeze 3.5 Compression Suite which includes Sorenson Video 3 Pro, Sorenson Spark Pro, and Sorenson MPEG-4 Pro video codecs, or Sorenson Squeeze 3.1 for Macromedia Flash MX.

The question is what is the difference between these products? If you are doing a diverse video work and want to compress video for Flash, CD, DVD, and other uses then the suite is a great solution. As an example, I was working on a children's CD that included video. The raw video was 6 gigabytes! Using the compression suite I was able to reduce the file size down to 500 megabytes and still had incredibly good looking quality. On the other hand, if you only need to compress video for Flash you can save several dollars by choosing Sorenson Squeeze 3.1 for Macromedia Flash MX.

SQUEEZE VERSION 3

To demo test this software go to
http://www.sorenson.com

When you first launch Squeeze you will be asked if you want to open an existing video file, batch process several files from a Watch Folder, or directly import DV into Squeeze.

In the following diagram I opened an existing video file. I then chose the File type and selected several different download speeds so I could see which one best met my needs.

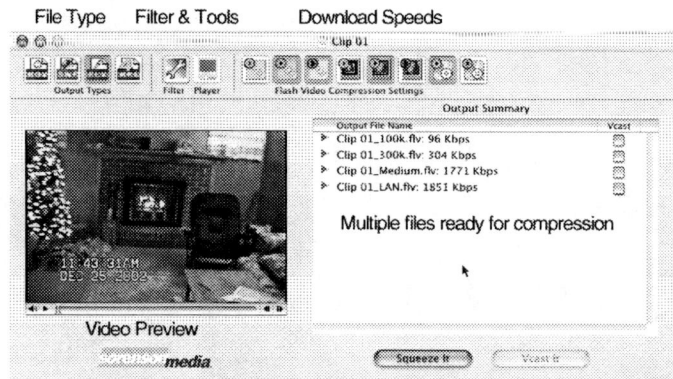

Download Squeeze Demo

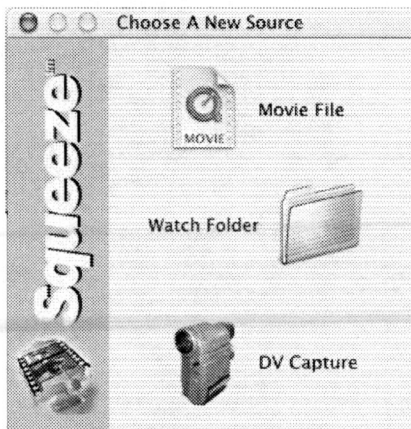

File Type: The pro version of Squeeze 3.0 provides four file types.
Quicktime movie, SWF, FLV, and MP4.

Quicktime is useful for Director or burning Video CDs.

SWF is useful if you want to create a video player with Flash and use the ActionScript loadSWF command to load different videos into your Flash player.

FLV is the format to use if you want to imbed the video into your Flash document for manipulation.

MP4 is a great option if you want to allow users to download the video, because it opens in the Quicktime player as well as others.

Download speeds: As you roll over each option you will note different download speed setting ranging from 56k modem all the way up to high end CD Quality.

A video compressed for 56k modem is going to be small in size and lose a lot of detail in order to accommodate slower connections.

My suggestion is to generate several different speeds, then import them into Flash and use control test movie to find the quality that works best for your needs. Once you find the quality that you like you will need to check the file size of the SWF file to determine if it will meet your needs.

The Filters button provides some great tools for quick video adjustments. As shown in the diagram on the right, you can change the contrast, brightness and gamma of the video clip. You can also set the highlights and shadows.

The feature I found incredibly useful was the cropping tool. To crop the video simply turn cropping on and move the cursor to the very edge of the video preview window and drag the crop lines in (as shown). With the crop border you can preview your video to insure your cropping works throughout the video. The one feature I would like to see with cropping is the final dimensions (width and height after cropping). Because each download speed setting has independent parameters, this might not be possible.

These are the basics of Squeeze and the results are wonderful. Sorenson has made this product incredibly easy to use. While Squeeze is easy to use it also offers in-depth controls for the technically savvy digital video expert. By double clicking on the download speed preset a variety of options are presented.

In the following diagram I wanted to strip the audio from the video, which was easy enough to do. As

FILTERS

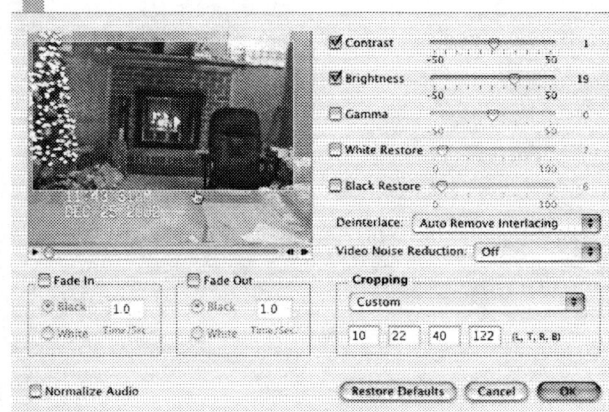

TWEEKING DOWNLOAD SPEED PRESETS

you can see there are a wealth of buttons, dials, and options to toy with.

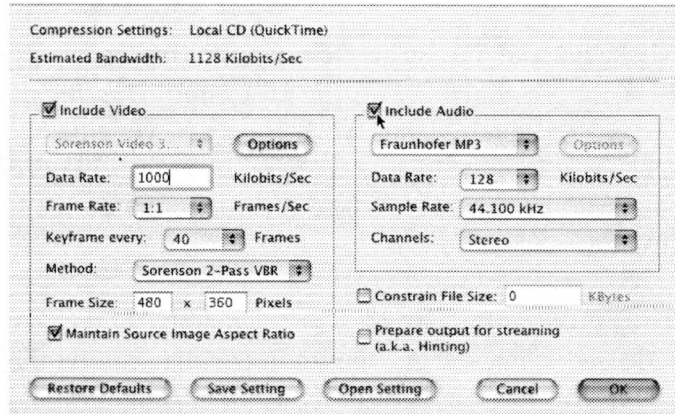

For those who want to go further click on the options button and even the most ardent technophile is overwhelmed with choices.

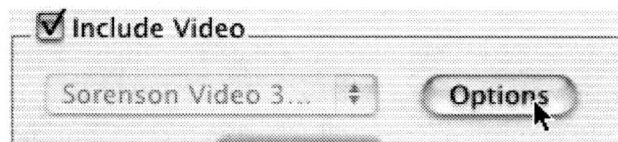

I am impressed with the results of this product and even more impressed with the interface design. At first glance it is an easy-to-use tool for video compression yet also provides in-depth control for those who want to fine tune.

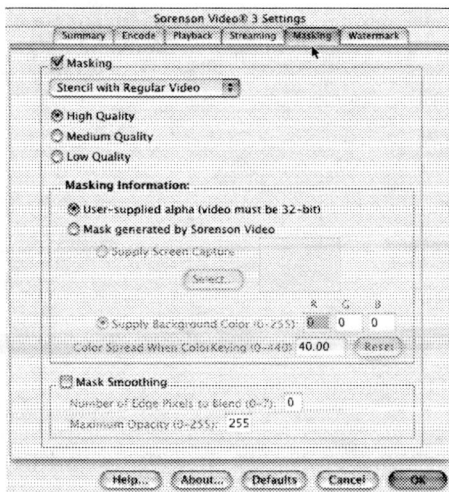

This short project is a simple effect that can make an interesting background or be used independently.

❑ Launch Flash and reset the palettes.

❑ Import raw video into Flash and use the Sorenson codec to compress it (or if you are lucky enough to have Squeeze compress your video as an FLZ for direct import into Flash).

❑ When Flash warns you that the video will require a particular number of frames choose yes.

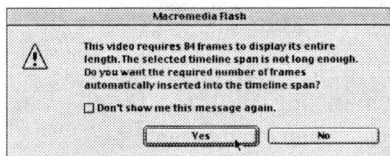

❑ If required, reduce the video size so it fills approximately one quarter of the screen.

❑ Convert the timeline video clip into a MovieClip.
1. Select all frames.
2. Copy Frames.
3. Insert New Symbol - MovieClip - Call it "Vidclip."
4. Click on frame 1 of the Movieclip Symbol and choose Edit Paste Frames.

❑ To avoid confusion, choose Window-Library, then choose File-New to create a new document.

PROJECT

CONVERT VIDEO TO MOVIECLIP

❏ Drag an instance of the video movieclip (VidClip) into the upper left corner of the new document.

PLACE VIDEO CLIPS ON THE STAGE

❏ Click on frame 40 of layer 1 and add a keyframe.

❏ Add a new layer (layer 2).

❏ Click on frame 5 of layer 2 and add a blank keyframe.

❏ Drag another instance of the VidClip onto the stage and place it in the upper right corner, as shown.

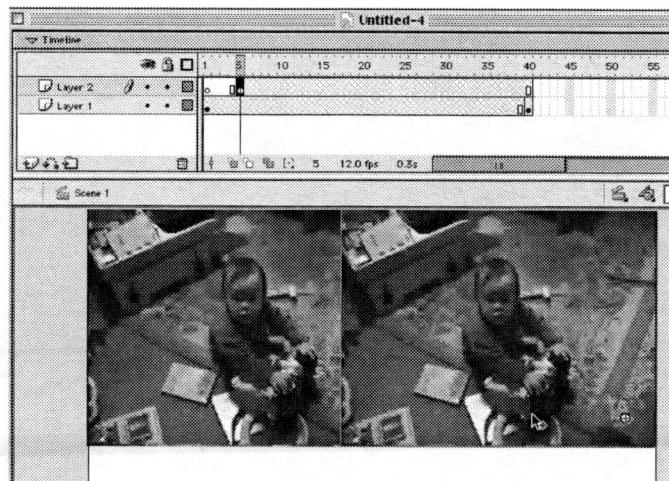

❏ Add a new layer (layer 3).

❑ Click on frame 10 of layer 3 and add a blank keyframe.

❑ Drag another instance of the VidClip onto the stage and place it in the lower left corner, as shown.

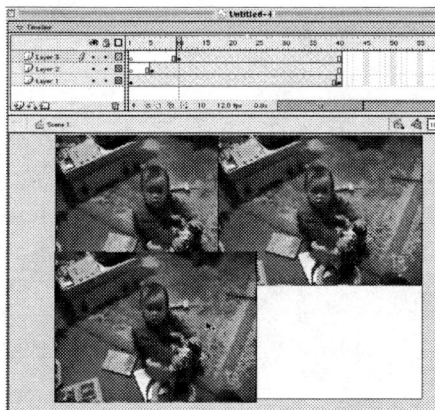

❑ Add a new layer (layer 4).

❑ Click on frame 15 of layer 4 and add a blank keyframe and drag another instance of the VidClip onto the stage and place it in the lower right corner, as shown.

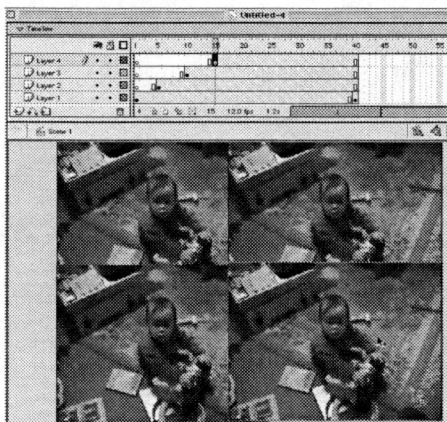

❑ Choose control test movie to see the results.

It is important to note that the file size of the SWF using four instances of the video clip is generally no larger than if only one instance of the video clip were used.

ADDITIONAL EXPLORATION

Additional Exploration:

1. Add a new layer for ActionScript. Insert a blank keyframe on frame 40.

Place the following script on frame 40.

```
gotoAndPlay(15);
```

This will keep the movies playing independently without a blank space once they have all loaded.

2. Click on any of the movieclips and choose the Color option on the Properties palette and experiment with the brightness.

Color: [Brightness ⬍] [12%] ▼

3. Click on another of the movieclips and choose the Color option on the Properties palette and experiment with the tint.

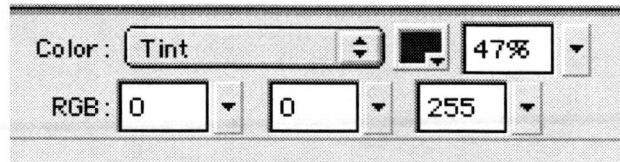

Color: [Tint ⬍] [■▾] [47%] ▼
RGB: [0] ▼ [0] ▼ [255] ▼

4. Click on another of the movieclips and choose the Color option on the Properties palette and experiment with the alpha.

Color: [Alpha ⬍] [70%] ▼

5. Click on another of the movieclips and choose the Color option on the Properties palette.

Play with the Advanced Settings.

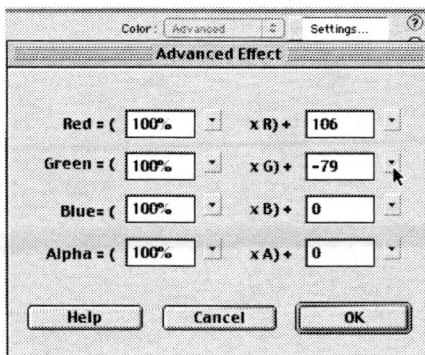

Color: [Advanced ⬍] [Settings...] (?)

Advanced Effect

Red = ([100%] ⬍ x R) + [106] ⬍
Green = ([100%] ⬍ x G) + [-79] ⬍
Blue = ([100%] ⬍ x B) + [0] ⬍
Alpha = ([100%] ⬍ x A) + [0] ⬍

[Help] [Cancel] [OK]

Swift 3D is an easy to use yet powerful application. This short chapter will discuss how to produce 3D content and export it for Flash. The next chapter demonstrates how to import into Flash and shows some fun code for allowing the user to control the 3D object.

If you have tried other 3D applications and found the learning curve too high you may be pleasantly surprised with Swift. If you have never used a 3D application then be prepared there is a lot to learn but the user manual that ships with the software does a great job of getting you started. Finally if you already have a lot of experience with another 3D application then you may want to check the website of the company that produces Swift, www.erain.com, to see if they have a plug-in to allow you to export for Flash.

The following is from the user manual for Swift: "We had an absolute blast creating Swift 3D V3, and my goal is to share the same excitement while learning the application." —Nicholas Petterssen, author of the user guide for Swift 3D.

To view the software manual and tutorials go to:
http://www.erain.com/support/tutorials/manuals/Swift3Dv3.pdf

PROJECT

CREATING 3D TYPE

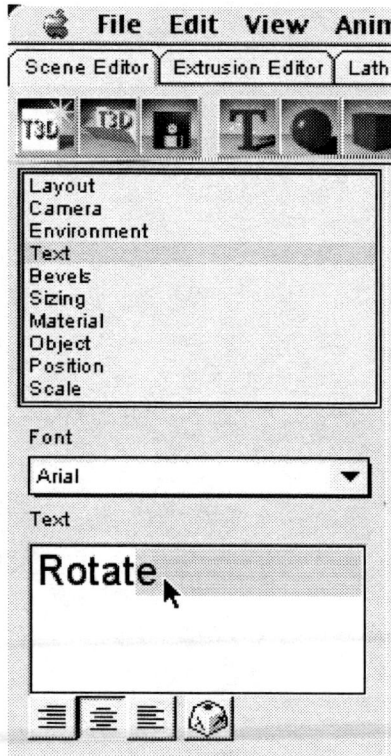

❏ Launch Swift 3D (version 3).

❏ On the main toolbar you will see the Create Text tool. Click on it to add text.

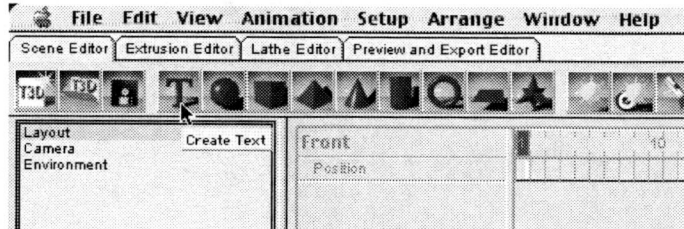

By default Swift places the word Text into the view windows.

❏ Change the text to the word you want to animate (see diagram).

The word "Rotate" does not fit into the Front View window.

❏ Click on the Top View window once to make it active, then click on the type object and drag it up (which actually moves it back). Keep it centered.

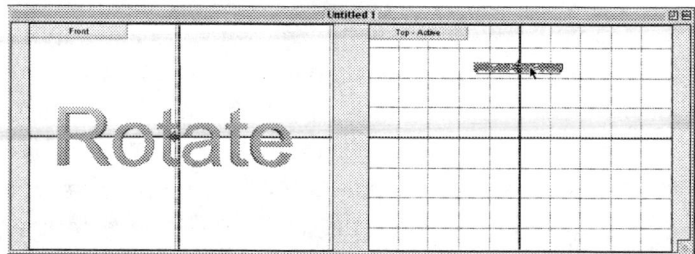

❏ Click once on the Front View window to make it active. Front - Active

Now to rotate the type.
In the lower right corner of your monitor you will see a variety of tabs. This is referred to as the Gallery Toolbar, see diagram.

❏ Click on the Animation Palette button.
While you can create your own animations in Swift it also provides several predefined Drag and Drop animations. This is just too easy!!

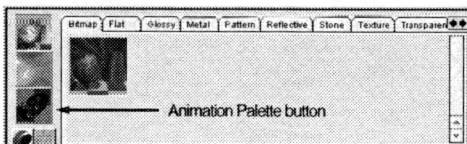

Animation Palette button

❑ Select the Horizontal Left spin and drag it on top of type object as shown.

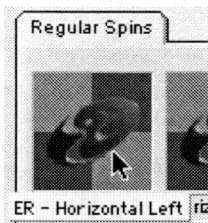
Regular Spins
ER – Horizontal Left

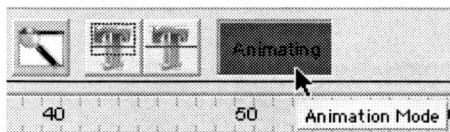

Note: While you are dragging the animation you will see the following cursor ⊘. Once you have positioned the animation directly on top of the type you will see the Apply cursor.

By default Swift applies a 20 frame animation. To extend the animation is a bit different than what you would do in Flash.

❑ Click on the Animating button which is in the upper right above the timeline.

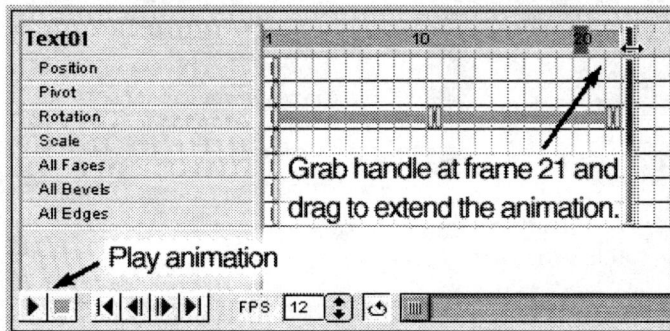
40   50   Animation Mode

❑ Click on the handle on frame 21 of the timeline and drag to the right to extend the animation. (Note that you are actually clicking on the number 21.) I recommend extending to 100 frames but use the Play button to preview and find a rotation you like.

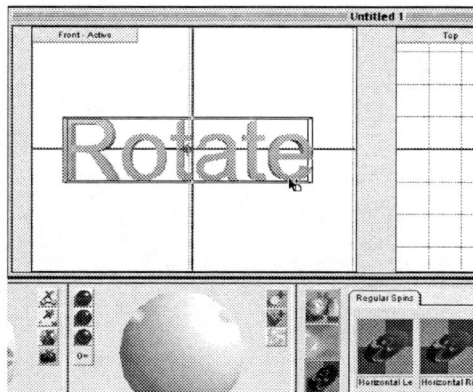

Text01
Position
Pivot
Rotation
Scale
All Faces
All Bevels
All Edges

Grab handle at frame 21 and drag to extend the animation.

Play animation

FPS 12

©BRADLEY KALDAHL 2003

The last thing to do in Swift is to export the animation for Flash.

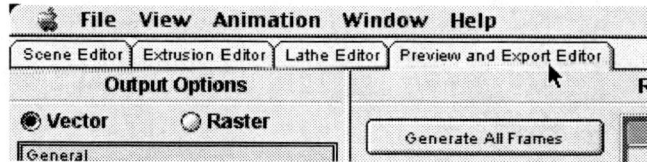

❑ Click on the Preview and Export tab (just below the menu bar).

❑ For this demo keep it simple, set the Output Options to Vector, then click the Generate All Frames button (as shown).

❑ Choose File Save-as to save the source file.

❑ Choose File Export All Frames to generate the .swft file for Flash.

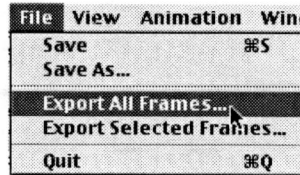

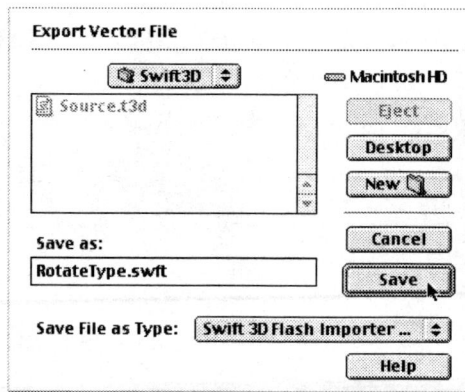

© BRADLEY KALDAHL 2003

ActionScript code by Josh Trout
http://www.amongtrout.com

You can import your swift 3D animation onto the main Flash timeline but the code shown below will only work on a movieclip so we might as well start by importing the animation into a movieclip.

❏ Launch Flash and reset palettes.

❏ Choose Insert - New Symbol.

❏ If you look above the stage you will see that you are inside the movieclip symbol editor.

❏ Choose File-Import and import the RotateType.swft that you previously created.

You will note that the animation fills the timeline.

❏ Click on the Scene 1 button.

❏ Display the Library palette using Window-Library.

❏ Drag an instance of the Rotate Movie Clip onto the stage.

❏ Test the movie to make sure the movieclip is rotating.

Now comes the cool part. Using ActionScript the user will be able to click and drag on the object to rotate it

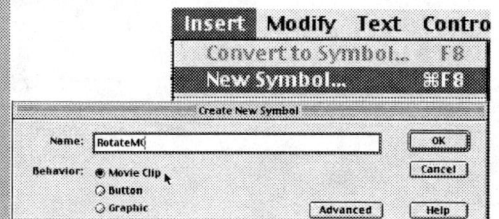

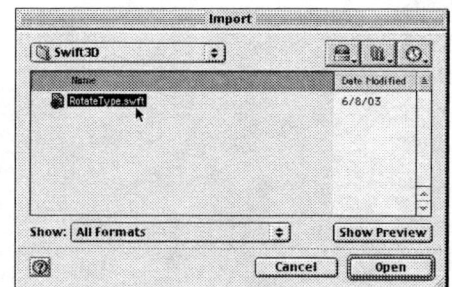

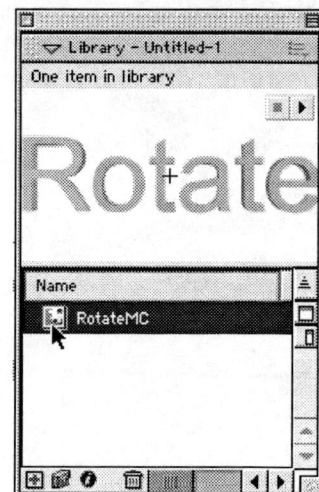

in the desired direction. The code is "Movieclip code" which has not been discussed in this book.

To understand more about movieclip code you will want to look for my book "ActionScript for Artists" due to be published in Fall 2003.

❑ Click on the graphic on the Stage and choose Window-Actions.

Rotate Code

❑ Set the ActionScript Editor to Expert mode and enter the following code...

```
//(Code developed by Josh Trout http://www.amongtrout.com)

onClipEvent (mouseDown){
        this.stop();
        manual = true;
}
onClipEvent (mouseUp){
        this.play();
        manual = false;
}
onClipEvent (enterFrame){
        rotate = oldx - _xmouse;
        oldx = _xmouse;
        if (manual){
                move = Math.round(_currentframe+rotate);
                move %= _totalframes;
                if (move <= 0) move = _totalframes;
                gotoAndStop(move);
        }
}
```

The ActionScript code for this chapter was developed by
Josh Trout
http://www.amongtrout.com
When I first played with Swift 3D I developed the 3D content easily but struggled to get the interactive rotation to work. I contacted a friend "Josh" who looked at it and in lcss then 2 hours had perfected a solution. If you are looking for a gifted developer either for consultation or for a permanent position you will want to contact him at: josh@amongtrout.com

This chapter provides a basic introduction to Fireworks, which is a scanned image application produced by Macromedia. If you purchased the MX Suite then you already have Fireworks.

Scanned image applications: While there are other applications used for scanned images, combining images, color corrections and many special effects, I will discuss only two, Photoshop and Fireworks. Photoshop, because it has been around since (almost) the beginning of the digital image revolution and is a standard tool for many professions. Fireworks, because it is part of the MX package, is designed to work with Flash, and as a result offers some advantages over Photoshop.

Vector graphics are defined mathematically and use lines and shapes for solid color or gradients. The result can produce substantially smaller file sizes. Bitmapped images are based on a resolution grid and each pixel increases file size. I am not suggesting that you avoid bitmapped images but instead that you use them judiciously. Generally you should avoid large bitmapped images on the first frame of your Flash animation.

Suggestions for using bitmapped images to get the most out of Flash.
1. Avoid using large bitmapped images in frame 1 of your animation.
2. Resolution: A resolution of 300 pixels per inch is recommended for print but is far more than you need

BITMAPPED VS. VECTOR

for computer monitor display. A resolution of 72 pixels per inch is ideal for the monitor, but that assumes you will not be stretching the image once it has been imported into Flash.

3. Managing Color Depth can also help to reduce file size, but for Flash it may not meet your visual needs.

PROJECT

❑ Launch Fireworks.

❑ Choose File-New and create a new document. Choose transparent for canvas color.

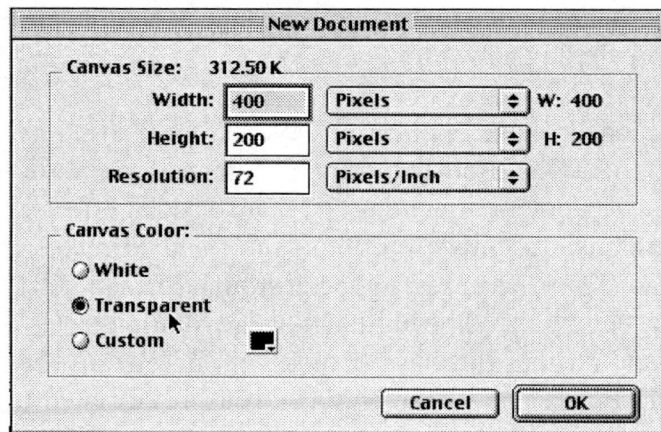

❑ Select the text tool from the tool palette then use the Properties palette to set the fill color to white, as shown.

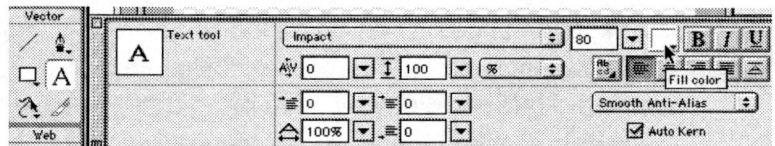

❑ Type in your text. Note that it should appear as white on a checkerboard (transparent) background.

❏ Choose Filters-Blur-Gaussian Blur.

❏ when you are warned that this operation will convert the type from vector to bitmap, choose OK.

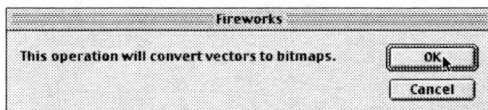

❏ Apply a Blur Radius of 3 and choose OK.

❏ In the image window choose the preview tab.

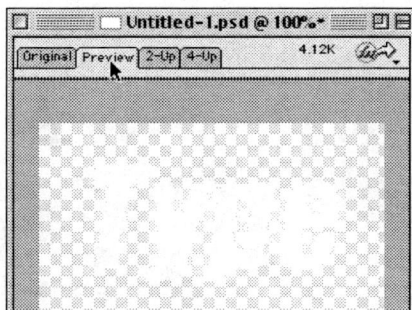

❏ On the right side of the screen set the Optimize settings to PNG 32. If you do not see the Optimize palette, choose Window Optimize (F6).

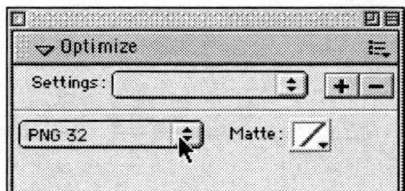

❑ For the Matte settings select the None option.

❑ There are a couple of ways that you can export this image for use in Flash. The easiest is to use Quick Export feature at the top of the image window.

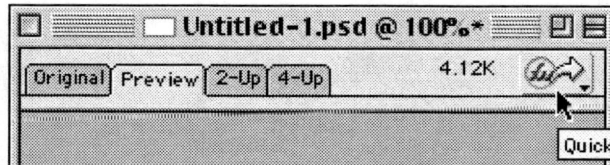

❑ Note that Fireworks will optimize for other Macromedia products. Choose Flash-Export SWF.

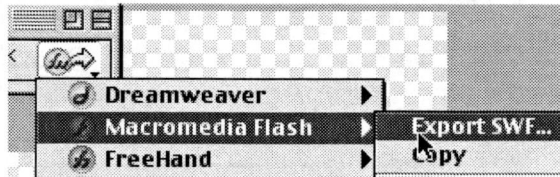

❑ In the Export Dialog name it and choose the location to save it.

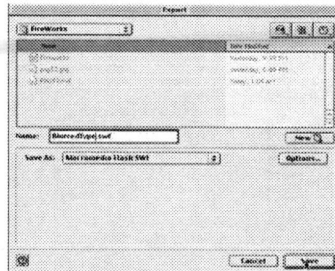

To import the image into Flash launch Flash and choose File Import or File-Import to Library.

If you have never tried Fireworks then hopefully this short demo provides a basic introduction.

© BRADLEY KALDAHL 2003

Fireworks for Flash

PHOTOSHOP 7

This short project will not make you an expert with Photoshop. The objective is to provide some ideas and cover the basics of exporting from Photoshop for Flash.

If you have grown with Photoshop then you know that each version upgrade offers fun and exciting new tools. If you have never used Photoshop before then a good course (or at least a couple of good books) is essential.

Some of the knowledge required to use Photoshop effectively (or any other imaging application) is a knowledge of image resolution and color depth, understanding how selection tools work as well as advanced selection techniques, how to combine images to create a believable result, how to "clone out" unwanted parts of an image, unsharp masking, file formats, color retouching using either RGB or CMYK, color correction theory and the list goes on.

If you prefer self-study then the first book you will want is one that covers the user interface of Photoshop. Once you are familiar with how the application works an excellent technical reference (not necessarily an artist's book) but definitely one of the best researched books on the market is "Real World Photoshop."

TOYS TO PLAY WITH IN PHOTOSHOP

Fun stuff to experiment with in Photoshop Ver. 7. Photoshop version 7 has some cool vector effects such as Warp Text, and some basic vector graphics.

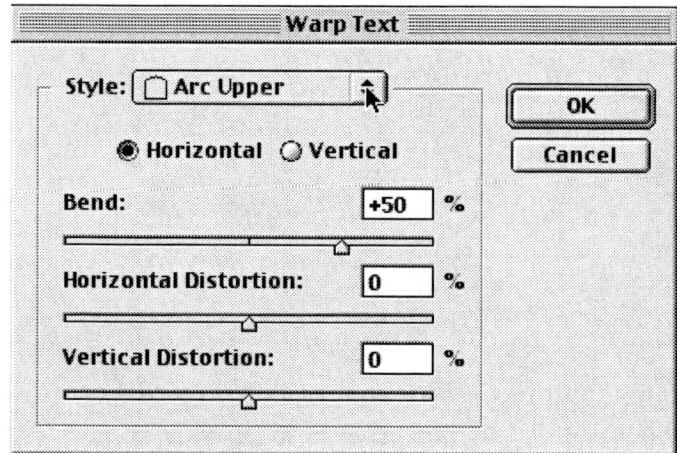

One filter that offers a lot of fun is Liquefy. It is like the smudge tool on Steroids.

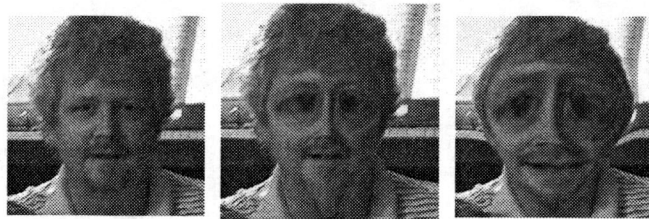

© BRADLEY KALDAHL 2003

Exporting images for Flash:
After you scanned or created your image choose File-Save for Web.

In the Save for Web window choose the Optimized Tab in order to visually see how changes will effect the image.

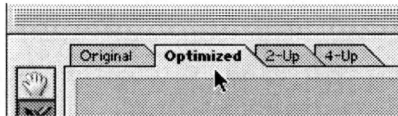

The settings area allows you to choose the file format you desire.
Flash will accept GIF and JPEG. My suggestion is to use the PNG 24 file format.
First, Flash prefers the PNG file format. Second, this format allows transparency and semi-transparency.

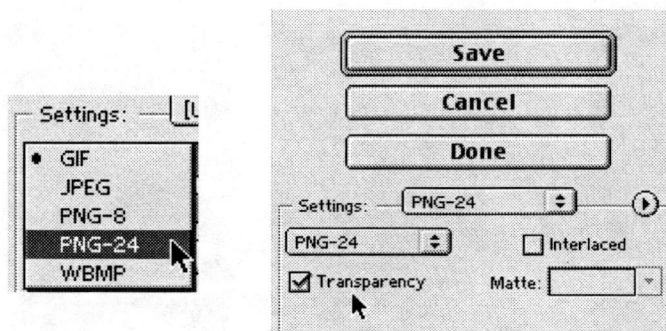

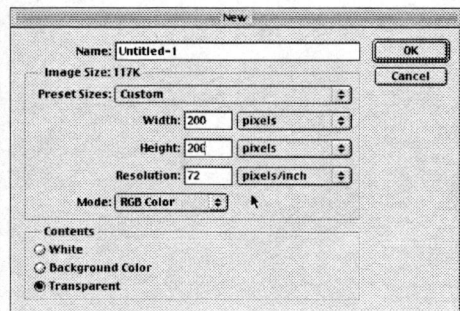

❏ Launch Photoshop and create a new document.

❏ Choose Window-Workspace-Reset Palette Locations.

❏ Select the type tool [T] from the Tool palette.

❏ Type a word in the document.

© BRADLEI KALDAHL 2003

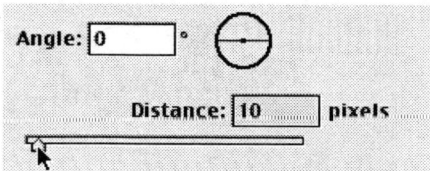

❏ Select the Move tool [icon] from the Tool palette to apply the type (and to reposition the type if needed).

❏ Choose Filter-Blur-Motion Blur. When the warning dialog appears choose OK to convert the type to raster.

❏ In the Motion Blur dialog choose an angle and distance that appeals to you.

❏ Use Save For Web to create one copy as a transparent GIF, then Save For Web again, to create another copy as PNG-24 with transparency turned on.

❏ Launch Flash and choose File-Import to Library and import the 2 versions of the image.

❏ Place the images on the stage and compare the results.

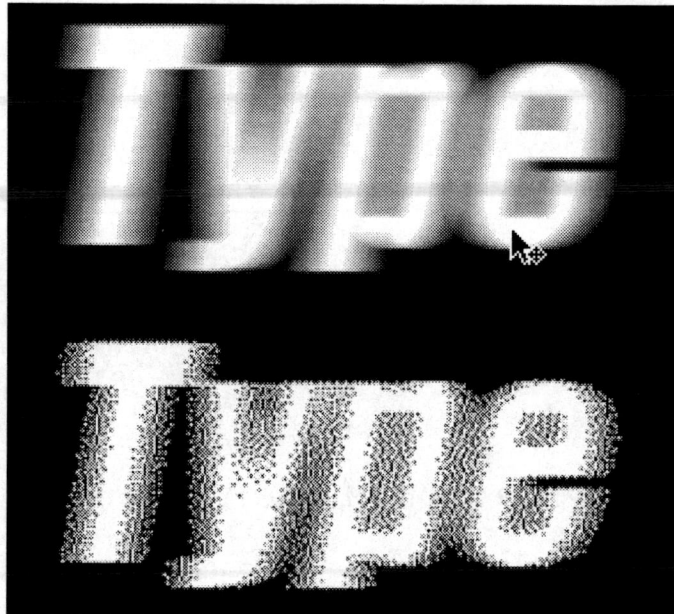

If all went well this short project should illustrate why a PNG-24 file is better in Flash than a transparent GIF.

Flash is a vector program. One of the things that I love about Flash is that it allows you to create vector information using a paint type interface. There are procedures that can easily be performed in Flash (with vector objects) that cannot be performed even in high end illustration programs. On the other hand there are times when you need the advanced control and sophistication of a high-end illustration application. Freehand is not only a high-end vector application but it also is designed to work with Flash and provides some easy-to-create yet very cool effects.

Note: The following is a simple demo to create cool effect using Freehand but to really get the most from a high-end illustration application requires quite a bit of road time.

ANIMATING TYPE IN FREEHAND

Project:

❑ Launch Freehand.

❑ Choose the text tool 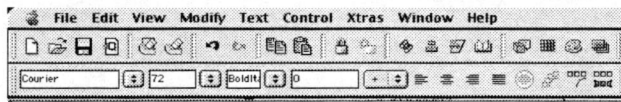 from the Tool palette.

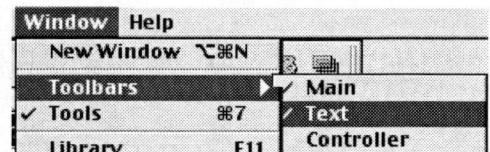

❑ Choose Windows-Toolbars-Text.

❑ Choose your text preferences.

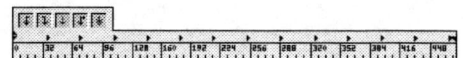

❑ Type some text on the page.

❑ Choose Xtras-Animate-Release to Layers.

Release to Layers

Animate: **Trail**

Trail by: 4

☐ Reverse direction
☐ Use existing layers
☐ Send to back

Cancel   OK

EXPORT FOR FLASH

File	Edit	View	Modi
New			⌘N
Open...			⌘O
Close			⌘W
Save			⌘S
Save As...			⇧⌘S
Revert			
Import...			⌘R
Export...			⇧⌘R
Export Again			

❏ For a bit of fun choose the Trail option and use a trail of 4 frames.

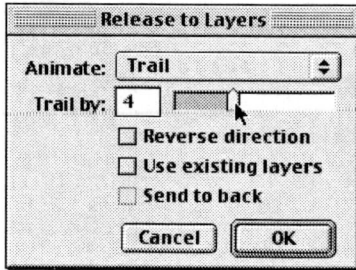

❏ Choose Control Test Movie to view the animation in the SWF player.
This is pretty cool stuff.

❏ Close the SWF window to get back to your original Freehand File.

Exporting your Freehand Graphics for Flash.

❏ Choose File-Export.

❏ Choose the SWF file format for export.

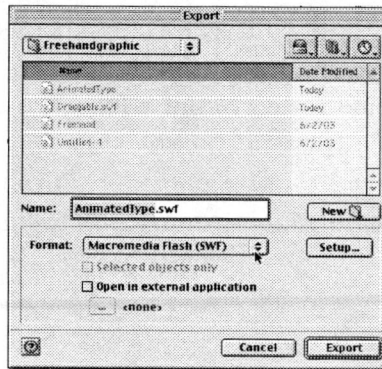

Export

Freehandgraphic		
Name		Date Modified
AnimatedType		Today
Draggable.swf		Today
freehand		6/2/03
Untitled-1		6/2/03

Name: AnimatedType.swf   New

Format: Macromedia Flash (SWF)   Setup...

☐ Selected objects only
☐ Open in external application
‹none›

Cancel   Export

Note: Set-up provides sophisticated features for optimizing your Freehand art or animation for Flash.

❏ Launch Flash and import the SWF file you created. If you import directly to the stage Flash will automatically add the frames required to display the animation.

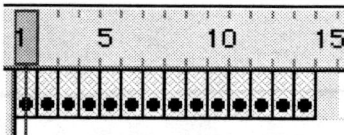

	5	10	15

Freehand also allows the capability to add some basic ActionScript commands to your objects. It is a cool feature that you might find useful. Personally, I would rather add my ActionScript inside Flash.

Using Illustrator 9.0 with Flash

This project will focus on how to export from Adobe Illustrator into Flash. Illustrator is a very robust application and, just as in the previous chapter, this project will not make you an Illustrator expert. It will provide additional options for creating images and artwork for use in Flash.

While Flash is an animation application that provides vector based drawing tools, Illustrator has been around for years and the primary purpose of this application is to produce vector art. While I have to admit that I am very impressed with some of the vector features in Flash, it is important to remember that it cannot, nor will it ever, do everything we might need. This project will focus on creating type on a simple path and exporting it as vector file for Flash. If you are a Photoshop 6.0 user you might be thinking that Photoshop can place type on a path and you are correct, but Illustrator offers much more control and has the huge added benefit of being able to export using vector as opposed to the bitmapped format.

If you know Illustrator you may wish to jump ahead to the section on export functions. If you do not know Illustrator, please remember, this project barely scratches the surface of this application. If you find the features in Illustrator exciting you may want to seek additional instruction.

Creating type on a path for use in Flash:

❑ Launch illustrator 9.0. (earlier versions of Illustrator do not have the export for Flash capabilities found in version 9.0.)

❑ Create a new document in the RGB mode, with an artboard size of 4" x 4".

❑ On the tool palette, select the fill swatch and set it to none, then select the line swatch and set it to none (as shown in the diagram at the left).

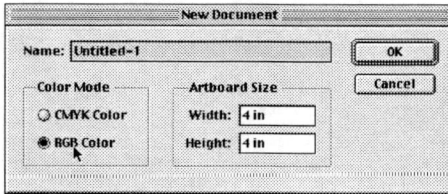

❑ Select the oval tool and draw a circle in the image window.

❑ Hold the mouse down on the Type tool, then select the Path Type tool from the pop-out menu, as shown to the right.

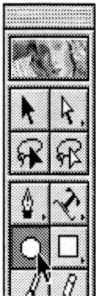

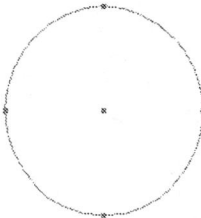

❑ Click on the circle to set the insertion point and type in some text, as shown below.

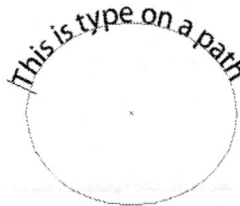

There are a huge number of effects that we could apply to this type but for this demo we'll keep it simple.

❑ Choose the selection tool from the tool palette, and click on the type to make it active.

❑ Choose File-Export to display the export dialog box.

❑ Select the Flash (SWF) format from the Format options.

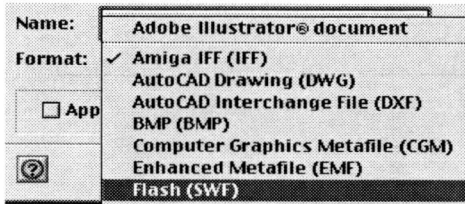

❑ Select your save location and name the file, then select the Export button to view the options.

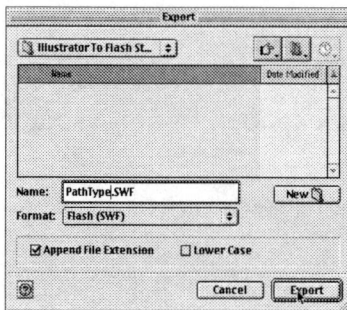

You may want to experiment with the export options depending on the artwork you're exporting. The following page provides some suggestions for selecting Export & Image Options.

I generally leave the Auto Create Symbols option off. Once the artwork is in Flash I prefer to have an opportunity to fine tune my artwork before creating the symbol. You may feel otherwise so do not hesitate to experiment with this option. I also like to crank the curve quality to the maximum setting of ten.

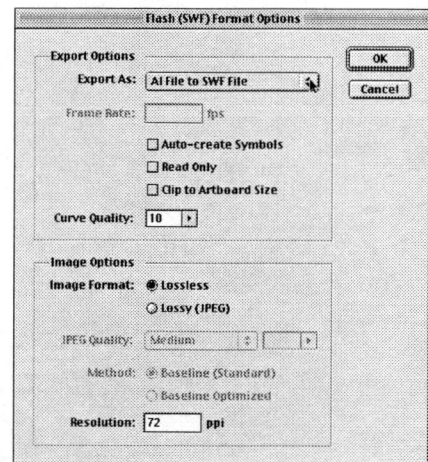

Illustrator is an interesting application. It is designed to create vector images but some of the styles, on the Style palette, and some of the filters, under the Filter menu, will convert your image into a bitmap or combine bitmapped information with vector in order to produce the desired effect. While this is not ideal for Flash, some of the options, such as blur, cannot be accomplished in vector format. Fortunately Illustrator provides some accommodation in the Image Options portion of the export dialog.

Image Options: The Image Options allow you to compress the file, if parts of it have been converted to bitmap. The text on a path image we just created will not contain any bitmapped information, so the image options with this graphic are not important.

In addition to exporting your images, you should always save a copy of the original Illustrator source file in the event you need to make changes or try other export options.

❑ To import the file launch Flash, choose File-Import and select the file you exported from Illustrator.

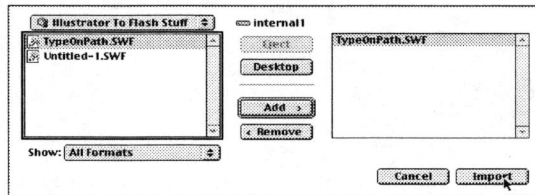

❑ To convert the graphic into a symbol, simply drag around the graphic with the pointer tool and select it, then choose Insert-Convert to Symbol.

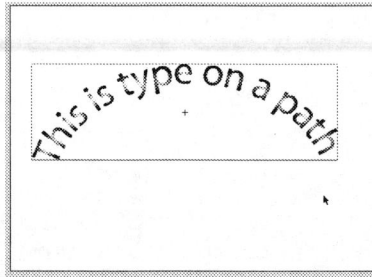

Further Exploration:
❑ Experiment with some of the different Styles, Strokes, and Fills, found in Illustrator, to see what types of effects you can create with your type.

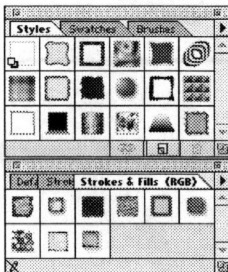

© BRADLEY KALDAHL 2003